THE MANAGEMENT GAME

THE MANAGEMENT GAME

Ardis Burst and Leonard A. Schlesinger

SIDGWICK & JACKSON
LONDON

First published in Great Britain in 1988
by Sidgwick and Jackson Limited
1 Tavistock Chambers, Bloomsbury Way
London WC1A 2SG

First published in the United States of America
in 1987 by Viking Penguin Inc.

Copyright © Leonard A. Schlesinger, Inc. and Ardis Burst, 1987
Illustrations copyright © Burst, Lazarus Associates, Inc., 1987

All rights reserved. No part of this
publication may be reproduced, stored in
a retrieval system, or transmitted in any
form or by any means, electronic,
mechanical, photocopying, recording or
otherwise, without the prior written
permission of the copyright owner.

ISBN 0-283-99651-X (Hardback)
ISBN 0-283-99718-4 (Paperback)

Printed and bound in Great Britain by
Butler & Tanner Ltd, Frome and London
for Sidgwick & Jackson Limited
1 Tavistock Chambers, Bloomsbury Way
London WC1A 2SG

To our families

Contents

Introduction 1
  1. Specialty Foods: The ConCom Challenge 3
  2. Making It in a Gourmet World 15
  3. Choosing an Advertising Campaign for Italiano 39
  4. Choosing a Sales Force Organization 63
  5. Establishing a Transfer Price for Salsa! 85
  6. Planning Italiano Production Systems 105
  7. Handling the Nubian Network Opportunity 123
  8. Balancing Corporate Reporting and Division Spending Needs 137
  9. Closing the Apple Products Production Facility 165
10. Choosing a New Group Product Manager 183
11. How It All Turned Out 207
12. The Year Ends: The Challenge Goes On 269

THE MANAGEMENT GAME

Introduction

Welcome to the international headquarters of Consolidated Commodities, Inc. ConCom, as it is known to its friends, is a Fortune 500 company located side by side with many sister corporations in the lovely county of Fairfield in the no-personal-income-tax state of Connecticut.

This book is about a year in the life of a member of ConCom's top management team. Ed Cunningham, who recently has risen to the position of senior vice-president of the corporation, heads Specialty Foods, a small but complex division of ConCom.

By following Ed's story, you will have an opportunity to see exactly what a manager does in the course of a year in the corporate life cycle. You will meet his superiors, his subordinates, even his press as he grapples with typical—and occasionally atypical—decisions a top manager has to make.

In order to develop an in-depth understanding of Ed's world, you'll first get an overview of Consolidated Commodities and the Specialty Foods Division in Chapter 1. In Chapter 2, you'll learn about the industry in which Specialty Foods competes: the gourmet or specialty foods area.

In Chapters 3 through 10 the real challenge begins. Each of these chapters describes a specific management problem that Ed faces and offers a number of "solutions" from which he can choose. In each of these specific management situations, there will be anywhere from two to five options. In addition, each problem is set in a different management discipline: marketing, organizational de-

2. INTRODUCTION

sign, accounting, and so on. At this point, you will have the same opportunity as Ed to make choices: you will have the same information he has, you will know of his personal concerns and needs. You can decide what he should do.

For each of the eight problem chapters, you'll get a "big picture" perspective on Ed's options, in Chapters 11 and 12. These chapters include a description of the key decision factors in each particular situation and how these factors affected corporate needs, division needs, and even Ed's personal career alternatives. Following each chapter's overview, you'll find out the outcome for each of the options that was available in that management situation. Here you'll share Ed's perspective. You'll know exactly what Ed would have found out if he had chosen a particular option.

At the end of each chapter review, each option will receive a score. If you keep track of the choices you make in Chapters 3 through 10, you'll be able to add up your scores and in Chapter 13 get an idea of how you did for the year.

We believe that if you work through all the decisions with Ed, not only will you have a good idea of what his life as a manager is like, but you will also find that you have gained some new management perspective from sharing his challenges.

Specialty Foods:
The ConCom Challenge

January 6, 1987

Ed Cunningham leaned back in his office chair with a deep sense of satisfaction. A 7:30 arrival at the office guaranteed him plenty of time to review the materials Irma Saloman had dropped off for their meeting at 9:00 A.M. It always paid to be ready for Irma. As executive vice-president of Corporate Relations, she was the only female top manager at Consolidated Commodities, Inc. Consequently, she seemed to believe that she had a duty to God, country, and women's rights always to be 100 percent prepared, buttoned up, and at least three steps ahead of everybody else.

Ed pulled out the bottom drawer of his desk, rolled his chair back, and propped his feet on the edge of the drawer. He picked up the stapled pile of papers and read the long note Irma had penned on the front page.

> Ed:
> Here is a draft of some sections of the upcoming Annual Report. This is the first time the Specialty Foods Division will be included, since it has come into existence during the past year. Consequently, it would be helpful to me if you'd read over the sections related to its structure and future. These include the letter from George Vulcani and Ralph Myerson and the section tentatively entitled, "Actions in the Eighties, Earnings in the Nineties," where

Specialty Foods is highlighted. Just so you won't be assessing these in a vacuum, I've included the drafts of some other sections that might be of interest.

Please do remember that all this is highly confidential at this stage of the game. I've numbered your copy and would ask that you not make photocopies of any section.

See you Tuesday.

Irma

Ed turned to the first page curiously. Any document that demanded that George Vulcani, chairman of the board and chief executive officer, and Ralph Myerson, president and chief operating officer, actually produce something together had to be interesting. Since becoming a division president and a corporate vice-president six months previously, Ed had had a number of opportunities to observe firsthand what, he confided to his wife, had to be the strangest marriage in corporate America.

First, George and Ralph were completely different in appearance, background, and style. George Vulcani, at age sixty-four, was at the peak of his form. His physical energy was evident from his tanned and lean physique. Every fitness buff at ConCom had at least one story of George passing him on a hike up a mountain or on the company indoor track at 5:00 A.M. (George already having worked up a sweat) or of having been beaten by George at tennis or handball or softball or even riding a horse. The man seemed to do everything.

Then, of course, there was George's marriage. His wife, Geraldine, was in her thirties. It was a second marriage for both. But Geraldine was not some beautiful empty-headed glamour girl. Rather, she was a plain but dynamic management professor at Yale who exuded brains, education, and an intelligent zest for life. Company scuttlebutt said George and Geraldine shared everything: they cooked gourmet meals together in their pied-à-terre in the Trump Tower, raised a huge organic garden in their country home on the Connecticut shore, and vacationed together regularly in a minuscule village in Tuscany where George had been born and where most of his family still lived.

On the other hand, there was Ralph Myerson. Ralph was as reserved as George was dynamic. With his thinning hair and skeletal frame, Ralph looked exactly like one of Charles Dickens's more woeful figures, perhaps a clerk who'd been chronically underpaid and overworked. In fact, Ralph had started his career at ConCom as a quality control clerk and the first twenty years of his employment had been in various areas of accounting and control. The only place ConCom employees ever seemed to have run into Ralph was in the corporate library, where he reportedly still read through every edition of *American Tax Accountant*.

Yet somewhere there must be more in the man than appeared on the surface. Ed seemed to remember that it was during the brutal recession of the early seventies that Ralph had been tapped to enter the ranks of top management. Reportedly, his conservatism and his grasp of accounting issues had helped ConCom weather those now almost forgotten days of "stagflation" and federal cost controls. Beyond this career information, nobody seemed to know anything about Ralph: where he lived, if he was married, even what kind of car he drove to work (could he possibly *walk*?). It was all a mystery.

Then, perhaps more important, there was a profound difference in how the two men managed. George loved to be involved in everything. He wanted to look at the people who worked for ConCom, shake their hands, ask them personal questions. For George, every business decision offered the drama of an episode of "Masterpiece Theatre." Ralph, on the other hand, preferred to look at the numbers, read the reports, and avoid having his assessments of what was going on sullied by the human element.

Of course, this led to some interesting situations for those reporting to the two men. Ed remembered an incident from his days as marketing manager of the Dry Groceries Division. Dry Groceries had a group of whole-grain products positioned as rice and potato substitutes that was going national after a very extensive and successful test market. The division had marketing plans and production plans and financial plans by the briefcaseful because they knew that was what it would take to get things approved by Ralph. Ed and the division president made their presentations and everything was "Go."

Then they went on to George to give him their sales pitch. But all George wanted to see was the packages the stuff would be sold in and the commercials they'd be using. After watching the first commercial, he had insisted it be reshot because the actor didn't have the right look on his face when he tested the bulgur wheat or whatever the hell it was.

Ed forced his thoughts back to the work at hand. He could think about those two forever and never understand how they worked together. Much more important now was his appointment with Irma.

> *To Our Shareholders and Employees:*
> *Fiscal 1986 has been a memorable and successful year for Consolidated Commodities, Inc. We have accomplished much and stand poised to evolve as a truly great marketing company through the end of the century.*

Well, this part certainly sounded like George at his most enthusiastic, thought Ed. All it needed was a bugle corps and a few baton twirlers. But undoubtedly Ralph's hand would be evident as he got to the numbers section.

> **Fiscal 1986 Highlights**
> *Highlights of the year included the following:*
> *—The largest acquisition in the company's history. In January, we purchased Scarborough Foods, Inc., for $1.3 billion.*
> *—Introduction of the greatest number of successful new products in any one year of the company's history. New products or line extensions were successfully introduced in the areas of cat food, main meal side dishes, instant cereals, novelty snack foods, and gourmet food products.*

—A continuation of our previously announced restructuring, focusing on two key areas: divestment of businesses unrelated to our areas of greatest strength with net proceeds of $1.1 billion; and internal reorganization of food products sold at retail, primarily focusing on the establishment of the Specialty Foods Division.

Financial Performance

Net sales for fiscal 1986 reached new heights at $7.8 billion. Primary and fully diluted earnings per share were $4.76 and $4.39 respectively. These earnings include $150 million of business realignment income having to do with the combined results of the divestment gains offset by costs which we believe will be incurred in our continuing restructuring and streamlining of ongoing operations, including those just acquired.

Ed skimmed through the next few paragraphs that focused on asset deployment and capital commitment, making sure Specialty Foods was not mentioned. Then he read the next section carefully.

Our Marketing Commitment

We believe that the strong and successful company of the twenty-first century will be that organization which knows its consumers, listens to what they have to say, and anticipates what they will need and want next. We plan to be that company.

As highlighted above, Consolidated Commodities has refined its business lines to focus on food alone. Our enormous Dry Groceries Division, with sales of $5.28 billion and earnings of $531 million, provides food to meet the basic needs of every American family through every major supermarket in the United States. Our International Division, with sales of $1.9 billion and earnings of $235 million, feeds millions of consumers throughout the free world. And our Food Services Division, with sales of $350 million and earnings of $75 million, gives ConCom a

> *meaningful position in the out-of-home dining segment without requiring strategic redirection into the restaurant business itself.*
>
> *This is how we measure our strength today; this is the basis for our strength in the year 2001. But this is not enough. Consumers of our products are changing. These changes are both demographic, for example, as the percentage of the population in older age groups continues to rise; and psychographic, for example, as people's attitudes toward what constitutes a satisfying meal are significantly altered.*
>
> *Consolidated Commodities has studied these changes and their implications for the future extensively. We are already repositioning products, adding new products and line extensions, and changing preparation requirements for many of our bedrock products. Within the past year, we have taken another important step: we have set up a new division in the corporation, the Specialty Foods Division.*
>
> *Specialty Foods is designed to look ahead into completely new areas, to respond quickly to what is going on today, and to investigate new distribution opportunities for ConCom. While Dry Groceries marches ahead in the battle for tomorrow's food dollar using its massive resources and highly developed firepower, Specialty Foods will supply our guerrilla fighters: a select few, a lean operation, designed to move ahead of the front line and keep us informed on what to expect two or five or even ten years from now.*

Who could have written this? Perhaps Ralph really spent his time in the corporate library reading the Roman historian Tacitus or some other expert on military strategy. Ed felt slightly embarrassed by the drama of the paragraph he'd just finished. His embarrassment rapidly turned to alarm as he realized that regardless of who the author was, he was talking about Ed's division.

Ed removed his feet from their resting place on his drawer, swiveled around in his chair, and looked out the window behind his desk. There was the lush rolling landscape of the Connecticut countryside which obviously, even in winter, was clipped and groomed and managed by innumerable gardeners and landscape experts. This in turn formed the jewel-box setting for the magnificent Consolidated Commodities headquarters building in which Specialty Foods was ensconced.

But rather than continuing comfortably as part of this corporate establishment, Ed was supposed to take his hearty band of men and women to crawl through the muck and slime of changing psychographics and slither up to spy through the windows of other corporate headquarters. And all in the name of figuring out what the average American housewife—who maybe wasn't even going to be around anymore—was going to serve her family for breakfast ten years from now.

Obviously he'd have to talk all this over with Irma. Perhaps these Annual Reports were always filled with purple prose at the draft stage and part of Irma's job was sanitizing and homogenizing them. But even if Irma changed the words, that would not change the unrealistic ideas either George or Ralph seemed to have about the objectives of the Specialty Foods Division.

Ed turned back to his desk. Oh, to be back in Dry Groceries where he knew what he was doing. This was like some crazy inversion of the Peter Principle: they kept promoting you until you got to the level of *their* incompetence, where they expected things of you that could never be done.

Quickly Ed skimmed the last two paragraphs of the letter—corporate social responsibility, equal opportunity—until he got to the summary of management changes.

> *During fiscal 1986, we added a number of fine people to our management group. These included three new senior officers: Edward V. Cunningham, corporate senior vice-president and president, Specialty Foods; Richard F. Lipping, corporate executive vice-president and chief financial officer; and Lewis Luison, corporate vice-president, Materials Planning. We sadly report the death of one*

> *of our most experienced and able directors, Zachariah Mallory III, who served for many years as chairman of the Corporate Affairs Committee. He will be missed for some time to come.*

Well, there I am, thought Ed. For better or for worse, probably until death did us part. Or early retirement, to be more realistic. Again urging himself onward, Ed turned to the next section of the draft, the Operations Review.

> **Specialty Foods Division**
>
> The Specialty Foods Division was formed this year in a reorganization that drew together a variety of products targeted or potentially targeted toward an emerging segment of the grocery-buying population: the consumers of specialty or gourmet foods.
>
> The basis of the Specialty Foods Division at this time is the Italiano line of imported food products. Previously part of the Dry Groceries Division, Italiano includes a variety of products ranging from such basic items as canned Italian tomatoes and tomato paste to gourmet items such as sun-dried Italian tomatoes and pignoli nuts. Sales of the total Italiano line were $26 million in 1986. Historically, the greatest part of the Italiano sales has been in supermarkets.
>
> The other major component of Specialty Foods is the Mountain Gourmet line of products. These products, all of which were acquired from Scarborough Foods during 1986, include maple syrup, apple products, cheese, and a large variety of jams and jellies. Mountain Gourmet products are distributed primarily through specialty food retailers, including gourmet shops, food departments of large department stores, and mail-order food merchandisers. Sales of Mountain Gourmet products were $10 million in 1986.
>
> Other Specialty Foods products include a limited selection of imports from the Consolidated Commodities International Division available under the Good Taste name.

> *Plans are to increase significantly the number and volume of these imports over the next few years. Good Taste products accounted for sales of $.5 million in 1986.*
>
> *In addition, Specialty Foods has a trial entry in the fresh foods segment of the gourmet food business, Salsa! Salsa! Salsa! This product, originally developed in the Institutional Foods Division, is available in limited distribution in the southwestern United States.*

That seemed straightforward enough, thought Ed, although it didn't address the important issues, such as how to combine all those different products and different salesmen and different retail outlets to make a sensible whole. But that wasn't the objective of the Annual Report; that was purely internal business, the kind ConCom would prefer shareholders didn't think about too much.

Ed stood up, stretched for a minute, and walked across to the door of his office. Perhaps he ought to have Madeline check the sales numbers for the different parts of Specialty Foods. He glanced at his watch. 8:20. She was probably in by now, plugging away at her calculator or her computer programs or some other analytic tool.

Ed paused in his doorway, momentarily considering turning right and heading for his secretary's office where the coffee machine might or might not be on, versus turning left and going straight to Madeline's office. He hesitated, trying to convince himself that for this meeting he could get by without those numbers.

Abruptly, Ed turned left toward his assistant's office. Dealing with Madeline at 8:20 in the morning might not be the most pleasant task, but he was simply not going to let that woman intimidate him into heading for the warmth and security of Ellie Vogel and her coffee machine.

As Ed walked purposefully down the hall, he found himself trying to figure out yet again what it was about Madeline Beauchamp Ballantyne that threatened to drive him crazy. He had been given a choice when it came to hiring her—sort of a choice, at any rate. When Personnel sent down her résumé, they had included a little note from Ralph Myerson saying that he knew the candidate and thought highly of her. That, combined with her credentials—MBA from Harvard, academic honors, training at a big New York City investment banking firm—led Ed to decide he should probably take her, sight unseen.

The problem came when she *was* seen, by Ed and the other people in the division. In a way, it wasn't Madeline's fault. Her height, her lush dark hair, the beautiful and elegant silk and cashmere clothes she wore, her Katharine Hepburn accent: these would be intimidating, no matter what a person's personality was like.

Ed knocked on Madeline's door. She was in, sitting at her desk with pale winter sunlight silhouetting her perfect profile and mass of auburn hair. "Oh, it's you," she said, looking up. "What can I do for you? I've almost finished this five-year financial analysis of the Italiano product line and I'd like to complete it before the early morning coffee klatch arrives."

Ed stood at the door, momentarily silenced. How the hell did this woman always end up making him feel like she was doing him a favor when *he* was the boss?

"Good morning, Madeline," Ed said, determined to regain the upper hand. "Lovely day for January, isn't it?" He crossed the room and sat down in a chair across from Madeline's desk.

"To be honest, I was so involved with my work that I hadn't noticed," Madeline replied, tapping out a command on the computer keyboard. "Let me save this file. Now. What do you need?" she asked briskly.

"I'm meeting with Irma Saloman shortly to review the sections of the Annual Report that have to do with Specialty Foods," Ed said, matching Madeline's tone. "Would you look over these numbers and make sure they accurately report our last year's sales? Irma's very security-conscious, so this is my only copy of the report."

"It would be a pleasure. I'll be there in fifteen minutes, if that meets your needs," replied Madeline efficiently. "That will still give me plenty of time to finish my analysis, which perhaps we can discuss after your meeting with Irma."

"Sure," said Ed, getting up and heading back out the door. "See you then," he added over his shoulder.

Back in the hall, he shook his head, thinking of that nursery rhyme his daughter had liked when she was young: "when she was good, she was very, very good and when she was bad she was horrid." That was Madeline. A good Madeline was a joy: she was prompt, thorough, brilliant in her analytic work, thoughtful, and rarely argumentative when they had professional disagreements. But her personal style . . . maybe he'd put her name in for one of those interpersonal development seminars Personnel was always pushing.

Ed walked back into his office. He had time to check a couple of things and get a cup of coffee before Madeline came down. Then was his meeting with Irma, and the day was rolling. Today, he told himself, he'd look at Specialty Foods as a challenge, not an impossible corporate dream. This was his big chance, his division, his future. Ed drew himself up straight. Guerrilla warriors, unite. Specialty Foods was a force to be reckoned with in corporate America and, at least for today, nobody could touch its leader, Edward V. Cunningham, senior vice-president, Consolidated Commodities, Inc.

2

Making It in a Gourmet World

January 9, 1987

Ed Cunningham looked up from the work on his desk as he heard his secretary's voice outside his door. "Right in here," she was saying. Ed stood up eagerly and walked to the door to greet the consultants from Foster, Weinstein. He'd been waiting for months for the report they were going to present and now finally they were ready.

Coming through the door and in front, as usual, was Amber Foster. She was reportedly the brains of the operation; she was certainly the salesman and the showman. Ed wondered again how old she was: thirty-two? forty-two? She seemed to have had about twenty years of experience as a market researcher, advertising agency executive, and with her own consulting company, but her skin still had the blossoming freshness of an English country lady's. This image was reinforced by her faint but noticeable British accent and the beautiful heathery tweed suits and capes she favored. Today she was wearing an almost lavender suit with a gray silk blouse and elegant gray leather pumps. Most becoming with her gray eyes and ash-blond hair.

"Edward, we're so delighted to be here," Amber chimed, shaking Ed's hand in a firm grasp and looking into his eyes sincerely. "Even a few days ahead of our original target date for the report." Amber never missed a chance to accentuate the positive when she was talking about her company's performance.

"Yes," added an American voice from behind Amber. It was Barry Weinstein, her partner, who was sometimes said to be also her husband or lover or something like that. Barry put out his hand, which Ed shook in turn. Barry's hand was smaller than Amber's. He was at least two inches shorter than she was, too. Surely this confident dynamic woman didn't need this little mousy man, Ed thought. Yet they'd been together for years, even before they started Foster, Weinstein, and there did seem to be some intimacy between them that was always hinted at in these meetings.

Barry and Amber were taking off their coats as Madeline came into the office. "I believe you remember my assistant, Madeline Ballantyne?" asked Ed. "Amber Foster and Barry Weinstein," he said to Madeline. Although they had all met in passing, Madeline had joined ConCom after the original report was commissioned. Ed was curious to see how Amber, who seemed rather to enjoy being the only woman in a meeting, would handle Madeline, who seemed in most meetings not to think of herself as being a woman at all. The two women nodded to each other and when Ed suggested that they get started right away, chose chairs side by side.

As soon as everyone was settled around the low coffee table, Amber took a stack of documents from her briefcase. "The results of our work," she said with a dramatic flourish. The measured way in which she handed a copy of the report to each person reminded Ed briefly of a duchess passing out cucumber sandwiches at a tea party.

After pausing to acknowledge the solemnity of the occasion, Ed spoke up casually. "It *looks* like a $100,000 report, Amber," he said, opening his copy of the report to the title page of the formally printed and bound document. " 'An Analysis of the Specialty Food Industry Prepared for Consolidated Commodities, Inc.,' " he read aloud.

"I must say, Ed," returned Amber, "that as it turned out, Specialty Foods is getting quite a bargain." In Amber's accent, "bargain" came across as almost a dirty word.

"This has been one of the most difficult and challenging studies we have ever taken on," she continued in a clipped tone. "We were aware before we began that the specialty or gourmet foods industry is quite fragmented but we were confident that research existed in the public sector that we could use as the basis of our study. Rather, we have found that we had to create everything from the ground up. We could only find one study—even in the proprietary sector—that at all defined and quantified the size of the market.

"Consequently," she went on, looking at Ed steadily, "almost the entire responsibility for the report fell on Barry and myself. We simply could not entrust the responsibility of establishing a conceptual framework for an entire industry assessment to anyone else. Furthermore, we had to spend a great deal of time in the field interviewing people, most of whom were appallingly egocentric. Each of them firmly believed that he was the most important link in the entire production, distribution, and retailing chain." She shuddered slightly.

"To be blunt, Ed"—she paused for a moment—"we did not make money on this project. It was only out of a deep sense of loyalty to you and to Consolidated Commodities that we were able to come in at our original quote at all."

"Well," said Ed, feeling slightly abashed, "all the more reason to get right into it." He turned past the title page. What else could he say? he thought to himself. Foster, Weinstein would probably end up getting one or more follow-up projects to this report—they couldn't possibly come out that far behind on the deal.

"I only want you to have the proper perspective, Ed," Amber replied in a more conciliatory tone, as she opened her copy of the report airily. "Shall we begin? We'll work through the Executive Summary now. Because the report is so complex, I've included a number of summary charts as we go along that will help us stay oriented within the total industry.

"You can find a great deal of additional information in the body of the report, including references to sources for your own follow-up, such as trade associations and trade journals. For today, we decided to present our basic findings and discuss with you how they impact Specialty Foods. We can then give you a written follow-up report that looks at relevant industry trends for the future, if you wish."

Ed raised his eyebrows questioningly. "Still within the $100,000, Ed," she said tersely. Ed smiled and nodded.

Amber then looked around the circle as if to make sure she had everyone's full attention. "An Overview," she began, after clearing her throat slightly.

> *The gourmet or specialty foods business is a dynamic, growing, and exciting business. It is extremely complex with many players whose relationship to one another and to the marketplace is constantly changing. No single company or product line dominates the industry. There is little consumer or retailer loyalty and there are many different and competing channels of distribution. Significantly, there is not even a clear definition of what constitutes a "specialty food."*
>
> *To date, no large corporation such as Consolidated Commodities has succeeded in gaining a completely successful position in this segment of the food industry. Volume, earnings, and return on investment have not fully justified corporate entries. Rather, large companies are entering this field on a trial basis, to gain experience in an area they expect to grow and to become less fragmented in the future. Reduced corporate earnings have been the price of these experiments.*

"You're sure of this, Amber?" Ed interrupted unhappily. This was not an auspicious beginning. Ed had always assumed that ConCom was taking a fairly conservative step in setting up the Specialty Foods Division, that this type of endeavor was a proven winner. But maybe he'd been wrong.

"We found that large corporate entries were either grocery-store fancy items, such as imported packaged cookies, or highly publicized entries that had quite small sales volume on rather large investments," Barry spoke up. "Of course, we can't be absolutely positive there's nothing . . . somewhere . . . ," he faltered.

"Quite so," Amber broke in smoothly as Barry fell silent and began fingering his tie nervously. "Only 99.5 percent sure." She looked at Ed challengingly. Ed returned her look but remained silent.

"I suggest that you turn to the next page," Amber finally resumed. "There you will find an outline of the text of today's report. This will be our road map for the presentation." She continued reading.

Summary Chart 1

Report Outline

1. Overview of the Specialty Foods Industry
2. Definition of "Specialty Foods"
3. Size of the Industry
4. Industry Structure
   —Sources of specialty foods
   —Size of producers
   —The distribution network
5. Specialty Food Retailing
   —Specialty food stores
   —Mail-order suppliers
   —Supermarkets
   —Department stores
   —Retail profit structure
6. Specialty Food Consumers
   —Demographic and psychographic trends
   —Consumer thumbnail sketches

"That is a summary of what we discuss today," said Amber. "Now we will get into the report itself. In each section, we will go through the text. Then there will be a summary chart you can refer back to later. The charts will not provide you with any additional information—they are simply there as a subset of our road map." She continued:

> *The last decade has brought about major changes in the specialty foods industry. As recently as the mid-seventies, "gourmet foods" referred primarily to processed foods, most of which were imported. Some of these seemed unusual to most American consumers: smoked oysters or*

white asparagus in cans, for example. Others were fancy and expensive versions of more familiar products, such as imported jams and teas. These products were purchased for special occasions or for gifts. Their high price made them unsuitable for daily consumption and their exotic qualities limited the consumers to whom they appealed.

Today gourmet foods are more varied. In addition to the canned or processed items, there are many fresh or lightly processed products, such as exotic fresh mushrooms and whole-bean coffee. There are also many more ingredients for home cooking, such as imported olive oils and balsamic vinegars.

Furthermore, specialty foods now extend beyond the exotic or strange to encompass a wide variety of ethnic foods that are staples in their culture of origin. For example, in San Antonio, Texas, a bagel is a specialty food item. In New York City, a fresh tortilla fills the same role. But in the end, both are simply types of bread.

Summary Chart 2

What Is a Gourmet Food?

Historically
—Processed foods (canned, preserved)
—Exotic or unusual items
—Fancy versions of familiar products
—Purchased occasionally, for special purposes
—Expensive
—Appeal limited by exoticness, price

Currently
—Processed food less important
—Many fresh or lightly processed products
—Ingredient items for use in cooking
—Increased representation of ethnic foods
—Individual items vary by geographic area
—Wider price range
—Wider appeal

As a result of these changes, the specialty foods industry has grown rapidly over the past ten years. But because of the enormous variety of product entries, this growth has been spread across many manufacturers and distributors that are located not only across the United States, but throughout many foreign countries as well. This fragmentation leads to substantial difficulty in estimating the size of this industry.

Industry Size

Prior to 1980, there were no published estimates of the size of the entire gourmet or specialty foods industry. Around that time, several large American corporations became interested in this industry and commissioned a study that attempted to quantify the size of this market and to predict future growth. We have used this study and extensive fieldwork to develop our own market estimates.

In 1980, specialty foods were found to constitute .75 to 1.00 percent of the volume of the U.S. grocery business, then $200 billion. Total sales at retail were, therefore, $1.6 to $2.0 billion.

More recent studies and our own research indicate that as of 1985, specialty food sales had risen 1.25 to 1.50 percent of total grocery sales of $280 billion. This puts current volume at $3.5 to $4.2 billion.

Summary Chart 3

Gourmet Foods Industry Size

	Total U.S. Grocery Business ($ billion)	Specialty Foods %	$ billion
1980	$200	.75–1.00	1.6–2.0
1985	280	1.25–1.50	3.5–4.2

One word of caution is important here: although the specialty foods industry has grown impressively over the past five years, we believe that a straight-line projection of this growth into the future is unrealistic. Demographic and societal changes have contributed to recent growth; these changes may not continue at the same rate in the future.

Amber paused and looked at Ed. Briefly he considered asking again if she was sure of her findings. Her answer would undoubtedly be the same. Sooner or later he'd have to dig through all the background numbers in the body of the report himself. For now, he just wanted the overview. "Fascinating, quite fascinating," he confined himself to saying. This seemed to satisfy Amber. She nodded her agreement and continued her presentation.

> **The Structure of the Specialty Foods Industry**
>
> *There are a number of ways of looking at the structure of the specialty foods industry. In this report we will review who makes these products, who distributes them, and who sells them. In a later section of the report, we will concentrate on who buys gourmet foods.*
>
> SOURCES OF SPECIALTY FOODS
>
> *Obviously, there are many sources of specialty foods because there are many different products in this category. The major sources are as follows:*
>
> *1. Manufactured/processed items. Traditionally, Europe has been the source of many products and this is still the case, especially for traditional "gourmet" items, such as jams and teas. However, other countries have become increasingly important as the demand for varied products has arisen. For example, Asia provides oriental products ranging from soy sauce to dried lemongrass; Africa and South America provide whole-bean coffee; the Near East provides spices and grain products: 55 to 60 percent of all gourmet products are imported.*
>
> *Meanwhile, U.S. manufacturing of specialty foods has increased. This is especially true for certain high-volume items that are frequently found both in supermarkets and in specialty food stores, such as Chinese products previously manufactured only in Asia.*
>
> *Finally, in an increasingly world-based economy, products traditionally sourced in one country are now coming*

from other areas. For example, more canned escargots are now produced in Taiwan than in France.

2. Refrigerated or short shelf-life items. *This is an area of specialty foods that has grown greatly over the last ten years. Included in this category are refrigerated items, such as cheeses, and items that require special handling and which have a short shelf life, such as dried or cured meats. Also joining this category over the past few years are items that were traditionally sold fresh only, such as certain baked goods.*

Many of these products are produced in the United States. In some cases, U.S. producers have entered markets that were traditionally supplied only by foreign manufacturers as demand for a product increased. In other cases, American manufacturers began producing products that could not be imported into the United States because of food laws, such as cheeses made in Europe from unpasteurized milk.

Summary Chart 4

Source of Specialty Foods

Manufactured/processed items
 —European companies (historically the biggest source)
 —Other overseas companies
 —U.S. manufacturers of products historically imported from overseas
 —U.S. manufacturers of typically U.S. products
Refrigerated/short shelf-life items
 —U.S. manufacturers/producers/growers
 —Overseas manufacturers/producers/growers

SIZE OF PRODUCERS

The size of the entrants into the gourmet food industry varies tremendously. At one end of the spectrum is the large European or Asian food manufacturer whose products are imported into the United States. At the other end is the local manufacturer of hand-dipped chocolates who makes the candy in her kitchen and delivers it to five local food shops from the back of her station wagon.

There are also further complications within even this broad range. For example, the large European manufacturer may have only a few products in the U.S. market, so the company is large but its position in the marketplace is relatively minor. Or a small manufacturer may be the only supplier in an area of a fast-selling item, so that company becomes important as a producer even though by total grocery industry standards it is quite negligible.

While there are probably fewer than 300 major U.S. manufacturers of gourmet foods, there are also thousands of small companies in the specialty foods business. Several large U.S. corporations have minor entries in the gourmet food industry, but these include things such as Grey Poupon mustard (Heublein) as well as true gourmet items such as Godiva chocolates.

Summary Chart 5

Size and Descriptions of Producers

—Large U.S. company with small specialty food business
  —Examples: Heublein, Pillsbury
—U.S. companies of various sizes that only produce gourmet foods
  —Can be a large company like Knott's Berry Farm
  —Can be a "cottage industry"
—Large overseas companies
  —May be major or minor entrants into the United States
—Small overseas companies

THE DISTRIBUTION NETWORK

Even more complex than the manufacturing of specialty foods is their distribution. This complexity reflects the multiple sources of specialty foods, their extensive variety, and the fact that they are sold in many types of retail outlets of many different sizes.

The major step in the distribution chain is getting products from the manufacturers or processors or growers (the "producer") to the retailers.

In the simplest case, the producer has a sales force who calls on retailers. Orders are taken; the product is warehoused with the producer until it is shipped to the retailer. Or if a producer does not have its own sales force, it may use a specialty foods **broker** who is really just a salesman for a number of different (often noncompeting) specialty foods producers.

In a somewhat more complex case, the producer does not handle any sales or warehousing itself. Instead, it uses a specialty foods **distributor,** who acts as salesman, warehouser, and distributor of different specialty foods items.

If the producer is overseas, it may also use a specialty foods distributor for sales and distribution plus importing services.

Summary Chart 6

Standard Distribution Flows

Manufacturer/Processor/Grower (usually U.S.)
(provides own warehousing and distribution)
↓
Own Sales Force
↓
Retailer

OR

Manufacturer/Processor/Grower
(small U.S., foreign, or large U.S. w/limited entries)
↓
Specialty Food Distributor
(usually provides warehousing and distribution)
↓
Retailer

Any part of the importing, selling, warehousing, and delivery process may be broken out of the whole chain and handled separately by a different person or company. In the most extreme case, a product could be imported by an importing company, sold by an independent specialty food broker, and warehoused and shipped by one or two other companies that contracted with the broker or the importer.

Summary Chart 7

Highly Fragmented Distribution Flow

Overseas Manufacturer/Producer
↓
Importer
↓
Specialty Food Distributor
↓
Warehousing Company
↓
Domestic Shipping Company
↓
Retailer

There are around 500 specialty food distributors in the country, but very few of these work nationally. Most of them are relatively small, with sales of $1 to $10 million, but at least one has volume in the $250 million range.

There are many food importers in the United States (over 700) but only about 150 handle products that could be considered specialty foods.

There are about 100 specialty food brokers, who are primarily salesmen for small or regional companies but who do not provide warehousing services.

Summary Chart 8

Number of Companies in Specialty Foods Distribution Chain

Category	Number
Specialty food distributors	500
—Usually local or regional	

  —Mostly $1–$10 million sales
  —Sales range up to $250 million
Specialty food brokers   100
  —Primarily sales for small- and
   medium-sized companies
Importers   150
  —Many others do not handle
   true specialty foods

  Each participant in the distribution chain is compensated based on how many services he provides. A full-line specialty food distributor might handle all services for a fee of around 25 percent of sales. A pure importer may receive 5 percent, a specialty food broker 5 to 10 percent. Warehousing and distribution services are not computed as a percent of sales but depend on volume and number of shipments.

Summary Chart 9

Fees for Services

Category	Rate
Full-line specialty food distributor	25% of sales
Importer only	5% of sales
Specialty food broker	5–10% of sales
Warehouser	Based on volume, storage requirements
Shipper	Based on volume, distance, carrier

  Amber paused and put down her copy of the report.
  "How do you like it so far, Ed?" she asked. "Are you beginning to see what I was referring to when I said this had been a difficult project?"
  "How did you get this information if there were so few published reports?" asked Madeline, before Ed had a chance to answer. "I've done some fancy analytical footwork in my time but this looks like it was an impossible task."

Amber turned to Madeline, who was sitting next to her. She looked deeply at the younger woman, seeming to register for the first time the full impact of Madeline's stunning appearance. Then she slowly smiled the warmest, friendliest smile Ed had ever seen on her face. "I would be delighted to share my little secrets with you, my dear," she said. "I do believe that it is so important that women professionals work together."

Ed was stunned. So much for his "Queen Bee" theory. Maybe all this time Amber of the stiff upper lip had just been waiting for the appearance of a female protégée.

"What an exciting prospect," Madeline said, returning Amber's smile. "Perhaps we could have lunch one day in the city? One of my favorite restaurants is quite near your office. It's called the Sow's Ear. You're on Park Avenue in the Thirties, aren't you?"

"A charming idea. The Sow's Ear is one of my favorite restaurants as well. Perhaps we could meet next week?" Ed stole a look at Barry. He looked a little left out. Or maybe a little put out. Ed certainly was starting to feel the latter himself.

"Ladies, ladies. We have a lot of report left here," Ed broke in before the social arrangements could go further.

"I beg your pardon," said Amber, somewhat frostily, focusing momentarily on Ed. She turned back to Madeline. "After this, my dear." To Ed's complete surprise, she actually patted Madeline's hand. Then she opened her report again. "Shall we continue?"

> **Specialty Food Retailing**
>
> Retail selling of specialty foods is as fragmented and diverse as is their manufacturing and distribution. There are a number of different types of retail outlets that specialize in selling specialty foods, plus a number of retailers who sell specialty foods as an add-on to their other business. In this report, we will focus only on the primary retailers.
>
> The vast majority of the retail business is done in four types of outlets. The largest volume is in specialty food stores, including cheese stores and coffee and tea specialists. Next in importance are mail-order houses. Then come

supermarkets, followed by the specialty food areas of department stores.

SPECIALTY FOOD STORES

These stores range from the giant Zabar's in New York City, which claims sales of over $10 million per year, to the small cheese store in a local shopping center with sales of less than $100,000 per year.

Some of these stores specialize, selling primarily cheeses or coffee or fresh produce or having an ethnic focus. Others offer a large variety of merchandise, including fresh take-home products prepared on the premises; fresh meat, fish, and produce; processed or canned items; baked goods; and even gourmet cookware and table linens. There are 3,000 or more specialty food shops throughout the United States, with a concentration on the East and West coasts. Less than 100 of the 3,000 have sales over $1 million a year. Total sales in all these stores is about $1.3 billion per year.

MAIL ORDER

Mail order is an old segment of the gourmet food industry, with products such as fresh fruit, fruitcakes, cured meats, and cheeses having been sold by mail for many years.

Air freight services have opened up new possibilities for mail-order firms. Vacuum packaging, shipping in dry ice, and overnight delivery have all made it possible to receive uncooked steaks, smoked salmon, chanterelle mushrooms, blue cheese, and fresh scones by mail. Mail-order houses can be located anywhere, though they must be set up to receive and ship out products where they are produced.

Besides the complete mail-order houses, some on-site retailers provide mail-order services secondarily.

Mail-order sales of specialty food products total $750 million per year.

SUPERMARKETS

In most cases, an individual supermarket is a fairly small purveyor of gourmet foods. Many supermarkets only have a section of one aisle or a small gondola devoted to specialty foods. Others only have ethnic specialties and some carry no gourmet items at all.

On the other hand, there are some large chains that have separate gourmet sections. These can consist of a large variety of specialty food items located together in a sort of gourmet boutique, or of gourmet items located in different sections of the store and shelved side by side with their less expensive, more mainstream counterparts. As supermarkets continue to attempt to differentiate themselves from one another and as they look for high-margin items, more are offering specialty foods.

Simply because grocery stores account for about 65 percent of nonrestaurant food sales in the United States, even chains with modest specialty food sections can account for a substantial dollar volume of sales per year. And it all adds up. In fact, grocery stores account for $450 million in sales of specialty food goods per year.

DEPARTMENT STORES

Department stores are the fourth major retailer of specialty foods. Specialty food areas are most likely to be found in the larger, full-line department stores located in larger urban areas. Perhaps the best known of these are Bloomingdale's and Macy's in their New York City stores. Here the boutique concept is very much in evidence. Macy's even has its shops laid out along a concourse in a mini-mall arrangement. There is a cheese shop, a pasta shop, a bakery, a deli, a gourmet cookware shop, et cetera.

In most parts of the country, full-line department stores are likely to have smaller areas devoted to gourmet foods. But again, the sheer number of outlets and the large overall sales of department stores lead these to add up to major sales volume, about $350–$450 million per year.

Summary Chart 10

Major Specialty Food Retailers

—Specialty Food Stores
  —Wide range of sizes, from less than $100,000 to over $10 million annual sales
  —May specialize, e.g., in cheeses, produce, coffee
  —May have an ethnic focus
  —Concentrated on East and West coasts
  —Number over 3,000
  —Total sales: $1.3 billion per year
—Mail Order
  —An old segment of the industry
  —Located across the United States
  —Mail order may be an add-on for another type of retailer (e.g., a department store)
  —Total sales: $750 million per year
—Supermarkets
  —Most outlets for limited item selection
  —Some have full-line "boutiques"
  —Large number of outlets plus overall high volume makes them important
  —Total sales: $450 million per year
—Department Stores
  —Specialty foods usually sold in larger full-line stores
  —Located across the country but primarily in larger urban areas
  —Large number of outlets plus overall high volume makes them important
  —Total sales $350–$450 million per year

MAKING A PROFIT

Different retailers have different pricing and profit structures for the merchandise they sell. Consequently, the same specialty food item may be priced differently by outlet.

Large supermarkets may underprice other retailers and still make money due to their high volume and relatively low overhead structure. The other major retailers, specialty food stores, department stores, and mail-order houses, are more likely to price products similarly. But since this is a fragmented product category with many types of retailers, differences in prices on individual products are probably the rule rather than the exception.

Summary Chart 11

Pricing and Profit Considerations

—Prices vary by outlet
—Supermarkets
 —May underprice other major retailers
—Other retailers
 —Usually price higher
 —But variations are common

Specialty Food Consumers

Who is the specialty food consumer? There is not one consumer type, just as there is not one specialty food category. In fact, rather than looking for the prototypical consumer, it is more helpful to look at a variety of trends that led to the emergence of these consumers.

First, the last twenty years have seen an increased interest in food itself. Beginning in the sixties, there has been an interest in natural, unprocessed, and organic food. Beginning in the seventies was an increased awareness of what constituted good nutrition and how this could affect health.

Second, there has also been increased interest in food variety. This can be attributed to a number of factors: the influence of people like Julia Child and James Beard, through their writing and on television; the fact that more Americans have traveled outside the country and thus experienced new cuisines; the continued influx of foreigners who brought their native cooking with them; the movement of people within the country who took their regional cuisines with them to new areas.

Third, more varied foods have become available. This trend goes back many years, to the time when fresh produce from California first was shipped East. Reduced shipping time, both within the United States and from other countries; new types of packaging and preserving; and the entry of new producers have all made previously esoteric products widely available. Retailers in search of new profit opportunities or ways of differentiating themselves from competitors have also played an important role in providing access to these products.

Fourth, there has been an increase in disposable income for many U.S. families. This can be attributed to both the continued growth of the U.S. economy and the continuing increase in two-wage-earner families. With more disposable income, there is more money to spend both on dining out, where new foods and recipes can be tried, and on buying more expensive and unusual foods to use at home.

Fifth, there has been a large increase in the number of people in the twenty-five-to-forty-year-old age group, the group most likely to try new foods and new ways of cooking. As the "baby boomers" have grown up and started their own homes, they have reflected the trends enumerated above in how they cook and eat.

Sixth, there have been major changes in family structure and in family eating habits. These have, in turn, led to more opportunities for trying new foods or new food forms. More women have joined the work force and are returning to work sooner after they have children. Consequently, there is less opportunity for families to sit down to traditional meals, and so there are more food-consumption opportunities within a family as different people eat different foods at different times.

When all these things are taken into consideration, it is possible to draw a picture of the stereotypical specialty food consumer. This person is age thirty, has a high disposable income, lives in New York City, is part of a dual-career family, and travels all over the world on vacation.

However, in reality the person is just as likely to be a seventy-year-old on a pension who immigrated to the United States as a child and still likes to cook the foods

> her mother made. So she frequents a local specialty food shop to buy mozzarella cheese/dark roast coffee/imported soy sauce/flour tortillas. There she rubs shoulders with the Yuppies who consider this same food exotic. Or perhaps the consumer is a two-year-old child whose mother buys an imported whole-grain cereal at the local specialty food store because she believes it is more nutritious than what she can get at the supermarket.
>
> **Summary Chart 12**
>
> **Who Is the Consumer?**
>
> —Demographic and psychographic issues
>   —Increased interest in food
>   —Increased interest in food variety
>   —Wider variety of foods readily available
>   —Increases in disposable income
>   —Changing demographics, particularly growth in 25–40 age group
>   —Changes in family structure and eating habits
> —Thumbnail sketches
>   —The "typical consumer" can be different from the likely consumer

As Amber delivered these last comments, Ed felt that she was watching him again for his reaction. Now she closed her report and put her copy down on the coffee table. Everyone else in the group did the same.

Ed leaned back in his chair thoughtfully. "I suppose," he said, "that the most optimistic conclusion I can draw is that there is a tremendous amount of opportunity in this business." He paused and laughed a little nervously. "Really I have to conclude that or turn in my employee ID card and walk out of here right now."

Amber and Barry looked solemn. Of course, Ed thought, this was befitting, after they came up with a $100,000 report that said they didn't know exactly what was going on in the area they'd just spent six months studying. He wondered fleetingly if somebody else could have done better. But Foster, Weinstein had always been superb at digging up information. Besides, Specialty Foods could only spend this kind of money once, so it was a moot point.

"I do think, Ed," Amber spoke up at last, "that you might find some helpful information in the rest of the report. It provides the kind of background numbers that ConCom is always good at using as a jumping-off point."

"Well, I'll certainly examine them before I do any jumping," replied Ed. "Meanwhile, I think what would be most helpful to me right now is to talk about how I see Specialty Foods in the context of this overview. I've been making some notes as you went along and I think I could test my understanding of what you said by discussing a few of these things with you now."

"Certainly," replied Amber graciously. "Go right ahead."

"Okay." Ed flipped back to the first page of a yellow pad he had propped on his knee. "Of course, the first thing that concerns me is that nobody like ConCom has made a lot of money in this business. However, to a certain extent the fact that we have established groups of products as the components of our division might help us. For example, Italiano has the basic grocery-store franchise, which we will retain. Mountain Gourmet comes to us as a successful full line with a long history as part of another major corporation. And Good Taste is basically the baby of the International Division, so any volume we add on is gravy to ConCom.

"On the good news side," Ed continued, "I think it is tremendously encouraging that this industry is growing so nicely. Jumping ahead to what you said about consumers, I can see from those sociological bits that the business ought to keep going extremely well into the future."

"Please, Ed," intervened Amber, "remember that we said at the beginning that we did not see the increase continuing at the same rate."

"Look, Amber," Ed answered matter-of-factly, "we're only talking about a sales objective for Specialty Foods of $50 million a year right now. In the total grocery industry, that's a rounding error." Amber's lips formed into a semblance of a smile but her eyes maintained a certain fixedness. Clearly her first objective continued to be to cover Foster, Weinstein's collective flank regarding such ticklish matters as market volume projections.

"I've got a lot more to worry about here than total market volume, at any rate," Ed went on. "First of all, I'm wondering if we've got the right range of entries when we look at all the different types of products, distribution channels, retail outlets, and so on."

"I was feeling quite good about our variety." Madeline spoke up now. "We have the traditional processed items, such as jams and jellies in both Mountain Gourmet and Good Taste. We have the ingredients for making our own gourmet dishes, with certain Italiano products. We've got some products that are considered healthy or nutritious, again in Mountain Gourmet—I'm thinking of the cider and the natural applesauces. And we've even got a refrigerated entry with that product which was recently spun off from the Institutional Division, the fresh Mexican table sauce."

"My, oh, my," it was Barry's turn to comment. "I had no idea you had so many, many things." Amber looked sweetly at Barry with an expression Ed usually thought of as reserved for babies and small dogs.

"Quite grand, isn't it?" she said to him. Barry smiled worshipfully.

"I guess you're right, Madeline," Ed intervened, drawing the group back to the business at hand. "And to continue that thought, we do have entry into just about every kind of retail outlet Amber described because we have such product variety. Although I'm not sure about department stores."

"I can look into that right away," volunteered Madeline.

"Good idea," replied Ed. "A wide variety of products. A wide variety of retail outlets." He ran his finger down his page of notes.

"Of course, the other side of that," he said, looking up, "is that we have a wide variety of people selling our products. Unfortunately, I didn't have much to learn about the distribution network. We already work with distributors, brokers, direct salesmen, and anybody else you can think of. In fact, the next thing on my agenda for the year is to try to bring some order to our selling situation."

Amber, Barry, and Madeline all nodded their agreement that this was clearly a wise step.

"I'm sure we'll have more questions as Madeline and I dig in to the report," Ed continued. "Meanwhile, Amber, I must say that I'm delighted to see that you and Madeline have so much in common, because she is the person who is going to do the most work with these numbers. Perhaps," he said thoughtfully, looking at Madeline and raising his eyebrows slightly, "you can talk more about them when you have lunch together."

Unfazed, Madeline returned his gaze and nodded unsmilingly. "Quite a good idea, Ed," she said.

"Quite," added Amber.

"On second thought, maybe we should *all* plan to have lunch together next week," continued Ed in his most sincere tone. "I'm sure that after Madeline and I go over this report on our own, we'll have a number of things we'll want to discuss further." From the corner of his eye, Ed thought he saw a look of gratitude cross Barry's face.

"All of us together," said Barry. He glanced quickly at Amber to see if she agreed.

"May I suggest that you call me and we will choose a mutually convenient date for all of us?" Amber replied. This seemed to represent her last word on the matter because she immediately stood up and crossed the room to where her coat lay. Barry quickly followed and helped her on with her coat. He rushed to hold open the office door and then stepped aside with a practiced gesture as Amber swept through the doorway and turned down the hall.

A few minutes later, Ed had seen them into the elevator, dismissed Madeline, and gotten his office to himself. He picked up his copy of the report, settled down behind his desk, and turned to the front page. Briefly he thought back to the Annual Report draft he'd reviewed a few days before. Perhaps the guerrilla warfare analogy wasn't so outrageous after all. Based on what Amber and Barry had said, the specialty foods business looked a bit like a jungle and he had been dropped into it—without the security of a golden parachute.

3

Choosing an Advertising Campaign for Italiano

January 22, 1987

The 3R-S conference room was filled to overflowing when Ed Cunningham and Madeline Ballantyne walked in shortly after lunch. Jack Bench, the AAM&N account supervisor, was standing right inside the door—waiting to pounce, Ed found himself thinking.

"Hi, Ed. Glad to see you. How was your trip to Florida? Took the wife and kids, I heard."

Ed took the proffered hand, returned the firm and manly handshake of Jack Bench, and murmured, "Fine, just fine." It was never a good idea to give Jack a chance to get going on his displays of good fellowship and personal concern. They could add as much as an hour to even a quarterly volume review meeting. Ed had decided early on that part of the account management training at AAM&N was a memory course: how to remember everything important about every client's life, right down to the name of the family dog. Jack in particular liked to display his skill in this area at the start of these big meetings.

"It looks like all our people are here, so let's get started right away," Ed said decisively, looking around for a place to sit.

"Fine, fine," Jack replied. "Well, we've got a nice spot for you here," he continued, edging past a pile of oversized art portfolios, a videotape machine, and two people Ed recognized as assistants from the AAM&N Media Department. "Right here. Good view, good company."

Ed sat down at the end of the table in the comfortable chair that had obviously been saved for him. He noted that Madeline was left to find a seat on her own, but a young man with a striking hairdo and a Hawaiian shirt jumped up as she squeezed into the room and gave her his seat.

"Sorry there's not more room," Ed felt compelled to say. "This is our biggest conference room, but somehow these agency presentations are always crowded."

"Well, we like to bring the whole team up for these reviews," replied Jack cheerfully. "And since we're talking about new copy, I've got the people who worked on that too. AAM&N likes the client to know that we're involved and that we care."

AAM&N cares about how big a bill they can submit, Ed thought to himself. These damn meetings. They always made him feel cynical about the advertising agency and it wasn't fair to them. They were doing a very good job on what was still, for them, a small account. In fact, they were doing Specialty Foods a favor. If AAM&N didn't have so much business in other divisions of ConCom they probably wouldn't be interested in this account at all.

But when they all appeared—the Media Department ladies with their hair in buns and the creative types in the outrageous outfits and the account staff in their three-piece suits—all he could think about was how much Specialty Foods would be billed for the six cars they had to rent to drive up from Manhattan.

"I think you know almost everybody," Jack began, taking his seat next to Ed. "Sandra Sullivan, the account manager on the Italiano line, will be making the presentations today." Sandra smiled at Ed.

"Matilda Mallory brought along several people from the Media Department." The buns nodded as a group. "Although we're not going to be going over media spending levels today, I thought she should come along just in case."

"And Josh D'Arcy brought the whole creative team that worked on the Italiano campaign alternatives," concluded Jack. "They're our stars today."

"Yo, we're here," called Josh from somewhere behind Ed.

"I don't need to tell you how excited we are about coming up with a new campaign for the whole Italiano line," Jack continued. "We reviewed literally dozens of ideas before we settled on the three that we'll be presenting. So let's get started. Sandra?"

"Thanks, Jack," said Sandra from her seat at the other end of the conference table. She was one of Ed's favorites among the account team and he was pleased that she was presenting today. Her ideas were always crisp and her presentations businesslike, but she was also an approachable and friendly person who didn't get defensive under pressure.

"Because this is the first time there has ever been an attempt to pull the entire Italiano line together under a single advertising umbrella, I decided that we should all review some salient features of the line before getting into the campaign approaches we propose. I'm going to be using this screen behind me to review some slides. Ralph, would you dim those lights?" The young man with the Hawaiian shirt jumped up and adjusted the rheostat.

A color slide flashed on the screen. They've gone all out, thought Ed. On a little business like Italiano the agency usually just used typed-up pages on an overhead projector.

Slide 1

The Italiano Produce Line
Products and History

Basic tomato products   Introduced in 1945–56
 —Tomato paste
 —Tomato sauce
 —Peeled whole Italian tomatoes
 —Crushed whole Italian tomatoes

"As this slide indicates," Sandra began, "Italiano originated after World War II. Constantine Arturi, the founder of the original company, had returned from military service in Italy and decided that American consumers might be interested in imported tomato products.

"He was right. These products fit right in with the kind of home cooking that housewives were doing in the late forties and through the fifties: casseroles, meatballs and spaghetti, meat loaves. The Italiano sales force was very successful in establishing relationships that gave them a foothold as small grocery stores gave way more rapidly to large supermarkets. In fact, it was largely the strong distribution network that made Italiano an attractive acquisition for ConCom in the middle sixties. At this point, ConCom bought out the founder of Italiano and added the basic tomato products to the extensive line of canned goods ConCom sold at that time."

The next slide appeared.

Slide 2

The Italiano Product Line
Products and History (continued)

Secondary tomato products   Introduced 1965–72
—Home-style spaghetti sauce
—Specialty spaghetti sauces
  —mushroom
  —sausage
  —fresh herb
—Pizza topping

"A year after the acquisition," Sandra continued, "ConCom began adding the secondary tomato products, correctly reading the beginning of the trend away from home cooking and toward prepared foods. This line also did very well and was gradually expanded, still through supermarkets."

Sandra clicked to a new slide.

Slide 3

The Italiano Product Line
Products and History (continued)

Gourmet tomato products   Introduced 1984–86
—Sun-dried tomatoes in oil
—Sun-dried tomatoes (dry form)
—Imported tomato paste in a tube

"As we see here, during the mid-eighties, ConCom recognized the emergence of another segment in the grocery area, the gourmet or specialty foods segment. At this point, Italiano was part of the Dry Groceries Division. Italiano was chosen as an experimental area for gourmet products and the first products were still in the tomato area. I believe these products were introduced into the California market and then rolled out across the nation. Is that right, Ed?"

"Yes," Ed answered. "In fact, it was the broker representing Italiano out there who first got some restaurant chefs interested in using sun-dried tomatoes in the California nouvelle cuisine movement. Now you can even get them on pizzas in Kansas City."

"Please, Ed, I'm *from* Kansas City." Sandra laughed. "At any rate, these products experienced modest sales, but that volume constituted success by gourmet food standards. So when Dry Groceries spun off the Italiano line as the basis of the Specialty Foods Division, it seemed logical to expand the gourmet food line by introducing some nontomato products. You can see from this list that the products were quite varied."

Slide 4

The Italiano Product Line
Products and History (continued)

Related gourmet products   Introduced 1985–86
—Italian olive oil
—Oil-cured black olives
—Peperoncini (mild golden peppers)
—Roasted pimentos
—Pignoli nuts
—Grated Romano cheese

"Now let me review how the advertising evolved on these products," she said as a new slide appeared on the screen. "First I'll talk about where the advertising appeared—the media placement."

Slide 5

Advertising Overview
Italiano Products

Basic tomato products
  Print advertising, primarily women's service books, 1946 to present
  Promotion-oriented advertising via annual cookbooks featuring Italiano products, 1945–62

"Not surprisingly," Sandra continued, "original advertising was modest since Italiano was a small company whose sales increases more than satisfied the owner. He concentrated on magazines like *McCall's* and *Woman's Day*, what we now call the service books, because space in these publications was cheap and they fit in with his homemaker orientation."

Slide 6

Advertising Overview
Italiano Products (continued)

Secondary tomato products
TV advertising, originally spot in 1965–67,
  increasing to national in 1967 to present

"When ConCom took over and introduced the new product lines, it used TV because that's what ConCom knows and loves. First it just bought spot TV—a series of ads in New York, say, then in San Francisco, then in Dallas. When this boosted sales in these locations, it decided to spend more and started buying advertising on a national basis.

"During the last year when Italiano was still part of Dry Groceries, the national advertising level had reached about a million dollars a year."

Sandra moved to the next slide.

Slide 7

Italiano Products
Gourmet Line Advertising

Gourmet tomato products
   Regional print advertising, 1984–85
   Food and wine print advertising, 1985 to present
Related gourmet products
   Food and wine print advertising, 1985 to present
   Specialty food dealer print advertising, 1985 to present

"Now things get a little complicated," she continued. "The gourmet tomato products were first introduced regionally, so we used magazines such as *Sunset,* which is mainly sold on the West Coast, to reach regional customers. As ConCom expanded distribution, we added magazines aimed at consumers across the country: *Gourmet, Bon Appétit,* and so on. These are not all targeted at women, like the magazines in which Italiano advertised the basic products. These are more 'upscale'—aimed at men and women who are more sophisticated and usually have higher incomes.

"When volume didn't take off as much as ConCom wanted, we changed our strategy and retargeted at the people who seem to be doing most of the gourmet buying. Now these aren't exactly the same as the people who do all their gourmet eating without ever cooking much of anything. So we went after them in *Metropolitan Home, Cosmopolitan,* and even *Gentleman's Quarterly.* These are magazines also targeted at the upscale buyers, but they don't have a food orientation, so they attract a wider variety of readers.

"Let's just get an idea of the volume of this advertising and how it ties in with total sales on the nongourmet items."

Slide 8

Advertising and Sales Volume
1965 to Present

(Millions of dollars)

	1965	1970	1975	1980	1985
SALES					
Basic tomato products	4.0	5.0	5.5	7.0	11.0
Secondary tomato products	.5	3.5	5.5	8.0	10.0
ADVERTISING					
Basic tomato products	.3	.3	.4	.4	—
Secondary tomato products	.3	.5	.9	1.0	.3

"This slide gives you an overview," said Sandra, "and you can see that basic tomato products kept building volume with very modest advertising. By advertising standards, this is almost token advertising. For example, it costs about $18,000 just to run one full-color one-page ad in a magazine like *McCall's*, so the whole $400,000 only bought about twenty-five pages of advertising a year.

"On the other hand, secondary tomato products built volume at a steeper rate and also built advertising more rapidly. Of course, a TV advertising campaign is usually going to cost a lot more than print advertising. One TV spot, for example, costs an absolute minimum of around $5,000 for thirty seconds. Thirty seconds during the Super Bowl, which has the most viewers of any TV show, can cost close to a million dollars! So even secondary products had a very modest budget.

"What this overview doesn't show you, however," Sandra continued, "is what happened during the transition of Italiano from Dry Groceries to Specialty Foods. Also we need to look at what happened on a more detailed basis when the new product lines were introduced. So that takes us to Slide Nine."

Slide 9

Sales and Advertising
1980–86

(Millions of dollars)

	1980	1981	1982	1983	1984	1985	1986
SALES							
Basic tomato products	7.0	8.0	9.0	11.0	12.0	11.0	10.0
Secondary tomato products	8.0	12.0	13.0	13.0	14.0	10.0	11.0
Gourmet tomato					.7	1.3	1.5
Related gourmet						1.7	2.5
TOTAL	15.0	20.0	22.0	24.0	26.7	24.0	25.0
ADVERTISING							
Basic tomato products	.4	.4	.5	.5	.5	—	—
Secondary tomato products	1.0	1.1	1.0	1.2	1.1	.3	1.0
Gourmet tomato					.1	.2	.2
Related gourmet						.2	.2
TOTAL	1.4	1.5	1.5	1.7	1.7	.7	1.4

"Very interesting, Sandra." Ed spoke up from his end of the room. "Could I say a little bit about this one?"

"Be my guest," Sandra answered. "Ralph, bring those lights up a little, will you?" Again the Hawaiian shirt jumped up.

"These numbers look a little crazy now," began Ed, "but it all made sense at the time. You need to recall the course of events.

"First, as Sandra said, Dry Groceries introduced some gourmet products. These were handled through the regular Dry Groceries sales force. They weren't a big hit with the supermarket buyers, who had never even heard of a sun-dried tomato. That led Dry Groceries to retain a specialty foods broker based on the West Coast because we—I was still in Dry Groceries myself then—wanted to see if we were running into problems with the products or the channels of distribution.

"As the nouvelle cuisine pizza story tells you, this broker did a good job of opening up new outlets for Italiano. We did some modest advertising spending to back her up, as Sandra indicated.

"Then Dry Groceries introduced the nontomato gourmet products under the Italiano name. The same broker got some nice placements for these products, but meanwhile we found that supermarkets wanted them too because they were more like the items they were used to carrying: nuts, cheese, peppers. They put them in their Italian section right next to the other Italiano products.

"Because these nontomato products got such good distribution, the volume for them took off quickly. So whereas the gourmet tomato products have sales of only $1.5 million in their third year, the related products are up to $2.5 million in their second year.

"When it comes right down to it, by the time you build up even a basic inventory in all those giant supermarkets, you can generate sales in the $2 million range. And that's what we're seeing here. The enormous distribution gives this part of the product line its basic momentum."

"Could I jump in here and say something about the advertising expenditures?" asked Jack.

"Please do, Jack," said Ed graciously. "You were much more involved with the decisions on the older Italiano products than I was."

"I was involved," said Jack, sighing slightly, "but I can't say I agreed with them. Dry Groceries got very enamored with the gourmet business and saw it as the way of the future. But 1985 was a very tough year in terms of the money the corporation had available to spend on building businesses. So when Dry Groceries decided to put advertising money behind the gourmet products, it took a chance on taking money away from the established line. Could we go back to Slide Nine for a minute?"

The slide clicked back on.

"You can see here that advertising was completely dropped for the basic tomato products in 1985. The $300,000 for secondary was all spent in the first quarter of the year, so for the last nine months advertising was dropped on these products, too. Meanwhile the advertising was built up for the gourmet products. But using typical corporate arithmetic, what was added didn't equal what was subtracted. Italiano ended up 'saving' a million dollars on advertising that year and the corporation was delighted to have that money."

"I'll have to add one thing, Jack," said Ed. "The advertising cuts took place at the same time that ConCom started planning to transfer Italiano from the Dry Groceries Division to the new Specialty Foods Division. During most of 1985, Italiano was in transition. The new division didn't get set up formally until 1986 and then it didn't have a president until I came on at the end of the summer. So it was easy to get away with cutting advertising. There was nobody in charge to say it wasn't a good idea!"

"And as those sales numbers show," Jack added, "for once the advertising agency appears to be earning its money. When advertising was cut from $1.7 million to $700,000, volume went down from almost $27 million in sales to $24 million in 1985."

"You've got to qualify that slightly," chimed in Sandra. "When advertising was cut on the *basic* tomato products from half a million dollars to nothing, volume went down somewhat. About 8 percent in 1985 and another 9 percent in 1986.

"But when advertising was cut on the *secondary* products—the spaghetti and pizza sauces, where there's a lot more competition—volume plummeted. There was almost a 30 percent decline in one year, and that was with three months of advertising."

"Which is why we started adding advertising back in 1986," said Ed. "But we've gone slowly because we knew we wanted to develop a total copy strategy for the full line. Consequently, volume is rebuilding slowly. We only got back to $11 million on the secondary products and since we didn't start advertising primary products again, volume slipped further, from $11 million to $10 million."

"Well, I'm glad we all agree on what's been happening," Sandra said. "But if we don't get on to the future instead of dissecting the past, we're never going to get through this part of the presentation and on to the real reason for this meeting."

"Let's hear it for Sandra. Storyboards. Copy strategies. The good stuff." Josh D'Arcy spoke up again from the back of the room and there was scattered applause from his area.

"Okay, okay, I can take a hint," said Jack. "Go ahead, Sandra."

"As you'll recall from an earlier slide," Sandra resumed, "Italiano's advertising is now rather fragmented. Basic tomato products aren't being advertised again yet. And their entire advertising history is in women's magazines. On the other hand, secondary tomato products are advertised on TV. Specialty foods are in other kinds of consumer magazines and at the suggestion of the specialty foods broker, we've even placed some ads in specialty foods trade journals, which are distributed primarily to gourmet food retailers.

"Not only is Italiano advertising in different places; it's also advertising with different messages. The secondary tomato sauces emphasize convenience, the basic tomato products focus on home cooking, and the gourmet products have a sort of life-style campaign that focuses more on image than on product characteristics.

"So Ed asked us to put together a campaign that would provide an umbrella for all the Italiano products. Here's a summary of what this campaign is supposed to do. Ralph, hit those lights."

Slide 10
Italiano Umbrella Campaign
Advertising Objectives

1. Provide consumers across demographic and psychographic segments with a unified and viable image of Italiano products
2. Convey the following concepts of Italiano products
    —imported
    —high quality
    —good value but not an economy product
    —variety of products
3. Let all consumers know of the full range of Italiano products
4. Develop a vehicle that provides future opportunities for different products or sets of products to be advertised individually

Sandra read aloud from the slide and then continued, "This is not a new advertising approach, of course. Many product lines advertise the whole group and then distinguish between individual products. On a macro level, there's Lee Iacocca talking about the Chrysler Company and then a lot of ads for individual brands of cars and even models within the lines.

"But other corporations' experiences didn't make it easier to develop a campaign for Italiano. What I'd like to do now is turn the meeting over to Josh so he can talk about the process the creative group went through in arriving at the three campaigns we have to present to you today."

After a momentary pause the room was suddenly flooded with light, showing Josh D'Arcy in his creative splendor in front of the slide screen. Ed found himself amazed anew that someone as unconventional in appearance as Josh could repeatedly produce work that could influence the most conservative housewives in middle America.

Today Josh seemed to have concentrated on arraying himself in the most flamboyant of what were probably the new colors for spring, though this season was still over two months away. Really, each article of clothing he wore was acceptable in its cut, though his jacket appeared to lack shoulder pads and Josh had pushed the sleeves up on his forearms. But the trousers were electric blue, the jacket was jonquil yellow, and the silk shirt, open at least two buttons beyond good taste, was a sort of paisley pattern of blue, yellow, and magenta.

"Good afternoon, ladies and gentlemen," began Josh jovially. With his bright colors and smooth style, Josh suddenly reminded Ed of a circus ringmaster.

"It's time for Uncle Josh's Show and Tell. I'll show and Ed will tell us what to do." Ed smiled tightly. Josh loved to get a rise out of clients and Ed loved to deny him the satisfaction.

"We sifted through many, many ideas as we considered an umbrella campaign for Italiano," Josh continued importantly. "We were very, very interested in finding an idea that was essentially Italian in nature. We wanted the most unsophisticated, untraveled viewer in America to look at this campaign and think 'Italy,' because, of course, it is only a short step from Italy to Italiano."

Josh paused thoughtfully for a moment, then continued. "We also wanted a campaign that conveyed food. The Creative Department, and in fact, everybody at AAM&N, has been appalled at some of the food advertising now appearing on television and in print. In these campaigns, image is everything. You'd never know anything good to eat was being discussed. We, on the other hand, want to get across the idea of mouth-watering, appetizing"—Josh looked around the room meaningfully—"you might even go so far as to say . . . yummy! . . . in every ad we run, regardless of whether it's in print, or TV, or even on a billboard of Interstate 10."

"And finally," Josh concluded, putting his hand over his heart as if to indicate his intense sincerity, "we wanted a campaign that would be *memorable*, that people would remember like they remember those old Alka-Seltzer commercials where the poor guy ate the whole thing." Again there was scattered applause from the creative types in the back of the room. "Yes, Ed, you always claim that the client is the one concerned with memorability. But the poor creative's only claim to fame is to have his work remembered. So we're just as interested as you are in how these ads score in the overnight recall ratings."

Ed felt an immediate response was called for. "Glad to hear that, Josh," he managed to say sincerely.

Josh nodded. "What we decided to do at this stage," he continued, "was to think through three campaigns and how they would appear in both print and on television. Initially we're going to present them to you as they'd appear on TV, that is, in storyboard form." He stepped to one side, revealing a large easel behind him.

"We all agree that we should choose one campaign, shoot the initial commercial, and test it on television for memorability and recall. Of course, we will use the usual numerical objectives for a ConCom campaign on the Burke ratings. But let me stress that we think *any* of these three ideas will do well and it's a question of your personal preference and corporate perspective as to which campaign you go with."

With a flourish, Josh removed a blank sheet of paper that had concealed the papers on the easel.

"So here, my friends," he said enthusiastically, "is the first campaign idea."

On the easel was a large cardboard sheet, about two by three feet. A series of pictures appeared on the sheet, each in a box that was shaped like a TV screen. Under each picture were words of text and, in parentheses, camera directions.

"We call this first one 'Italiano Dining Map.' As you can see in frame one, we have Italian violin music to open and a map of Italy with the Italiano logo overlaid. In the first scene, we have an American housewife standing in an American kitchen, though it is decorated with Mediterranean-style tiles. Through the window behind her, you can see a sample of magnificent southern Italian scenery. Mount Vesuvio or some such thing. The voiceover says, 'Whether it's Italiano tomatoes or tomato paste, Italiano brings you the ingredients for the finest homemade foods in the southern Italian tradition.'

"Then we dissolve to an American family out on their southern California deck—perhaps a hot tub—you know the scene. Behind them are the Italian Alps. The mother is serving a platter of spaghetti. Voiceover: 'You can also choose our carefully prepared sauces for spaghetti and pizza using authentic imported Italian ingredients.'

"And a third scene: the young upscale couple in their hi-tech American kitchen making white pizza with pignoli nuts, sun-dried tomatoes. Grape arbors and underprivileged Italian peasants picking grapes in the field we see through their window. 'Or our unique gourmet tomato products and other Italian specialties.'

"Finally dissolve back to the opening scene with the voiceover plus the message written out: 'Italiano puts your dining on the map.' "

"Our second campaign has a slice-of-life focus." Josh removed the first storyboard and handed it to a young woman dressed completely in orange—including her shoes and stockings—who Ed guessed was another member of the creative team. A second board was behind the first.

"Here's the storyboard. We open with the same Italiano reference, then dissolve to a typical upper-middle-class kitchen. Two people, WASP types, not Italian, are in the kitchen. We can tell from the fact that they look alike that they are brother and sister.

"And we can tell from all the things out in the kitchen that they are getting ready for a big family party—several charming little children in the background, a dog. Very informal. But you can see in this frame a certain tension between the two.

"In the third frame here, the sister says she's brought a great appetizer: miniature pizzas made with Italiano pizza topping. Dissolve to a close-up of these. They look delicious—gooey melting cheese, sliced mushrooms.

"Then in the next frame her brother says, 'You're mistaken, sis. *I* brought the appetizer. Look at this antipasto!' We come in close on a great platter filled with Italian olives, peperoncini, roasted peppers, fresh vegetables. Pull back to the brother. He's mugging—pidgin Italian, kissing his fingertips.

"Then in this frame Mom comes in. She's comfortable but elegant. She sees what's going on. She says, 'Some things never change,' and shakes her head at twenty-five years of sibling rivalry. Then she picks up a huge platter of spaghetti with tomato sauce. Her two children stand on either side of her, we get a brand identification from a view of Italiano products on the counter behind her, and

THE MANAGEMENT GAME . 55

① ("BROTHER AND SISTER" CAMPAIGN)
② (PAN OF KITCHEN, ZOOM IN)
③ (WOMAN) LOOK, ANDY. I BROUGHT THESE TERRIFIC MINI-PIZZAS FOR OUR APPETIZERS TONIGHT.
④ (CLOSE UP OF PIZZAS AND ITALIANO PIZZA SAUCE)
⑤ (MAN) YOU'RE MISTAKEN, SIS. MOM TOLD ME TO BRING THE APPETIZER. JUST LOOK AT THIS ANTIPASTO.
⑥ (CLOSE UP OF ANTIPASTO AND ITALIANO PRODUCTS)
⑦ (OLDER WOMAN) SOME THINGS NEVER CHANGE. YOU TWO HAVE BEEN COMPETING SINCE ANDY WAS BORN!
⑧ (MAN) THE BEST THINGS NEVER CHANGE, MOM, LIKE YOUR SUNDAY DINNERS.
⑨ (VO) ITALIANO PRODUCTS—NEW OR TRADITIONAL. SOME GOOD THINGS NEVER REALLY CHANGE.

in the last frame the son says, 'The best things, Mom—like your Sunday dinners.' She smiles. The camera pans back, we dissolve to the opening scene. Voiceover: 'Italiano products—new or traditional. Some good things never really change.'

"And now, the finale," said Josh dramatically, as he revealed the third storyboard. "The celebrity pitch. We use a celebrity who is not Italian but who obviously loves good food. He's robust, passionate, flowing with the juices of the good life. He's the same age as our target group—in his late thirties. He's known as someone who likes to cook, or plays a character on TV who likes to cook.

"Here in frame one we have the same lead-in. Then we see our man in what we think of as his own kitchen—warm, earthy, very upscale. He's confiding in us, talking to the camera. 'I love life. And some of the best parts of the good life are cooking and eating great food.' We zoom in on what he's cooking—a big pot of spaghetti sauce, another pot of pasta. He sprinkles some fresh herbs into the sauce.

"In the next frame, he walks over to the counter. There he joins a beautiful woman: hopefully, his wife. 'Even doing simple things, I like to go for it all.' She is putting Italiano prepared pizza sauce on a homemade pizza. The jar with the label is on the counter beside her. They smile at each other.

"He picks up a tray of antipasto—all the Italiano products, like what the brother had in the previous ad—and walks out the kitchen door onto the deck. View of the Pacific Ocean behind him. His friends are gathered around, sipping whatever they are sipping in California these days. He holds the tray out dramatically, saying, 'Another Italiano masterpiece,' and the friends break into applause, toast him, et cetera.

"In the last frame, we pan back, and we have the voiceover: 'Italiano fine imported Italian products. When you go for the best, go for Italiano.'

"And—that's it from the creative team," Josh concluded. Suddenly he looked tired in his bright clothes, as if the presentation had been more of an effort than even he had realized.

"Wonderful copy. Great ideas," spoke up Jack in the momentary heavy silence that followed.

"Thanks, Josh," added Ed. "Nice going." The storyboards were always such a dramatic part of these meetings that it was hard to get things rolling after their presentation. Such a massive effort on the part of the agency called for an enthusiastic response, but more than once Ed had seen an off-the-cuff comment at a time like this lead to the wrong campaign choice or hurt feelings among the creative team or other unexpected problems.

"Let's run through them each again," said Sandra tactfully. "That will give everybody a chance to absorb these ideas and then we can have an informal discussion of the pros and cons of each."

"I'll second that," said Ed. Sandra did know how to handle these meetings.

"Maybe Ralph could pass around those plates of delicious ConCom

THE MANAGEMENT GAME   .57

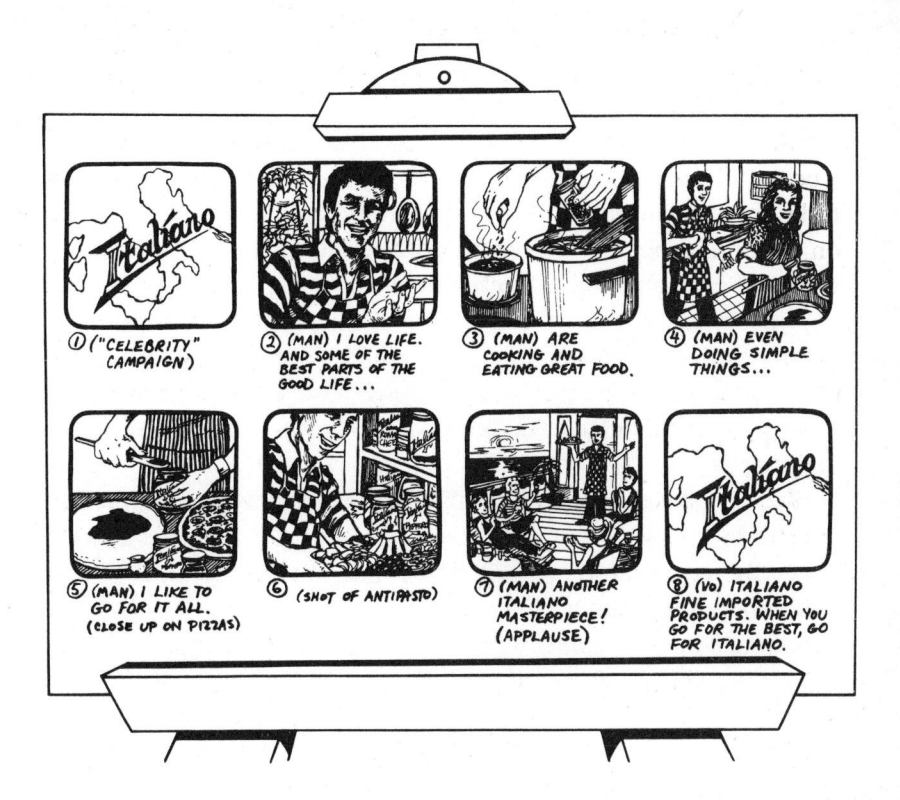

① ("CELEBRITY" CAMPAIGN)

② (MAN) I LOVE LIFE. AND SOME OF THE BEST PARTS OF THE GOOD LIFE...

③ (MAN) ARE COOKING AND EATING GREAT FOOD.

④ (MAN) EVEN DOING SIMPLE THINGS...

⑤ (MAN) I LIKE TO GO FOR IT ALL. (CLOSE UP ON PIZZAS)

⑥ (SHOT OF ANTIPASTO)

⑦ (MAN) ANOTHER ITALIANO MASTERPIECE! (APPLAUSE)

⑧ (VO) ITALIANO FINE IMPORTED PRODUCTS. WHEN YOU GO FOR THE BEST, GO FOR ITALIANO.

cookies I see back there, too, and open some sodas," Sandra continued. "Let's celebrate this terrific creative work." She smiled at Josh. Josh smiled back.

"Hear, hear," added Ed, relaxing. The tricky moment had passed and now they could dig in and get some work done.

After the meeting broke up an hour or so later, Ed checked in with his secretary, returned a few urgent phone calls from her phone, and walked down the hall to the office of the Italiano product manager. The assistant product manager was already there and the three new storyboards were propped up on the floor opposite the PM's desk.

"Ed, glad to see you." Grady Jennings, the product manager, stood up from behind his desk. "We were just discussing these boards and what we thought the next steps should be. You've met

Mary Gale, haven't you? She just joined us as assistant product manager on the secondary products line."

Ed and Mary nodded to each other. "And what are your group's thoughts so far, Grady?" asked Ed, moving a chair over so he could see both Grady and the storyboards at the same time. Grady sat back down behind his desk.

"I like all three of these campaign possibilities," he began slowly, "at least enough to consider them. But I can't say I'm sure that any one of them is head and shoulders above the others. They all appear to have the potential to meet our objectives: they can be executed in print or on TV, they can focus on different products in the line, and they emphasize quality and the fact that the products are imported.

"We're talking about a $2 million-a-year advertising campaign, potentially," he continued, leaning back in his desk chair and looking at the ceiling thoughtfully. "That's a good bit of money to spend behind a new campaign."

"I sense you're leading up to something here, Grady," Ed said. Grady bumped his chair down.

"I'm leading up to the possibility of doing some pretesting," Grady replied. "We've been talking it over and Mary got some numbers on testing together in advance but it's not that easy a decision. If we were in Dry Groceries, there'd be no problem. There's plenty of money to test everything and with their multimillion-dollar spending levels, they *have* to test. But on Specialty Food's limited volume and profit contribution, testing involves enough money that it's going to end up having to be your call."

"Let's try to make that *our* call, Grady," replied Ed. "Maybe we can work it out together right now."

"I'd like that," said Grady. "Mary, give Ed a copy of that memo. We can start there."

"I wanted to make sure I looked at everything," said Mary apologetically, as she handed the memo to Ed. "There's probably a lot of stuff in here you know with your eyes closed."

"I can almost always learn something new in a case like this," answered Ed kindly, thinking that what he'd probably learn was something about Mary herself.

"Okay," said Mary. "Here goes."

> *In order to pretest commercials, two steps are necessary. First, a cost-reduced version of the commercial is filmed. Second, this commercial is given limited TV exposure and viewers are polled to determine the extent to which they recall the commercial and the messages they took away from it.*
>
> *Whereas a finished commercial costs anywhere from $100,000 to $1 million or more to shoot, test commercials can be filmed for $5,000 to $20,000 apiece. Three techniques are available for making test commercials.*
>
> *The least expensive is* animatics. *The visuals are artwork, usually animated somewhat, with the soundtrack being just about the way it would appear in a finished commercial. Animatics cost $5,000 to $9,000 each. They are the cheapest and quickest type of test commercial. However, they are the least like the finished product.*
>
> *This means that there is always a question of whether a commercial that doesn't do well would have done better if it had looked more like the "real thing."*
>
> Photomatics *are similar, but the visuals are still photographs rather than artwork. They can cost more, depending on whether you use stock photos or shoot on location. The usual cost is $8,000 to $10,000 each.*
>
> Livamatics *use live talent in a setting with minimal propping. Photographs can be used for the background and/or a minimal set can be built. These are the more expensive test format, costing $10,000 to $20,000. However, they are the closest to the finished product, so they raise the fewest questions about how accurate their test results are.*
>
> *In addition to the cost of producing the commercial, there is the cost of the test itself. Market research fees are*

about $2,500 per commercial exposure. Media cost is about $5,000 per placement.

Putting all this together gives us this range of costs, assuming a middle-of-the-range production cost for each vehicle.

Animatics	$7,000 production $7,500 research Total: $14,500 per commercial or $43,500 for 3 commercials
Photomatics	$9,000 production $7,500 research Total: $16,500 per commercial or $49,500 for 3 commercials
Livamatics	$15,000 production $7,500 research Total: $22,500 per commercial or $67,500 for 3 commercials

"So we're talking a low of $14,500 to test one commercial in the cheapest way to a high of $67,500 to test all three in the most expensive way," summed up Grady.

"And there are some complications that arise from the campaign ideas themselves," said Mary, sounding anxious. "We couldn't test the celebrity campaign unless we use livamatic because the person is the important thing. We'd have to use the actual celebrity and that could cost any amount of money, though I'd guess he'd do a test commercial for a standard fee in hopes of more money if the campaign flies.

"The Italian dining map campaign, on the other hand, would probably do best with photomatic because it uses all those Italian background scenes. The brother and sister campaign could be done any way."

"But if we're going to test all three commercials, the Market Research Department would never let us do it with one in one format and another in another format. They'd say we have to do them all the same way," said Grady wearily.

"So our first option," Ed said, "is to test the campaign we think is best using the appropriate production device. This would basically be trusting our judgment but with the addition of a disaster test just to make sure we hadn't chosen a real bomb. In this case, we ought to use the hurdle rates for recall that Dry Groceries uses. A minimum of 15 percent of the people we talk to have to be able to recall the commercial without interviewer prompting. With prompting, it's got to be 26 percent. And they've got to give us back a reasonable approximation of the message we're trying to get across.

"Our second option," said Ed, "is to test all three campaigns using livamatic, adding the actual celebrity for the third campaign. Then we could compare recall scores and see which one the most people remembered. This is definitely taking the conservative approach, not just relying on judgment. But we'll be paying $67,500 for our caution.

"Or, of course, there's the third option: don't test any of them. Let's follow our judgment and save all our money to buy TV time.

"I'm willing to play devil's advocate on the 'don't test' option," Ed went on. "You'll recall that Josh D'Arcy said he thought the celebrity campaign was the best of the three. I disagree. If I chose just one right now, I'd go for the brother and sister. It's simpler and cheaper than the celebrity campaign. And it gives me a warm and friendly feeling I don't get from that Italian sight-seeing campaign."

Grady looked over at his assistant as Ed finished talking. "I'm afraid we reached a different conclusion," he said. "Both of us really like the map campaign because it emphasizes the variety of Italiano products and their multiple uses. In the other campaigns everything was more or less lumped together in one big confusing meal."

"Interesting observation," said Ed thoughtfully. "You like the first campaign, I like the second, and Josh likes the third. At least if we tested, we'd know whose judgment we could rely on for the future. Then we could really save money."

Grady laughed.

"Well, if we do test, I can guarantee one thing," Ed concluded. "That money will come out of the media budget and we'll be able to spend that much less of the $2 million on advertising itself. So what choice shall we make here?"

Indicate your choice here:

_____ Option 1. Test Italian Dining Map only.
_____ Option 2. Test Brother and Sister only.
_____ Option 3. Test Celebrity only.
_____ Option 4. Test all three.
_____ Option 5. Don't test anything. Shoot Ed's favorite, "Brother and Sister," and get it on the air as soon as possible.

4

Choosing a Sales Force Organization

April 3, 1987

"Good morning, Ellie," said Ed Cunningham jauntily as he stopped at the door of his secretary's office. It was a few minutes after 9:00 and Ed felt ready for anything after a good night's sleep, an early game of tennis, and a long hot shower.

"You've been out taking advantage of this lovely weather," said Ellie. "Every year about this time I see you cheer up. Was it tennis?"

"Correct, as usual, Mrs. Vogel," Ed replied. "The good weather's just in time, I might add. Have you happened to take a look at my calendar for today?"

"Yes, I was just going over the schedule," said Ellie, "and thinking about what a time I had setting up all these different meetings. We've got someone coming in from California and somebody else from New Jersey and that nice Mr. Spencer from the Sales Department."

"So we have," said Ed, "and I've got to get ready for all of them. What I need right now is a cup of coffee and the presence of Madame Madeline. If you could provide those things, what I'll need next is an hour or so with no phone calls. The first meeting is scheduled for 10:30, I believe."

Ellie nodded. "You just go right down to your office," she said reassuringly, "and I'll take care of everything." She stood up and started shooing Ed from her office. "Go on now—time's flying."

Ed continued down the hall to his office and was just hanging up his jacket when there was a tap on the door. Madeline Ballantyne walked in.

"Did Ellie find you already?" asked Ed pleasantly.

"Ellie didn't need to find me," said Madeline impatiently. "I've been waiting for you since 8:30. We've got an enormous amount of material to go over here."

"And we've probably already been over most of it at least twice," answered Ed, settling down behind his desk. "*And* we'll be hearing even more from the broker and the sales manager and the distributor. As I've said before, sometimes the best preparation for a demanding day like today is to get a little exercise and eat a nourishing breakfast. I suppose you did eat a healthy breakfast?" Ed asked solemnly. The only way to deflect Madeline on the days she was especially task-oriented was to put her slightly on the defensive.

"Ed, please. You know I never eat breakfast and I can't say that I really see what my eating habits have to do with the performance of my duties." Madeline was still standing near the doorway, holding a large stack of papers. She was beginning to look a tiny bit awkward there.

"All right, all right, sit down and we'll get to work." Ed motioned to the chair across the desk. There was another knock at the door. "And there's Ellie with the coffee. Now we can really get busy."

For the next fifteen minutes, Ed and Madeline pored over the first part of the material Madeline had brought in. "That's the Italiano line," Madeline finally concluded. "Most of the information is what we saw a couple of months ago in that agency presentation."

"The important thing for today's meeeting is how the stuff is sold," Ed said in turn. "Almost everything is still handled by the Dry Groceries sales force. Their effort is supplemented by that specialty foods broker from the West Coast who concentrates on marketing to retailers other than supermarkets."

Ed sighed. "And of course the whole thing is being coordinated by Billy Burke. Billy's a nice enough guy, but I get the feeling that maybe Stewart Spencer wasn't too sad to see Billy go when our division was set up." Madeline tactfully said nothing but instead handed Ed the next page of her report.

"Well, let's continue," said Ed. "This is Mountain Gourmet."

"Yes," said Madeline, "and I've taken the same approach: a brief review of Mountain Gourmet and how we got it and a description of the sales setup we've got now."

She began reading the page aloud.

> **Mountain Gourmet**
> HISTORY
> —Founded 1962 as counterculture cooperative for small independent food producers in Vermont. Grew to be a large, sophisticated organization but remained a cooperative, adding paid management as size warranted.
> —Bought out by Scarborough Foods, Inc., in 1981 as part of its expansion program. At that time sales were approximately $5 million.
> —Scarborough Foods, Inc., acquired by ConCom in January 1986. Mountain Gourmet assigned to Specialty Foods Division in mid-1986. Scarborough management has gradually been reassigned and/or phased out by ConCom throughout the past year.

"So now we've got a group product manager who came from Scarborough and that's about it," interjected Ed.

"Yes, for the marketing people," replied Madeline. "But there are all the same Scarborough people in manufacturing and sourcing. In fact, I've gotten the impression that a lot of them are the same people who came from Mountain Gourmet. I know Scarborough kept the same factories and didn't change the product lines."

"Scarborough was big on keeping things the same," said Ed, swiveling his chair so he could look out the window. "That's why they ended up being acquired by ConCom," he said to the window. "They had turned into a sitting duck." He turned back around. "However, that's not our focus for the day. Please go on."

Madeline resumed.

PRODUCT LINES

—Maple products: syrup, sugar, candies
—Apple products: apple butter, jelly, home-style sauce, dried apples, pasteurized cider
—Jams and jellies: raspberry, blackberry, wild strawberry
—Cheddar cheese
—Crackers: oyster crackers, water biscuits

Most of these products are processed dry groceries. However, the Cheddar cheese requires special handling, including temperature control and careful attention to expiration dates. Most of it is prepackaged in foil wrapping but it is also available in ten-pound wheels.

The pasteurized cider must be refrigerated, though it does have a longer shelf life than unpasteurized apple cider. It is packaged in clear plastic beverage containers.

DISTRIBUTION

Mountain Gourmet products are available throughout the United States with the most extensive distribution on the East Coast.

The Mountain Gourmet name had become identified with high quality and retained its nonconventional image even after the acquisition by Scarborough. Products are sold primarily in small specialty food/gourmet shops, including those specializing in cheeses, where the wheels of Cheddar have provided an entrée. But the "honest Vermonter" image has been helpful in giving Mountain Gourmet a strong position in certain sophisticated, upscale outlets including Bloomingdale's and Balducci's on the East Coast and in many gourmet greengrocers on the West Coast.

On the other hand, its maple products, which are marketed at a very competitive price, have given Mountain Gourmet a strong position in several specialty food chains and larger mail-order houses.

SALES STRUCTURE

Historically, Mountain Gourmet's cooperative members were interested in growing and processing food and not in distributing or selling it. Consequently, early on Mountain Gourmet entered into a relationship with a large specialty food distributor, Marvin Gross Foods, Inc. This company, headquartered in Hoboken, New Jersey, is one of the oldest and largest specialty food distributors. With annual sales of about $10 million, Mountain Gourmet is one of Gross Foods' major clients.

"And that explains why Marvin himself will be representing his company at our meeting today," said Ed, as Madeline came to the end of her report.

"Quickly followed by the person advertised as Marvin's number one competitor," added Madeline, tidying the papers in front of her. "The other oldest and largest specialty food distributor: Henri Margolis, founder and president of Margolis Specialty Products, Inc. Shall we move right along to the products Mr. Margolis handles? I've got the report right here."

"There's obviously no stopping you this morning," Ed acknowledged, taking a copy of the next report and leaning back in his desk chair as Madeline resumed.

Good Taste, Ltd.

HISTORY

Good Taste, Ltd., is a British corporation that was acquired by Consolidated Commodities during the 1960s. Its sales in Britain, now under the management of the ConCom International Division, totaled approximately $25 million last year.

In 1984, when Dry Groceries began investigation of the specialty foods business, it arranged with the International Division to import certain Good Taste products into the United States on a trial basis. These products were to be sold to specialty food retailers. Because Dry Groceries did not have experience selling through this channel, products were assigned to Margolis Specialty Products, Inc., a large and well-established specialty food importer and broker located in Rheems, Pennsylvania.

PRODUCT LINE

The entire Good Taste line is as follows:
—Jams and jellies: 20 varieties, including seasonal
—Biscuits (cookies): 10 varieties
—Teas, bags and loose teas: 6 varieties
—Savories: mustard (3 varieties), anchovy paste, chutneys (3 varieties)
—Cheeses: Double Gloucester, Stilton, others on a seasonal basis

All the products are nonperishable except the cheeses, which are available solely in bulk for distribution through cheese shops or retailers with fresh cheese departments.

At this time, only the jams and jellies have been introduced into the United States.

DISTRIBUTION

Good Taste is a very prestigious line in Great Britain, with flagship distribution in Harrods and London specialty shops. However, the line is also carried by smaller retailers throughout England, Scotland, Ireland, and Wales. Traditionally, only one retailer carries the products in a given geographic territory.

Distribution to date in the United States has been upscale. Margolis has excellent contacts in the major department store chains and has obtained distribution in Bloomingdale's, Macy's, Neiman-Marcus, and high-end regional department stores with large food sections.

SALES STRUCTURE

Margolis Specialty Products, Inc., has retained complete responsibility for importing, selling, and distributing the Good Taste products to date. Currently, this distributor *reports into the Specialty Foods Division through Billy Burke, Specialty Foods sales coordinator.*

"And that's Good Taste," Ed said, as he put the last part of the report down thoughtfully. "These reports are very informative, Madeline. To be perfectly honest, I'm not sure I'd ever heard the whole history of all of these things."

"I'm glad I could be of help," said Madeline sweetly, "but I'm afraid we're not quite through."

"Please, Madeline, this is no time for jokes," Ed said sternly. "Stewart Spencer and Billy Burke are scheduled to arrive in about ten minutes."

"It's Billy's baby we've got to talk about," rejoined Madeline.

"Of course, how could I forget? My favorite little tidbit in the Specialty Foods smorgasbord—Billy's Salsa."

"You're inspiring confidence again, Ed," said Madeline, nodding. "There's not much to review. Just take a look at the last page of my report."

Ed took the paper Madeline handed him. "I'll read this one to myself, thanks. Go out and see what happened to the coffee and doughnuts the dining room was supposed to send up for this meeting, will you? I can tell I'm going to need fortification." Before Madeline could question the appropriateness of her errand, he turned back to the window and began reading.

Salsa! Salsa! Salsa!

Salsa! Salsa! Salsa! was developed and marketed in 1985. It is a traditional home-style salsa like that first used in Mexican, Tex-Mex, and Caribbean Creole cooking. The ingredients include tomatoes, onions, various peppers, garlic, and citrus juices.

The original product was distributed by the Food Service Division throughout the Southwest and in parts of Florida and New York that had large Caribbean populations. It was used both by ethnic restaurants and by several large regional chains, which offered it in their "condiment bars."

Many customers in these restaurants asked if the salsa

> could be made available for them to take home. Salesmen from the Food Service Division reported these requests and they came to the attention of Billy Burke, who was then chairman of an interdivision Sales Task Force.
>
> Working with the same Dry Groceries group that was investigating marketing specialty foods (Italiano and Mountain Gourmet products in particular), Mr. Burke almost single-handedly developed a product that could be sold through traditional retail outlets.
>
> After the product was developed and was extremely well-received in consumer tests, no appropriate means of distributing the product could be identified. Again working on his own, Mr. Burke set up a relationship with a distributor in Texas who now handles the product throughout the Southwest.
>
> In its first year of distribution, 250,000 one-pint containers of the product were sold at $1.98 retail. ConCom continues to manufacture this product through the Food Service Division at a cost of about $.10 per pint. Fully allocated cost including retail packaging is $.25 a pint, and ConCom sells the product to the distributor for $.80. He in turn has been selling the product for $1.30 wholesale.
>
> In December 1986, the product was assigned to the Specialty Foods Division.

The best news about this product is that we don't have this small-time operator from Texas coming in for a meeting today, too, thought Ed. Although it was my own idea to take a look at all these characters in the flesh.

Ed opened his desk drawer that doubled as a file cabinet and took out a thick folder labeled SPECIALTY FOODS SALES OPERATIONS. He found himself thinking wistfully of how simple the Dry Groceries sales operations were in comparison. The key to Dry Groceries wasn't in any file. It was just one person: Stewart Spencer. As U.S. sales manager, Stewart was on top of everything, could answer any question, knew every salesman. A superb sales manager. Oh, to have a Stewart in Specialty Foods.

Of course, Specialty Foods didn't generate enough business to pay Spencer's salary, much less his bonus, his travel expenses, and the salaries of all those busy salesmen Spencer directed flawlessly. But under Ed's leadership, all that was going to change. Specialty Foods would move from its frail and confused infancy through a robust and well-focused childhood into a $100 million-a-year manhood. And top management expected it all by last week, he thought ruefully.

The step to take now was to consolidate the sales efforts, to choose a structure for selling that would reduce expenses, eliminate overlapping responsibilities, and correct the fragmentation plaguing Specialty Foods. The costs of selling each product today were all here in the bulky folder. Madeline had given him the historical perspective he needed. Now he'd take a look at the players and their proposals. He pressed the buzzer on his desk and heard Ellie's "yessir."

"I'm ready," Ed said firmly. "When those sales mavens show up, send them right in. And tell Madeline that if necessary she should go down and get the coffee herself. When she says it's not in her job description, tell her I said that she should keep in mind that we've got an enormous amount of material to go over here."

During the next six hours, Ed met with one of the salespeople after another. By 4:30 that afternoon when the last salesman had finished the last presentation, Ed felt as if he could be sure of only one thing: every one of them could sell. Each option had sounded very good as it was presented by its creator. But now he had to choose among them.

However, this choice clearly required a fresh start. Ed decided to clear off his desk, sort through the pink telephone slips Ellie had given him, and make a decision tomorrow.

By 10:00 A.M. the next day, Ed was ready to tackle the Specialty Foods selling issues. He asked Ellie to hold all calls, took out his now even thicker file on selling, and started piecing it all together.

The first option he had was to set up a Specialty Foods sales force. At yesterday's meeting, Spencer Stewart had made it quite clear that he didn't think Dry Groceries could handle the kind of selling Specialty Foods required. He'd backed up his thoughts with a description he and Billy Burke had put together of how they saw the selling tasks differing. Ed took this out and read through it.

GROCERY CHAINS

—Big, buy in large quantities, focus on discount prices and special deals for the trade.

—Sophisticated about accepting and declining products: daily inventory and sales information mean they know how everything is moving.

—Consequently not very loyal to individual products or lines but over time can develop loyalty/personal relationship with salesman.

—Fairly homogeneous group—more similarities among chains across the country than differences.

SPECIALITY FOOD RETAILERS

—Very fragmented group—lots of different types of stores. Different retailers have different needs. Department store buyer vs. local cheese shop, e.g.

—Generally small. Even a big operation is small compared to a supermarket chain.

—Individualized approach to running the business. Often seat-of-the-pants or relatively unsophisticated management. May rely on salesman for help and advice on a variety of business issues.

—Small retailers are constantly evolving and changing based on what their consumers want. Therefore, also not very loyal to individual products or lines. May be on cutting edge as far as what they sell so may be more interested in new products, quicker to drop old products.

—In some ways less price-conscious because they don't expect volume discounts and deals. But more price-conscious in other ways because relatively small volume doesn't leave as much margin for error.

OTHER CONSIDERATIONS

—There is the potential for Specialty Foods and Dry

> Groceries product sales to overlap. The biggest example is Italiano: this product is under Specialty Foods but most volume is through grocery chains. Looking at other Dry Groceries products, some may be attractive to specialty food dealers. This needs to be examined.
> —On the other hand, specialty food retailers may not want to carry products carried by big grocery chains because chains can undercut their prices due to lower overhead. This could be a problem, particularly for Italiano.

"I know you have a lot of respect for my sales force," Spencer had concluded, "and we've done a good job filling the gaps so far, but obviously we can't give you what you need long-term."

"So Spencer and I worked up a plan for a Specialty Foods Sales Force," Billy had added. "Spencer would help us recruit and train the salesmen; we even have his permission to hire some of his people."

Ed took out Billy's proposal.

> **In-House Sales Force**
> —65 salesmen covering 50 states with concentration in major metropolitan areas, especially on East and West coasts.
> —Average compensation $30,000 plus 30 percent in benefits, or $39,000 each.
> —Travel and related expenses range from $5,000 for local salesmen (75 percent of sales force) to $15,000 for those with geographically dispersed territories (25 percent of sales force). Average expenses per salesman are $7,500.
> —Sales support is relatively high due to start-up nature (heavy training, close supervision, etc.): 6 supervisors at $65,000 salary and benefits; $15,000 travel and related expenses each. Plus national sales manager at $104,000 salary and benefits, $20,000 travel and related. Total $604,000.
> —ConCom charges (administrative, burden, etc.) estimated at 10 percent of total budget.

> —Total cost: 65 salesmen × ($39,000 salary + $7,500 expenses) = $3,022,500
> 6 supervisors × ($65,000 salary + $15,000 expenses) = $480,000
> 1 national sales manager × ($104,000 salary + $20,000 expenses) = $124,000
> Overhead (at 10%) = $362,650
> Total, all expenses $3,989,150

Ed turned to the page of notes he'd made while Billy and Stewart were talking. This sales force was designed to handle the total projected Specialty Foods volume of $50 million annually. The fact that Specialty Foods sales were not yet up to this level meant that there would be time to build the sales force up gradually. Since Spencer had offered some of his people, there would also be an opportunity to transfer the contacts and skills that were needed to keep selling the Italiano line. On the other hand, Specialty Foods would not be starting out with anybody who had sold firsthand to the specialty foods retailers. There was only Billy, and he'd only provided "coordination."

Ed put his notes down and thought about the person into whose hands he'd be putting the complete sales effort. Billy was around the same age as Stewart Spencer, but while Stewart had ended up as national sales manager, Billy was the guy who'd never quite made it to the top. He'd spent a long time as southern region manager for Dry Groceries, though Ed remembered that he'd also worked outside the southern region for quite a while. Throughout all, Billy had retained what could tactfully be called his "regionalism." Stewart was more sophisticated, a man of the world, while Billy was a good ole boy.

At one point, Ed thought, Stewart and Billy had probably been in head-to-head competition on the sales ladder. Now that Stewart had won, he seemed to be trying to figure out what to do with Billy. High-level staff jobs apparently had been Stewart's solution. So when the opportunity came to move Billy out of his division, no wonder Stewart had jumped at it. And Ed, who knew very little about specialty foods at all, was happy to get what expertise Billy had, even if it was limited.

Now Ed probably had Billy for good. With Billy's seniority and personal contacts in the corporation, Ed wouldn't have a chance of getting anyone else as Specialty Foods sales manager.

Ed rubbed his temples as he thought more about Billy. He'd always known Billy wasn't the manager Spencer was. But after yesterday he wasn't happy with Billy for another reason. Ed had asked Billy to fill him in on the Salsa! product and Billy had described how his major coup was setting up his brother-in-law to handle all the distribution. Obviously the brother-in-law was doing a good job. He'd sold over $300,000 worth of Salsa! last year. But he'd probably made close to $100,000 on the sales. That was a lot of money between brothers-in-law, and apparently it didn't bother Billy in the least.

Well, the sales force prospect looked reasonable from a numbers point of view and he could work on Billy's ethics while Spencer helped Billy on the sales front. Ed decided that he'd keep his proposal as an option while he reviewed the other possibilities.

He took the next set of papers out of the file folder. On top was a nicely bound report titled "Specialty Foods and Marvin Gross Products, Inc.: A Partnership for the Year 2000." Now here, thought Ed, was the answer to *everything:* importing, warehousing, distribution, sales, PR. Marvin Gross had made it crystal clear that he could and would do everything Ed needed, wanted, or could dream up over the next decade.

Ed started thinking back about his meetings with Mr. Gross, which had been followed immediately by a meeting with Mr. Margolis. Ed felt the headache he'd developed during the meetings threatening to return. Scheduling the two men back to back had definitely been a mistake. He'd been careful not to have them run into each other, but it had been an unnecessary precaution. Each man had said almost at once that he knew the other was coming. Small world, specialty foods.

Physically and in terms of background, two men couldn't be more dissimilar. Marvin Gross had grown up in Queens, New York, was a high school dropout. He'd started off working in his father's neighborhood grocery store. One thing had led to another and now he lived in a mammoth estate in Upper Saddle River, New Jersey, and ran a mammoth company that imported, warehoused, distributed, and sold about half the gourmet products available in the United States.

Henri Margolis, on the other hand, had immigrated from France to the United States to attend Harvard Business School. Once in Boston, he had spent more time eating than studying. When he threatened to abandon his MBA and enroll in the Culinary Institute of America to become a chef, his father had bought out a New York food-importing business for Henri to run in a compromise move. Once he had the business, Henri had gone at it with a vengeance and now ran a mammoth company that imported, warehoused, distributed, and sold the *other* half of the gourmet products available in the United States.

Despite the differences in their backgrounds, however, the two men now had companies that were very similar. After both meetings, Ed had concluded that there was no real difference in what they could offer Specialty Foods. Gross had a long working relationship with ConCom. In fact, he was probably making about $1 million a year in fees for his services, which covered complete sales and distribution for the Mountain Gourmet line. Margolis, on the other hand, only had a small piece of the action. He was handling the Good Taste experiment, which was only generating about $500,000 in total sales per year, for commissions of about $100,000.

Probably either company could do equally well in the long run for Specialty Foods. But Gross would hit the deck running, while Margolis would need more time to handle the sheer increase in physical product that would pass through his company. Ed decided that although Henri had been more charming and urbane, the focus here should be on business expertise, not social skills. At least for the time being, Marvin's company was his first choice.

Ed opened Marvin's report. The first page was titled "What Marvin Gross Foods, Inc., can offer Specialty Foods."

Marvin Gross Foods, Inc., is a full-service specialty foods company. As one of the biggest corporations in our field, we sold over $250 million worth of fine foods and related goods last year. Our products range from triple-crème cheeses produced by a tiny California farmer to high-volume maple syrups produced by one of the oldest specialty food co-ops in the nation. The retailers we serve vary from the only gourmet food shop in Fort Dodge, Iowa, to the gourmet food buyer for the biggest grocery-store chain in the Pacific Northwest.

The Marvin Gross client and the Marvin Gross customer both benefit from our full-service approach. For clients, we import products if required, provide full warehousing and distribution services, and handle all sales and sales support functions through our 200-person sales force. For customers, this sales force is the key: salesmen are highly trained, generally have been with Marvin Gross for many years, and can help customers not only with reviewing and ordering products, but also with inventory management problems, product mix issues, and even short-term working-capital crises, through our variable payment terms policies.

How would Marvin Gross best be able to adapt our special skills to meet Specialty Foods' special needs? Taking a broad perspective over the entire product line you now have or have the ability to market, here's what we could do for you.

—Sales. What Specialty Foods needs most is a consolidated sales effort that can reach its target customer: the true specialty food retailer. Marvin Gross has worked with these retailers for many years and has grown with the industry. Our well-established and trusting relationships can smooth the way for Specialty Foods' entry into these outlets. And we can make sure that once Specialty Foods gains distribution, it keeps distribution, because we know exactly what these retailers need and how to provide it.

> —Distribution. Specialty food retailers have very special distribution needs. The average store, while relatively small in square feet, carries an enormous range of products. This variety can't be backed up by the retailer alone, however. Most retailers have limited storage space and tight working capital budgets. Therefore, retailers have come to rely on the distributor to ship odd lots and mixed packages and to provide quick turn-around on orders. This is the opposite of the kind of distribution that is a strength of a large company like ConCom.

Ed stopped reading for a moment. Marvin certainly had a point here. Which ConCom logistics specialist would be responsible for sending out twelve jars of jam split between strawberry, blueberry, and kiwi when he'd spent his career thinking in terms of boxcars full?

> —Warehousing. Closely related to distribution needs are warehousing needs. Gourmet food products are quite varied in their warehousing needs: some require refrigeration, some require dry storage, others have no special requirements. Marvin Gross has the capacity to provide these different types of storage across the country. Our regional warehousing means that products can be provided to retailers quickly and in peak condition, regardless of what kind of warehousing they require.
> —Importing. Although an organization like ConCom has an extensive importing network, its sheer size and economies of scale render it less than ideal for importing specialty food items. The Good Taste line, for example, consists of forty-three separate items plus cheeses. High-volume importation of these products, whose individual sales potential has yet to be proven, could result in problems for the British producer as well as for the American warehouser and distributor. Marvin Gross has the ability

> to import these products in coordination with other European goods, thus making it economically attractive to import more appropriate-sized quantities. Also, by locating importing in the same organization as selling, it will be possible to monitor and update demand efficiently, and, long term, very economically.

Ed put the Marvin Gross report down on his desk and got up to stretch his legs. He didn't need to consult his notes to recall the next part of the conversation with Marvin. He'd asked Marvin how much these wonderful services would cost Specialty Foods and Marvin had not hesitated for a second: "14 percent and it's a bargain."

It probably was a bargain, Ed thought, as he walked slowly up and down his office. The Foster, Weinstein report had said that the usual fees charged by distributors were around 20 percent of sales and that importers added up to another 5 percent. He'd also found in the background material Madeline had left him on Mountain Gourmet that Marvin's company had been making 18 percent on that line for years.

He sat down in the chair Marvin had occupied the day before and thought about what else he'd said.

"I didn't come to nickel and dime you," Marvin had added. "I thought about handling $50 million worth of Specialty Foods products and worked out all the economies of scale I could pass on to you. Besides, as you undoubtedly realize, it would be a PR dream for us to work out a deal with you. What credibility! What feature articles! Sure, I'd be making money. That's why I'm in business. But you'd be making money, too."

Ed got up and walked back to his desk. Marvin Gross Foods would hit the deck flying. But when all systems were go, its momentum would be costing Specialty Foods $7 million a year. There was one more set of numbers he ought to take a look at before he moved on from the Marvin Gross proposal. Ed opened his file folder and took out a memo he'd had Billy bring in with him the day before.

Warehousing and Distribution Costs
Dry Groceries Products 1985–86

	$000	% of sales
Total sales, dry groceries	1,592,992	n.a.
Fully allocated warehousing costs	11,948	0.75
Fully allocated distribution costs	34,249	2.15

Estimated Importation Costs
International Foods Division 1985–86

	$000	% of sales
Finished goods imported into U.S.	1,229	n.a.
Fully allocated importing charges	13	1.00

For Dry Groceries, warehousing was running less than 1 percent of sales, about .75 percent. Distribution was a lot more: 2.15 percent. So if total Specialty Foods sales were $50 million, these two charges could add up to 2.9 percent or $1,450,000 a year.

Importing was less predictable. These numbers looked like 1 percent of sales, but right now there probably weren't many economies of scale being realized. Still, there was no way to get a better number for now. If Good Taste sales were $10 million out of the $50 million, importing charges would be about $100,000. Peanuts, really . . . if the numbers were accurate, of course. Even if charges were twice as much, though, Ed reasoned, this would still be only $200,000. Still peanuts.

So to provide all the Gross services in-house would result in considerable cost savings over Marvin's best number: $3,989,150 for sales; $1,550,000 for everything else, for a total of $5,539,150, or a savings of $1,460,850. That was the equivalent of 2.9 percent of sales, if sales were $50 million.

If sales were $50 million. There was a real possibility that Marvin was right on at least some of his points. How long, realistically, would it take Specialty Foods to develop the expertise in selling, warehousing, and shipping to get sales up to the $50 million mark?

Would it happen faster—maybe even much faster—with the help of Marvin Gross?

Ed decided to look at the cost comparison one more way, from the point of view of a break-even point. How much extra money in sales would Marvin Gross have to bring in to make up for the extra expense he would be to the division?

Very roughly speaking, every $1.00 of product that Specialty Foods sold cost about $.60 to make. About $.03 more went to shipping and warehousing. That meant that for every $1.00 of sales, there was $.37 of profit contribution. This could go toward offsetting Gross' charges or to meet overhead expenses for the whole division or to pay for advertising: for anything, really.

The extra cost of using Gross was $1,460,850. At $.37 on the dollar, Specialty Foods would have to sell $3,948,243 more to offset his extra expense. This was almost $4 million, or 8 percent of the sales target. Was it realistic to think that Marvin could generate an extra 8 percent of volume? Ed sighed. He'd have to be honest with himself: he didn't know and couldn't think of any way to be certain. This was going to be a judgment call, but it did help to use the numbers to test the basic feasibility of the options.

Of course, there was one more option he should think through. This would be to give some extra support to an in-house sales effort. This would cost money, too, though undoubtedly not as much. Ed laid aside the notes he had just made and took a neatly printed light-gray brochure out of his file folder.

"Sarah Spotsworth and Partners: Specialty Food Sales Consultants" was italicized across the front of the brochure in blue ink. All in all, Ed mused, this brochure was very nice, very professional, but more interesting than most things of this type he ran into. Rather like Sarah. She had definitely been the high point of his meetings the day before.

Ed opened the brochure and reread Sarah's biographical note. "Principal, Sarah Spotsworth and Partners, 1975 to present." This made her practically a pioneer in the specialty foods areas. "MBA, Stanford University; B.A., Italian, Scripps College." Well-educated and intelligent—though that had been clear in the course of their discussion. She had told him how she'd gotten interested in gourmet foods when she spent her junior year abroad studying Italian and had gotten her MBA so she could learn how to turn her interest into a paying business proposition.

Ed squinted his eyes at the very small picture of a very professional-looking Sarah that accompanied her biography. Her fantastic good looks didn't show in that picture. Just as well for her, probably. In fact, the day before, Ed had been highly distracted when Ellie showed her into his office: the archetypal California blonde, deep tan, a figure that demanded a bikini. But a mature woman of thirty-five—maybe even more?

Well, Ed reminded himself, what he was thinking of now was her professional credentials and expertise. Sarah was the independent broker who had been handling the gourmet extensions of the Italiano line. She had done very well in obtaining placements and had played a part in expanding the line to the nontomato products. They had talked about her experience with Italiano over lunch the day before, but the more interesting part of the conversation had been when Sarah described other services her company offered in addition to acting as brokers.

"I would be doing both of us a disservice if I told you that my company could sell your whole line," Sarah had said over dessert. "Brokering is the bread and butter of our operation but what I like to do most is consulting. From what you're telling me about Specialty Foods, I think that I could offer you some consulting services that would be invaluable in setting up a well-coordinated sales and marketing effort for all these different products."

Ed thought about the services she had gone on to suggest might be helpful: help with sales recruiting and training, consultation on volume and product planning, help to Ed in developing a better understanding of the needs of each set of consumers Specialty Foods would need to deal with. The more Ed thought about it, the more it sounded like Sarah would be an invaluable asset if he decided to go the in-house route.

He turned over the gray brochure and looked at the notes he'd made on the back. Compared to the kind of fees big consulting companies like McKinsey charged, her rates were very modest: $1,000 a day plus expenses for Sarah, with rates for the other consultants going down from there. She had mentioned a new associate the company had recently hired who had an extensive background in sales training and who was being billed out at $400 a day. McKinsey didn't even walk in the door without a team of four people who added up to $3,000 a day. Even adding in plane fares from the West Coast, Sarah still looked like a good bargain.

Wait a minute, Ed, Ed thought to himself, leaning back in his chair. Are you sure you're not guilty here of either trying to pass the buck because you don't know what you're doing or trying to make a pass at Sarah because she's so damned attractive and lively? His uncertainty could cost Specialty Foods as much as $75,000 or $80,000.

But if he could go to the in-house sales function and save $1.5 million over Marvin Gross' charges, and if he could set up something very good that would keep him from having to make a commitment to Gross or his competitors for years to come, spending the extra money on Sarah's services could be easily justified.

So it all boiled down to three choices, Ed concluded. First was Billy Burke to build up a sales force plus a lot of work to get the warehousing and distribution system to fit with the division's needs. Second was the same setup with Sarah as a consultant to alert them to the pitfalls and problems they were likely to encounter. And third was what would be more of a sure thing in the immediate future but a financial burden for years to come: a commitment to the Marvin Gross organization.

Indicate your choice here:

_____ Option 1. Set up an in-house sales force without outside consulting support.
_____ Option 2. Set up an in-house sales force with consulting support from Sarah Spotsworth.
_____ Option 3. Contract for all sales, warehousing, importing, and distribution with Marvin Gross.

5

Establishing a Transfer Price for Salsa!

May 12, 1987

Ed Cunningham sat, temporarily speechless, in an armchair beside his conference table as Arnie Clowder, his counterpart from Food Services, stormed back and forth across the room.

"For Christ's sake," Arnie shouted, "it's only a lousy nickel. What kind of a cheapskate are you, Cunningham, to make such a big rotten stink about a crummy nickel? Ever since you moved up to this fancy job with this fancy office"—he waved angrily at a painting behind Ed—"you've forgotten your old friends. I knew you when, buddy"—at this he stopped dead in front of Ed and glared into his face—"and you would have given old Arnie a nickel then, by God."

As Arnie towered over him, Ed noticed with a kind of bizarre detachment that sweat had broken out across Arnie's shiny forehead and that his hair looked slightly askew. Arnie's eyes were bloodshot and his eyelids looked puffy and inflamed. Suddenly Ed knew that Arnie was in some kind of trouble and that the screaming and yelling in his office had a lot less to do with the cost of tomatoes than with whatever else Arnie's problems were.

"I'm sorry you feel that way, Arnie," said Ed evenly. If he could just get Arnie to sit down and stop yelling maybe he could figure out what was wrong. "I'm not completely opposed to your idea. If we could talk about it more—"

"What's there to talk about?" Arnie said, even more loudly. "I want that nickel. I need that nickel." He was shouting right into Ed's face. "And you're going to give it to me!"

Arnie began reaching toward Ed to hit him or grab his shoulders or do something. With a quick duck under Arnie's raised arms, Ed was out of his chair and headed for a safe spot behind his desk. Even as he escaped the chair, however, Bart Small, Arnie's administrative assistant, had left his uneasy position standing against the door jamb and dashed across the room. Now Bart had his arms around Arnie, restraining him. Arnie fought him off roughly, then slumped into the chair Ed had just vacated.

"All right, all right," he said harshly, shoving Bart away from him. "Get your hands off me, you young upstart. I can make my own way here. I can handle myself."

Bart backed off but stood poised to one side of Arnie. Arnie seemed to decide to ignore his waiting there and turned his vituperation back to Ed.

"I've been making this stuff for you, practically giving it to you, because I felt sorry for you," he spit out. "Starting up a new division, starting all over like some thirty year old."

He stopped, then continued in a disgusted tone. "And that has-been Billy Burke, he wanted it bad. He thought it was his last chance to make his tiny little mark on this company. I sell the damned stuff in five-gallon containers, for Christ's sake, but I started putting it into these dinky little pints for you. Oh, we get ten cents for it, but if it weren't for my loyalty, Food Services wouldn't even bother!" Arnie looked at Ed challengingly.

"Arnie, I appreciate what your division has been doing for us," Ed said, deciding to try a conciliatory tone. "Salsa! may not account for a lot of our dollar volume yet, but it plays an important role in the division."

"You're damned right it does!" said Arnie, somewhat irrationally. His voice had dropped a little and he was shaking his head slightly, like someone who'd just gotten up from a bad fall.

"And I'd be more than happy to sit down with you and go over all the numbers in detail—"

Suddenly Arnie reared up out of the chair. "Like hell you're going to go through all those numbers!" His voice rose. "Those are private information in my division and I'm not giving them to you without a fight!"

For a moment, Ed, who was now standing behind his desk, thought Arnie was going to cross the room and go for him again. But suddenly, for no discernible reason, Arnie seemed to have had enough.

"You'll be hearing from me!" he shouted. "Old buddy!" he added, with heavy sarcasm. He turned and lumbered toward the door. "And you'd better listen"—he paused heavily—"or some other people at Consolidated Commodities will be hearing about your attitude," he threw back over his shoulder.

As Arnie lurched out into the hall, Bart Small followed. At the door, Bart turned back and mouthed to Ed, "I'll call you." Then they were both gone.

Ed dropped down into his desk chair. And who said managers' jobs were dull? He'd been at ConCom for twenty years and he'd known Arnie for nineteen of those twenty. But who would have ever expected such a violent scene as that which had just transpired? And over a nickel increase in the internal transfer price of a product! It was unbelievable.

Ed picked up the sheet of paper that Arnie had put on his desk when he and Bart had first come into the room. He'd even put down the paper in a challenging way, Ed realized. Ed's first unconscious attempt to defuse the tension had been to step from behind his desk and invite Arnie to join him at the conference table where they could talk more informally.

The paper was a one-page memo. Probably it said the same thing Arnie had just talked about, but maybe there was more information that could help Ed understand what was going on.

Memorandum
To: *Ed Cunningham, President, Specialty Foods*
From: *Arnie Clowder, President, Food Services*
Re: *Transfer price for Salsa! Salsa! Salsa!*

Effective immediately, the base manufacturing price at which the Food Services Division provides Salsa! Salsa! Salsa! to

> Specialty Foods in containers suitable for retail sale shall increase from $.10 per pint to $.15 per pint.
>
> In addition, the overhead allocation for the product shall also increase, from $.15 to $.25. Consequently, the fully allocated transfer price (base manufacturing cost plus overhead allocation) will now be $.40, up from $.25.
>
> These increases reflect higher costs of raw materials and higher production costs.

Ed put the paper down impatiently. This memo said absolutely nothing. No wonder Arnie had brought it over himself. If he had simply sent it through interoffice mail, Ed would have turned up immediately in *his* office.

Ed picked up the memo again, crumpled it into a ball, and threw it into his wastepaper basket. Really, he thought to himself, this was completely absurd. Suddenly one division president jacks up the price of what he's selling to another division president without a word of real explanation and expects the poor victim to pay up without saying a word. Furthermore, Arnie was trying to pull a fast one with his storming on about a nickel when really he was talking about charging Specialty Foods an additional $.15. This amounted to a 60 percent increase in the internal price of the product. Ridiculous!

And what was Ed supposed to do? Go straight out and double the price he charged to the wholesalers he sold to? This was not the way things got decided in a company like ConCom, and Arnie was in as good a position to know that as Ed was.

Ed stood up and walked toward his door. He'd go down the hall, get a cup of coffee, maybe talk to Grady Jennings about how the Mets looked for the season. Anything to take his mind off the scene he'd just been an unwilling part of. Then later he'd figure out how he was going to address this little problem.

Just as he got to the door, the phone rang. Ed thought briefly of just letting it go. Ellie Vogel would pick it up and take a message. Oh, the hell with it! he thought with annoyance, and turned back to pick up the phone himself.

"Hello, Ed?" said a slightly unfamiliar voice. "It's Bart Small.

Arnie Clowder's assistant. I thought maybe I could shed some light on what just happened in your office. Do you have a few minutes?"

I can understand this craziness in a few minutes? Ed thought, but aloud he said, "Sure. Thanks for calling." He walked around his desk and sat back down, ready for a long story.

"Let me tell you the business situation first, as it relates to Specialty Foods," said Bart. "Although even that has its complicated elements." He sighed. "After that part, I was hoping I could tell you some more of what's going on and maybe you could help me figure it all out."

"I'll try," said Ed. He swiveled his chair around so he could look out of the window at the spring vista the view provided. The beautiful scene outside would be a good balance to whatever strange tale Bart was about to tell.

"Okay," Bart began. "Let's start with the easy part, the $.05 increase in the basic manufacturing cost of Salsa! Of the $.25 per pint Specialty Foods paid Food Services, $.10 was to cover the cost of producing the basic product. Now this will go up to $.15. There are two key components to the $.05 increase. First of all, there are general inflationary price pressures on the raw materials we use, the tomatoes, onions, peppers, and also on the chemicals, you know, the preservatives, coloring agents, and so on. I'd guess this accounts for $.03 of the increase."

"That makes sense so far," said Ed. "It sounds very high, especially in this economy, but at least I understand what you're talking about. Now what about the other $.02?"

"Well, the $.02 can be accounted for by a seasonal increase in the fresh ingredients."

"Wait a minute," Ed interrupted. "A seasonal increase in May? I mean, if you'd told me in December or January that it was going to cost more to buy fresh vegetables I'd have understood what you were talking about. But this is *spring*. They're harvesting tomatoes in the Rio Grande valley and in California. Why an increase now?"

"I know it sounds unlikely," said Arnie patiently, "but it's real, I can promise you that. What most people don't realize about Salsa! is that one of the major ingredients of the product is citrus juices, mostly lemon and lime juice. That's what gives it that sort of soft consistency and the tart flavor. After the severe frosts they had in central Florida early in the winter, the supply of lemons and limes has been seriously reduced. We didn't have to make price adjustments earlier because ConCom's central purchasing office had made a good investment in juice futures to cover exactly this problem. But they didn't buy out quite far enough, and now we're running up against the shortage that lots of other suppliers have been dealing with for months."

"I see," said Ed resignedly. "All right. That's Arnie's nickel. Now what about the additional $.10 increase that is showing up under the 'fully allocated transfer price' heading?"

"That's where it starts to get a little complicated," said Bart. "But I'll tell you about that as best I can."

"It's your call, Bart," Ed replied. "I'm starting from ground zero here and the memo Arnie left on my desk didn't help a bit."

"Oh, the memo." From Bart's tone, Ed knew he hadn't thought much of Arnie's approach either. "You're right, it didn't say much. But I can do a little better.

"First of all, keep in mind that the $.10—soon to be $.15—we've just been talking about as 'manufacturing cost' has only covered the cost of raw materials and of preparing them. The additional $.15—soon to be $.25—that we've called the 'fully allocated cost' includes not only costs that are allocated back, like various types of manufacturing overhead, but also the other costs involved in getting the bulk product into the wholesalers' hands.

"Let's see," Bart said. Ed heard the crinkle of papers as he apparently went through his notes. "Of the $.15 of overhead allocation, a nickel was for the packaging materials: the semi-rigid container, the cover, and the labels that are pasted on. Another $.01 was for getting the stuff into the package; $.03 was for shipping. I know that shipping cost sounds high relative to everything else, but we're talking about a refrigerated product and that accounts for the cost. That leaves $.06. That was for manufacturing overhead: supervision, depreciation, other divisional expenses. Really, both direct and indirect manufacturing overhead, I guess you'd have to say."

"This is getting complicated," said Ed. "Just a minute. I'm going to write each thing down and compare old and new as we go along."

He laid the phone down for a minute, took Arnie's crumpled memo out of the wastepaper basket, smoothed it out, and wrote on the back.

Costs to Make Salsa!
BASIC MANUFACTURING COST
—*$.10 raw materials (vegetables, chemicals)*
—*$.05 to be added*
　—*$.03 increased raw material costs due to inflation*
　—*$.02 seasonal increases (citrus juices)*

ALLOCATED OVERHEAD
—*$.05 container*
—*$.01 packing into container*
—*$.03 shipping*
—*$.06 division manufacturing overhead*
—*$.10 to be added*
—WHAT FOR?

"Okay," Ed said, picking the phone back up. "How's this?" He read the list to Bart.

"That's right," said Bart. "Shall I give you the components of the $.10 increase next?"

"I can't wait," said Ed, with a grimace.

"Well, $.03 of it is pretty simple. An extra penny each to container purchasing, putting it into the container, and shipping."

"That's an increase of anywhere from 20 percent on the container to 100 percent on the packing," replied Ed. "I mean, it sounds simple but that seems like a lot, especially on the packing."

"I agree," Bart said, sighing again. "But I've just been over all those numbers Arnie didn't want to share with you and it really is costing us that much more to do each of those things."

"Let's let it go for a minute," said Ed wearily. "What's the other $.07 out of this dime?"

"That's less straightforward," said Bart. "Listen, are you sure you don't want me to come back over and talk about this? Maybe it's better than trying to sort it out over the phone."

"I appreciate what you're saying, Bart," said Ed, opening his calendar. "But I've got another meeting coming up. I didn't expect to see you or Arnie today, you know. You just sort of showed up."

"Yeah, I see what you mean," Bart said. "Let me just get to the point then.

"Really, the other $.07 is all increases in division overhead that Arnie wants allocated to Specialty Foods. They are not amounts that can be tied directly to your products. It's just a bigger share of our costs, which have been rising fairly rapidly."

"What share have we been paying so far?" asked Ed. "Was it reasonable?"

"I'd say so," Bart replied. "We originally looked at the total annual production run of Salsa! For ourselves, we make 1 million pints a year of the stuff. For you, we make an additional 250,000 pints. That's a total of 1.25 million and you get 20 percent of it, so you have been paying 20 percent of the overhead allocated to that product.

"But what Arnie came up with," Bart continued, "was a new way of looking at things. His thinking was that he could look at Food Services manufacturing as having two clients for Salsa! One is Food Services *sales* and the other is Specialty Foods. Since there are two clients and each one requires a certain amount of special packaging, types of shipments, and general administrative attention, he's proposing that the two clients split the overhead costs equally."

Bart continued, after a thoughtful pause. "That adds up to the whole $.07 we hadn't accounted for. Arnie was pretty sure that you'd hit the ceiling if he told you that rationale for that part of the increase. So he was trying to put it all together and focus on the raw material and specific manufacturing cost increases instead. I guess that's how he got stuck on the nickel. He really wanted you to think about that instead of getting into why allocated overhead was going up so much."

Ed sat for a moment without replying. His thoughts were whirling. Three cents here, seven cents there, stick them all together.

This he could follow in a way. But the whole business about two clients and half the overhead. And the cost of putting the product into the containers going up 100 percent. They were getting into the realm of funny money here and Arnie was obviously trying to do something that he knew Ed wouldn't think too highly of.

Then one idea came to the forefront of Ed's thinking.

"Why are you telling me all this, Bart?" he asked bluntly. "You've worked for Arnie for two years. You've been in Food Services how long?"

"Six years all together, sir," was Bart's quiet reply.

"Hmmm," Ed replied. "It is not like a seasoned ConCom employee to tell someone in another division who he hardly knows that his boss, the man he's worked for for two years, is trying to do something that the stranger isn't going to like. If anything, I've always found the people in your division unusually loyal to one another. If somebody makes a mistake, everybody else would go to amazing lengths to cover up for him, to make it come out all right, to present a united front. What's going on with you?"

"Are you sure you don't have a few minutes for me to come over there, sir?" Bart said after a long pause. "I really need to talk to you about what's happening here."

The plaintive tone of Bart's question brought to Ed's memory the vivid picture of Bart leaping across the room to restrain Arnie. He had been surprised by Bart's action. Bart was so tall and skinny, his long face rising morosely above his tight white collar and polyester jacket. He didn't look like a man who'd jump into a physically critical situation and yet he'd taken action. He must be worried, thought Ed. Or under a lot of pressure. He's obviously a man who is having to take steps that he finds unusual and that even run counter to his basic values and professional beliefs.

"All right," said Ed in a more kindly tone. "It sounds like there's something complicated going on here. Why don't you come by my office at the end of the day, when things have quieted down. About 5:30?"

"That would be great," said Bart, though his somber tone contrasted with his enthusiastic words. "Arnie usually leaves at 5:00 or 5:15 at the latest, so I won't have any trouble getting away."

"See you then," said Ed. He hung up the phone slowly. After a moment, he resolutely put Arnie's memo into his IN box and turned to his other work.

The day went quickly and Ed had almost forgotten about Salsa! Salsa! Salsa! when he heard a sound at the door and looked up to see Bart step in quietly. Bart appeared to glance over his shoulder, then closed the door behind him.

"Thanks for letting me come over," he said sincerely, quickly crossing the room. "Once I started talking about what was going on, I realized how much I needed to talk about it some more. I've been feeling like I was losing my mind and I didn't know what to do about it."

"Have a seat," said Ed. He'd just let Bart talk for a while and maybe he'd end up with some idea of what Arnie was up to.

Bart sat down across the desk from Ed. "I feel really bad talking about Arnie this way," he began, "but there comes a time when you've got to think it's for his own good." He ran his hands over his hair, which responded by standing straight up in back, increasing the artlessness of his appearance.

"What first tipped me off to the fact that we have a problem," he said, "was that a lot of the costs of getting things done in Food Services were going up for no particularly good reason. In your case, for example, there's the cost of packing the product. That's not a made-up increase. The pints are coming off the line slower, there are more rejects, more cracking of containers, more misaligned lids. Everything's kind of falling apart." He shifted in his chair, looking uncomfortable.

"And it wasn't just on Salsa! The canned goods that we pack for institutional sales, the little packets of condiments we sell to fast-food chains, the costs of having our salesmen travel around the country, everything, but everything was going up.

"I talked to some of the guys I know in other divisions," Bart continued, looking at Ed earnestly, "just to make sure it wasn't something to do with the corporation or the general economic picture." He paused dejectedly.

"It wasn't. . . . It was just us."

After a moment he continued. "Then I tried to figure out if there was any theme, sort of, to what was happening. If it wasn't financial, what was it? I thought and I thought. I went over all the numbers—my main job for Arnie has always been to keep the numbers straight—and I finally reached a conclusion that was pretty indisputable."

"Well?" Ed said impatiently. "What did you decide?" This was getting interesting.

Bart swallowed. "The theme—the problem—the common denominator—well, to be perfectly honest, it was Arnie." He looked down at his shoes, apparently unable to continue.

"What do you mean?" Ed said quietly, after a minute. He didn't want to scare Bart into silence but he did wonder how Bart had reached such a broad conclusion about a man who was a successful ConCom veteran.

"It was really a question of leadership, I guess," Bart finally said. "Of setting priorities and getting things done. Whenever I looked to see why things were going wrong, it was because somebody had made a decision last week or last month or even occasionally last year to take the easy way out, to let things slide.

"Whenever I found a person out on the line who was slacking off or making so many mistakes that it slowed everything else down, it turned out that person had been identified before and that nobody had done anything about him, that he was just allowed to drift along. Equipment hadn't been replaced in time, people hadn't been fired, people hadn't even been promoted or given raises.

"Do you know," Bart said, the picture of complete frustration, "that of the sixty people who are directly assigned to our division, not one single person has had a personnel review in almost two years? It's not going to be long before all the good people just leave in disgust. Then we're going to see even bigger problems."

"I see what you mean by calling it a failure of leadership," Ed replied slowly. "Have there also been cases of the kind of dramatic behavior we saw today?"

"Not really," said Bart. "Maybe what Arnie did today is what finally convinced me that my thinking about all this was right.... Although, you know, in a way this was the first time Arnie has been outside our division, has had to deal with somebody who wasn't his subordinate, in quite a while. I've noticed that he's handled more and more things with memos—usually he's asked me to put them together over his signature. And when meetings have come up where he'd have to interact with the other people at his level, he's called in sick or been out in the field that day."

Suddenly a surprised look crossed Bart's face. "There's another funny thing about the field trips! It just dawned on me," he said. "Arnie always asked me to file his expense reports for those trips, to put all the receipts together and fill out the forms. Lately, I just assumed he'd decided to start doing them himself. I haven't filed a report for months. Maybe"— he paused, his eyes opened wide in disbelief—"maybe—he hasn't been on those trips at all."

Ed looked at Bart. Bart looked back. After a long moment, Ed pushed his chair back, got up, and walked to the windows across the room. He looked out again, stalling for time. Here was a man he had known for nineteen years, a man who had been at ConCom his whole professional life, a man who was probably looking at retirement just a couple of years down the line, and this man seemed to be falling apart.

Obviously the man's problems were affecting his business judgment. And now these problems were spreading outside of Food Services. Arnie's problems, whatever they were, were threatening to affect the ability of Ed's division to sell a promising product at a competitive price.

Finally Ed turned back to Bart, who'd been sitting silently, apparently as lost in his own thoughts as Ed had been in his.

"Thank you for sharing this with me," Ed said kindly, but firmly, returning to his desk chair. "I know it must have been terrible for you. To watch the division eroding, the problems developing, to see a man whom you began by respecting become a caricature of himself. Am I putting it too strongly?" he asked, as Bart looked almost on the verge of tears.

"No," murmured Bart.

"Look," said Ed, "I think you've come to the right person. I've been here a lot longer, I've known Arnie a lot longer than you have. I want to spend some time thinking about what you're saying. To be perfectly honest, I have to look at two problems here. One is what you're telling me about Arnie. Somebody has to do something to help him and I'm not even sure who that person is. The other problem is that Arnie's apparent mismanagement of Food Services forces me to try to figure out what I should do in order to take care of my own business needs.

"It might turn out," Ed continued, "that there is some way to use the business situation to force Arnie to look at himself and his personal problems. At this point I'm not sure. It's something I need to think about more."

"You mean there might be something that can be done for Arnie?" asked Bart hopefully. "Something that might save our division and help him too?" After a minute he added generously, "And of course help Specialty Foods also?"

"I hope so," said Ed. He stood up and walked over to Bart's chair. "Look, Bart, it's getting late and I'm sure you've had as long a day as I have. Give me a couple of days to look into the alternatives and I'll give you a call."

"Okay," Bart said, standing up and walking with Ed to the door. "Meanwhile, we won't say anything to Arnie, right?"

"Right," Ed agreed. "I'll leave a message with his secretary tomorrow saying I'll be tied up at some meetings out of the office for a few days and that I'll get back to him on these price increases as soon as possible. Does that sound good to you?"

"Yes, very good," Bart replied. He reached out to shake Ed's hand. When Ed put his hand out, Bart pumped it up and down almost as if he couldn't stop himself. "Thank you, thank you, Ed," he kept saying. "I feel like a great weight has been lifted off my shoulders."

Ed finally managed to disengage his hand. "Good night," he said and subtly nudged Bart out the door. "I'll give you a call."

Ed turned back into his office. "Damn, damn, damn," he said aloud. "The weight is off of your shoulders, young man, because it's now squarely on mine!"

He took his suit jacket off its hanger behind the door, threw it over his shoulder, switched off the light, and left the office. This was not the night for a briefcaseful of work. He'd need the whole evening just to figure out what his alternatives were with Arnie

Clowder and the little problem he'd passed on to Ed. Then—he shuddered slightly at the unpleasant prospect—he'd have to do something about the whole mess.

After dinner that night, Ed's wife, Claire, asked him if he wanted to watch an old Fellini movie that was showing on cable TV. The children were both upstairs doing their homework and it looked like a quiet evening. Ed considered Claire's invitation longingly. They'd watched a lot of Fellini movies together when they were younger. It had been one of those quirky interests that always made Ed feel that he and Claire were made for each other. But if he put off the Arnie dilemma until tomorrow, when there were a million things going on . . .

"I'm going to spend some time in the study," he finally said to Claire. "With luck, I'll be able to get in for the end of the movie. I need to sit down and think about something that happened today that made about as much sense as one of those weird scenes in $8\frac{1}{2}$."

"I'll miss you," said Claire, giving Ed a hug. "Don't feel too bad about the movie. They always show them again. Anyway, we've got fifty years of movie watching ahead of us!"

Ed laughed as he went into the study. It wasn't that often that he brought problems home from the office, but Claire was always understanding when he did.

He sat down at the rolltop desk he used at home and decided just to think about the whole situation for a few minutes. First and foremost, Ed said to himself, I am president of the Specialty Foods Division and I have to think about what is good for my business. Unfortunately, I also have to think about what is good for ConCom because I have an obligation, as a high-level employee, to think about the total corporation and its future. On top of everything else, I'm a human being who has an opportunity—maybe even an obligation—to help somebody else who is in trouble. Now, how can I put those three things together and come up with some idea of the options I've got in this particular case?

Ed stood up and paced the room. He let his mind drift from one idea to another. After a dozen or so laps across his study he felt that things were falling into place. He went back to his desk, took out one of a large stack of note pads he kept there, and opened a Cross pen Claire had given him for his forty-fifth birthday. Somehow if he put some things in writing, it might help.

> *First alternative: put Specialty Foods first*
> —*We don't want to raise the price of Salsa! if we can possibly avoid it. Five cents per pint is the maximum increase I'm willing to pass on. Less would be better. None would be best.*
> —*Even the proposed increases for things like raw materials are too high: these probably reflect the poor management and neglect. E.g., if Arnie had done a better job of informing Central Purchasing of volume projections, they could have bought more citrus juice futures and we wouldn't be paying more.*
> —*Arnie is under pressure and he will not do what I want unless someone makes him. He could even turn things on me if I refuse to pay the increase.*
> —*Arnie is running his division into the ground. Somebody above him in ConCom needs to look into this.*
> ACTION: *Blow the whistle on Arnie rather than try to work things out with him.*

Ed put his pen down and read back over what he had just written. In a lot of ways, this made sense. He would be taking care of himself and his people. He'd be doing ConCom a favor by letting Ralph Myerson or George Vulcani know what they'd managed to miss so far, that Food Services was in trouble. And maybe he'd be doing Arnie a favor by forcing him to confront his mismanagement.

On the other hand, Ed thought, could he be fooling himself? ConCom was first and foremost a big corporation. Big corporations were not noted for their sympathy toward individuals with personal problems, and Arnie certainly appeared to be one of those individuals. It was perfectly possible that they'd take a look at the chaos Arnie had created and simply throw him out. God knows, the corporation wouldn't suffer. There were plenty of bright young stars waiting to replace a man nearing retirement age.

Ed decided to try to think through an option that took Arnie's needs into account more. He mulled over the situation for a few minutes, then picked up his pen again.

> *Second alternative: help Arnie and protect Specialty Foods*
> —We can raise the price of Salsa! $.05 without major harm to the franchise (probably). Tell Arnie I'm willing to go this far.
> —Tell Arnie I know about the problems that are developing in his division and I'll have to do something about it if he doesn't. (Don't let him know about Bart's involvement.)
> —Offer a compromise: I'll pay $.05 more if he'll get help. If necessary, go to $.06 or $.07 temporarily. Important thing is to put some pressure on him, but not so much that he goes crazy.
> —Before talking to Arnie, find out about help inside ConCom: Employee Assistance program, health insurance coverage for psychotherapy, etc. Provide him with this information as part of discussion of what I know about problems.
> ACTION: *Meet with Arnie, make a deal. Try to work things out with him by myself.*

In some ways, this looked more like it, Ed realized. He'd still be largely protecting his business. Even if he had to give up $.02 a pint in profit contribution, on the current volume of 250,000 this would only be $5,000. Wouldn't it be worth $5,000 to save a man's career?

Wait a minute, Ed, he continued to himself. Nobody said Arnie's career is shot if I go for the first option. Come to think of it, George Vulcani is the person who pushed for the whole Employee Assistance program in the first place. Didn't he have some nephew who worked for ConCom who had a drug problem or was an alcoholic or something and that led George to get interested in ConCom helping its employees? If I went to George—with whom I get along pretty well—maybe I'd have a lot better chance in the long run of helping Arnie.

And yet, Ed thought further, I don't have anything hard and fast to tell George. Maybe I *would* be better off handling this myself. I've only seen one violent scene and the rest is Bart Small's idea of what's going on. Could I explain all that to George?

Ed sat quietly thinking back over the two choices he'd identified so far. Maybe, he decided, he ought to look at a third alternative. Maybe it would be better to stay out of the whole thing. He turned to a fresh sheet of paper and began writing again.

> Third alternative: dump Food Services, buy Salsa! outside
> —*It would probably be possible to get Salsa! for less than even current price of $.25 a pint by going to a regional supplier (closer to raw materials, lower shipping costs).*
> —*Need to build a good case for this because corporate policy heavily favors purchase between divisions wherever possible. Arguments: lower price, ability to alter recipe for product according to regional needs (if varied suppliers), no need for ConCom to make capital investments in production facility if volume increases.*
> ACTION: *Start looking at external suppliers immediately. Don't challenge Arnie's increases but use them as a basis against which to realize cost savings.*

Ed read back over the last alternative, put the cap on his pen, and leaned back in his chair. This really looked good, in a lot of ways. First of all, it was possible—likely even—that volume on Salsa! would be going up. A lot of big corporations were starting to get into the fresh foods sections of grocery stores and, although Salsa! was only sold in specialty stores now, it could be the entrée into supermarkets for ConCom if it did well. By keeping Food Services as the sole source of supply, Ed could argue that he was doing the corporation a disservice. The product was more expensive and there was less opportunity to produce more product easily.

Besides, this would completely avoid the Arnie problem. What could he really do for Arnie anyway? In these cases where somebody had such an obviously serious problem, they usually had a very strong defense system. It would be almost impossible for Ed, who had no training or expertise, to confront Arnie and accomplish anything.

On the other hand, Ed thought somewhat guiltily, he would certainly be letting ConCom down if Arnie was doing as much damage in the Food Services Division as Bart Small seemed to think he was doing. Could Ed really side-step the whole issue this way and feel comfortable with himself? It was a difficult decision.

Ed's thoughts were interrupted by a knock on the door. Before he could say anything, the door opened and Claire came in.

"I don't want to disturb you"—she laughed—"but I really do! There are a couple of commercials on right now, but they're just about to get to the part where Giulietta Masina waves good-bye to Anthony Quinn and he drives off with the circus."

"You mean that scene where she gives that heartbreaking little backhanded wave and tears stream down her face?" asked Ed.

"That's it." Claire came over and put her arms around Ed's shoulders. "Are you finished here yet, Mr. Division President?" she asked, nuzzling his ear playfully.

"I am now," said Ed decisively. He put down his pen and stood up quickly. "Let's go." He took Claire's hand and pulled her out of the room. There were times when real life had to wait. Bart Small, Arnie Clowder, George Vulcani, the company shrink—they'd all be there tomorrow and the day after that. Giulietta Masina and Anthony Quinn, however, would only be there after the McDonald's commercial—and right now, with Claire's company, Ed wanted to be there too.

Indicate your choice here:

_____ Option 1. Do not deal further with Arnie. Set up a meeting with George Vulcani, describe the situation in Food Services and its implications for Specialty Foods, and request his intervention.

_____ Option 2. Meet with Arnie and, using information from Bart but without revealing the source, get him to admit

Food Services has some problems. Make a deal: if he will seek professional help with his personal problems, Specialty Foods will pay $.05 to $.07 more per pint of Salsa!

_____ Option 3. Find an outside supplier for Salsa! who can make the product more cheaply. Convince ConCom management that Specialty Foods should source this product outside.

6

Planning Italiano Production Systems

June 30, 1987

As their taxi driver pulled to a leisurely stop in front of the massive brick factory building, Ed Cunningham, Madeline Ballantyne, and Grady Jennings, Italiano product manager, began scrambling around for their raincoats, briefcases, and hanging bags. Ed barely restrained himself from hurrying the other two along, especially when Grady opened his wallet and meticulously began counting out eighteen $1 bills to pay the taxi driver.

First, the flight from LaGuardia had arrived in New Orleans almost an hour late. Then there were no taxis. When an ancient rattling Yellow Cab finally pulled up, its trunk wouldn't open so Ed had squeezed into the back seat with Grady and Madeline while the bags rode in front. To top it all off, the taxi driver had assumed that they were tourists there for a good time. With a strong sense of civic pride, he described every point of interest all the way from the airport to the factory, which was situated on the Mississippi River where it swept past downtown New Orleans. For the time and effort that had gone into this trip so far, Ed felt, he could have relocated the entire Specialty Foods Division to Sri Lanka.

Even in the two or three minutes it took to walk from the taxi to the front door of the factory, Ed felt sweat break out all over his body. He'd heard that the temperature and humidity in New Orleans were brutal at this time of year, but no amount of mental preparation could be adequate for the reality. With a great sense of relief he plunged into the dark and cool entryway of the enormous building, almost crashing into Madeline, who had stopped abruptly in front of him. "God, it's dark in here," she was saying.

"Just in comparison to that Gulf Coast sunlight," Grady answered mildly. "You might try removing your sunglasses," he continued, stepping from behind Ed to take the lead. "I think we go down this hall. There's a receptionist and she'll call Dwight. That's how it was last time I was here, anyway."

When they neared the receptionist's office, Ed noticed a heavyset man in a rumpled blue work shirt standing by the desk. The man began walking toward them, hoisting up his trousers, which threatened to escape the grasp of the narrow belt that barely secured them below his generous belly.

"Dwight!" said Grady warmly. As the man reached them, he stuck out a large hand to shake Grady's, clapping Grady on the shoulder enthusiastically with his other hand. "Grady! I thought you all would never get here!" The man turned to Madeline, a wide smile cracking his deeply tanned and wrinkled face. "Pleased to meet you, ma'am. Dwight Rochambeau, at your service." Then he smiled at Ed. "Ed Cunningham! Grady has talked about you so often." Ed returned the man's strong handshake as firmly as he could. "My pleasure," he replied. "I've heard a lot about you too."

"Let's just run on down to my office," Dwight said. "I'll have somebody bring us a couple of Cokes and we can get down to work. We've gotta get this meeting out of the way so I can show you all the sights." He shepherded the three visitors down a dingy hall. "I promised Grady I'd take him back to my favorite eating place out on the Lake. They boil up the best crabs and shrimp and crawfish around these parts! They keep the oysters and the beer ice cold and the fried catfish and hush puppies red hot. I gotta tell you"—as they reached Dwight's office, he lapsed into a moment of lip smacking—"boy, oh, boy!"

At the door of the office, Ed almost ran into Madeline again. When he looked over her shoulder into the office itself, he could see why she'd come to such an abrupt stop. It looked more like the office of the plant maintenance man than that of the factory manager. An old wooden desk in the middle of the room was piled high with papers, folders, and loose-leaf binders. But filling most of the rest of the room were what looked like odds and ends from every piece of equipment in the Italiano plant.

"Don't be shy, little lady," said Dwight from behind Ed. "There's some comfortable seats in there. You just need to figure out where they are. And believe me, it's cool in here. I've got myself the best little air conditioner Consolidated Commodities can buy."

Madeline stepped into the room and Ed followed. A blast of frigid air washed over him, causing him to break out in goose bumps. From hell to the Arctic Circle, he thought, in five minutes. This must be how people contracted fatal respiratory diseases in the middle of summer.

Dwight came into the office and steered everyone to a group of chairs that had been hidden by the clutter on his desk. "Now," he said, settling down in a creaking desk chair on wheels that immediately molded to his generous proportions. "I've got me my favorite chair and I'm ready to talk turkey."

"I really appreciate your agreeing to have us all come down," Ed began. "From up there in headquarters, we can get a funny perspective on what goes on out here in the real world." Dwight nodded and smiled. "We've got a situation here where we may have to get a lot of product out the door in a hurry and the only person I know who can tell us how to do it is you." Dwight smiled again and then spoke up.

"But the only person who can tell me what I'm gonna have to do is you," he said to Ed. "With help from my good friend, Mr. Jennings, of course. And this charming young lady, I presume."

"Oh, I'm mostly here to learn," said Madeline modestly. "I've only been Ed's assistant since the beginning of the year and I've never even been out to one of our factories before."

Ed looked at Madeline carefully. It was not like her to be so self-effacing. Perhaps she too found something disarming in Dwight's easygoing approach. Or maybe she was just playing some sort of a game with Dwight. Ed put his speculation aside temporarily. It was time to get the meeting rolling.

"Here's what we need to do this afternoon," Ed began as he opened his briefcase and took out a folder labeled PREPARED SAUCES.

"I want to pull together the marketing thinking and the production thinking for the segments of the Italiano line that come out of this factory. We've got a problem here that needs to be solved. But it's the kind of problem that as president of the division, I'd like to see more often. Shall I go back to the beginning just to make sure we're all on the same wavelength before we start analyzing possible solutions?"

"Good idea," said Dwight, creaking back in his chair comfortably. "We can get some pretty funny notions down here in the bayous about what's going on."

"I'll take some notes," said Madeline helpfully.

"All right, good," said Ed. He opened the folder, glanced at the first page briefly, and then looked at the others pensively. "The way I see it is the basic problem is sales of the Italiano line are starting to respond to our return to national advertising support. For over a year, the line was slipping through the cracks as Italiano was restructured, repositioned in the corporation, and so on. Earlier this year we put together an umbrella campaign for the line, which provides advertising support to every Italiano product, from the canned tomatoes we started importing in the 1940s to the pignoli nuts we started selling in 1985. You've seen those ads, Dwight?"

"Yessir, and mighty nice they are," Dwight said cheerfully.

"I'm glad you like them," Ed replied. "They've only been on the air a short time, but as they've run, we've found that true to marketing theory, there are certain products that are more advertising-sensitive than others. We have definitely seen volume growth starting on the primary tomato products—the paste, the whole Italian tomatoes. And there should eventually be substantial percentage increases on the gourmet products, as awareness and trial increase. But it's on the products made in this factory, especially the prepared spaghetti sauces, where the real increases will take place.

"These products have always been advertising-sensitive," he went on, glancing at Dwight, who appeared to be following the marketing shoptalk with interest. "When Mrs. Average Housewife is thinking about an easy dinner, she is more likely to pick up a jar of prepared spaghetti sauce if somebody on TV just reminded her that it exists. If they reminded her of Italiano, she's more likely to choose us.

Now we're out there on the air, reminding her all the time, and the results are showing up in our sales figures.

"While pizza toppings definitely have a cap in terms of total demand," Ed concluded, closing his file folder, "we really don't know what the ceiling is for the spaghetti sauces. We can do quality improvements, line extensions, more advertising. It's an open question right now: exactly how high is up for these products?"

"But we do know one thing for sure," Dwight said, dipping his chair forward and looking at Ed solemnly. "Every jar you sell has got to come out of old Dwight's factory sooner or later."

"Absolutely right," Ed agreed as Dwight eased back in his chair again. "It's only a short step from 'They want it!' to 'How are we going to make it?' This factory was built a long time ago, back in the 1920s. The conversion to the current manufacturing setup was made in 1965, the first year Italiano began selling prepared tomato sauces. That was a successful period for ConCom and it invested a lot of money in renovating this plant. It was farsighted enough to provide basic manufacturing capacity of 6 million equivalent units of prepared sauces a year."

"But now," Grady spoke up somewhat worriedly, "we are selling almost 6.4 million units. And some of our preliminary projections show that volume could rise over 8 million equivalent units per year in 1988. How are we going to turn out the additional product? What alternatives are available? What are the cost implications? That's what we have to figure out."

"Well, we know it's not hopeless," said Ed reassuringly as he looked at Grady. "It's just a question of choosing between alternatives. Let's start with reviewing what demand might really be for these products. Grady, get out your numbers, will you? When we've talked it out, we'll all feel a lot more comfortable about exactly what we're up against."

"You're right, Ed," Grady answered as he took a very small note pad out of his jacket pocket. Ed looked at the size of the pad and marveled again at Grady's extremely controlled style of keeping himself organized. The notes in there must look like the fine print of an insurance contract.

"I've had my people working on a variety of assumptions," Grady began. "Of course, we had to look at the wide range of Italiano products, which come from many different sources. The products made in this plant are only a part of the line, but they're the main part, so I wanted to concentrate on them first.

"Let me take you through our assumptions," Grady continued, squinting slightly as he glanced through the note pad looking for the right page of notes. "I did assume a cap on pizza topping demand. Right now we are selling 1.7 million topping equivalent units, that being 16-ounce cans. My information shows that even with a 25 percent increase in demand, which seems high according to market research data, we'd still have plenty of capacity in the current production-line setup. Is that right, Dwight?"

"Yessir," Dwight answered.

"Good. So we're not worrying about that right now. I mean, things can change, but we have no reason to think they will.

"But meanwhile," Grady continued, sounding nervous again, "we've got the real concern. Right now we're selling 3.6 million equivalent units of the home-style spaghetti sauce and 2.7 million of the specialty sauces: mushroom, sausage, and fresh herb. I know that it makes a difference here in the plant as to which of these you're running at a given time, but for gross planning purposes, I've grouped all the different products together."

"Yup," said Dwight, leaning forward to look at Grady. "It sure can make a difference. We run into our little problems here with the French mushrooms and the Italian tomatoes and the Spanish onions but we've got things worked out pretty well. Helps keep it interesting. Keeps me from taking early retirement." He slapped his knee and laughed, apparently at the absurdity of his ever leaving the plant before he absolutely had to.

Grady smiled at Dwight briefly and then resumed. "Dwight, tell me if I'm wrong, but I understand that right now the plant has a basic capacity of 6 million equivalent units when we run a standard two-shift operation five days a week."

"Excuse me," said Madeline, "but what is an equivalent unit on the sauces? I know you said toppings were a 16-ounce can, but aren't the sauces in glass jars? I want to make sure I get this right."

"Want me to fill you in on this, honey?" asked Dwight helpfully. Ed felt his goose bumps return as he waited for Madeline to say something awful to Dwight about his sexist, patronizing, demeaning form of address.

"Thank you, yes," said Madeline. Ed raised his eyebrows and looked fixedly at Madeline, but she was already focusing demurely on Dwight, waiting for his explanation.

"All of the spaghetti sauces anybody makes," began Dwight in a kindly tone, "are sold in glass jars. The industry standard is a 32-ounce jar. This is about enough sauce to serve a family of four, at least where the daddy can eat like I can." He stopped and chuckled again, patting his stomach appreciatively. "Anyway," he went on more seriously, "that's what people want, so that's what we give them. The sauces are also sold in other sizes. There is the smaller jar, 16 ounces, which feeds two people. There is also the economy size, 48 ounces, which is sold at a little bit lower price per ounce than the smaller sizes.

"Now, what we do here isn't fancy. Mostly we have to mix and cook the sauce. I'll take you all on a tour of the plant after we finish here. You're just gonna love it. I do, even after twenty years here. But as you'll see, the size of the bottle we put the sauce in is very easy to change. All of our bottling lines can be run for 16 ounce, 32 ounce, or 48 ounce. So we don't worry too much about end jar size when we do our production planning. Instead, we think in terms of that basic 32-ounce jar I was talking about. We call this the basic or equivalent unit. So a jar that holds half that much—the 16-ounce jar—is .5 equivalent units and that big jar, 48 ounces, is 1.5 equivalent units. Of course, the 32-ounce jar is 1.0 equivalent units."

"Thanks. That's pretty clear," said Madeline. She turned back a page on the pad in her lap. "You said earlier that capacity is 6 million equivalent units of prepared spaghetti sauce a year. Right?"

"Right," chorused Grady and Dwight.

"On a five-day, two-shift schedule," she added.

"Right," they replied again.

"So all we have to do is add a shift and we'll be able to turn out

9 million e.u.'s, which is more than enough to meet the highest demand we projected." Madeline looked up from her notes questioningly.

For a long moment nobody said anything. Madeline looked at Dwight, then Grady, and finally at Ed. She sighed.

"A nagging doubt in the back of my mind told me I ought to keep my mouth shut," she said ruefully. "I guess that's why you brought me to this meeting, Ed. Live and learn."

"Madeline usually doesn't take making a mistake so well," Grady said in an audible aside to Dwight. "You must be having a good influence on her."

Madeline gave Grady what Ed considered a more typical Madeline response: prolonged silence accompanied by an icy stare.

"Well, ma'am," intervened Dwight tactfully, "I wouldn't call it exactly a mistake. There are two problems with just running the factory more hours. Want me to tell you about them?"

"Please," said Madeline, in a gracious tone.

"First," Dwight said, "this factory is just plain old. ConCom put money into it, but equipment doesn't last forever. The plant has never run more than sixteen hours a day, even though we have gone into overtime on weekends now and again. There's a real possibility that with the type of machinery we have here and the age of the place, going to twenty-four hours a day on a permanent basis would give us a big increase in breakdowns.

"I also worry," he continued, leaning back in his creaking chair again and looking up at the ceiling thoughtfully, "that we'd run into some bottlenecks we never identified before. Right now, with the extra eight hours a day, we're kind of taking it easy and probably making a lot of little adjustments we don't even think about."

Madeline nodded. "I see. And the second thing?"

"Well, that's kind of unique to New Orleans," said Dwight, settling back even farther in his chair but looking at Madeline again. "It has to do with the labor supply and the labor unions." He creaked his chair down slowly. "First, we're right next to the oil and gas region. There's a lot of men who drift in and out of that business. When the oil and gas industry is going strong, we can't get them to work for us for love or money. When that industry hits a snag, the men are there but it's not the easiest group in the world to put on a production line. They're used to heavy labor and a rough life. Stirring up mushroom and tomatoes . . ." He shook his head sadly. "Sometimes it's just plain hard to get them to take it seriously."

Dwight rolled his chair toward Madeline slightly and went on with his explanation as if she were the only person in the room. "Then there are the workers in this area who don't have skills in the oil and gas business. These folks are always worried about the roughnecks getting laid off and coming in and snatching up their jobs. So we see more unionization than you would normally expect down here. Our whole factory is unionized and they stand behind their leadership 100 percent.

"Actually, this presents a little problem for us right now that the gentlemen ought to know about." Dwight rolled back a foot or so and turned to Grady and Ed. "We just signed a new three-year contract with the union about six months ago, before we knew we'd be wanting to make a lot more sauce. There was a new clause in that contract that prohibits compulsory overtime. With so many people coming from families where everybody works, it looks like they'd rather have weekends off than be making extra money."

"I'm getting some insights into the situation here, Dwight," Ed said when Dwight stopped and waited for his response. "Let me be sure I understand it right. On one hand, you can't be positive you'd get anyone to work one or two extra days a week if we did go to a six- or seven-day schedule. On the other hand, if we opted for a three-shift operation five days a week, we could find the new employees to gear up, since the oil and gas business is in a slump. But they're hard to handle and if the other industry turns around, they're gone in a minute."

"You've got it, son," said Dwight. "We *could* have a devil of a time turning out more sauce if we've gotta run the lines more hours. I'm not saying it couldn't be done, especially if we all decide that the volume increases are short-term. For a while—maybe even a year. But beyond that—well, I just don't know." He shook his head regretfully.

"Let's go back to those volume projections," said Ed. "That should help us decide if adding shifts or days is the answer. How about it, Grady? I know you just did an update based on the most recent sales figures. How great are the demand increases going to be and how long are they going to last?"

Grady looked uncomfortable. "Gosh, I feel bad saying this," he began slowly. "I don't want to let you all down, but to be perfectly honest, I'm not sure."

"Not sure?" Madeline broke in. "You're the group product manager. You're the one who always tells me how to figure out everything. How can you not be sure?"

Everyone looked at Grady questioningly. "Well," he said apologetically, "it *is* complicated. Italiano just went back on the air. Volume is just starting to increase. It's too early to be sure *what* is going to happen. That's the frustrating part of the whole thing. Maybe Italiano volume will only go up 10 percent and we can run the plant every other Saturday and be fine. On the other hand, maybe volume will return to the old highs or even go farther. That would mean volume increases of 30 to 40 percent. That calls for something a lot different if we're going to keep up."

"Hmm," said Dwight. "That's quite an increase. What about next year?"

"Another 20 percent?" Grady looked at Dwight apologetically. "I'm really sorry. I hate to do this to such a nice guy. But the early response on this umbrella advertising is pretty amazing."

"Look, I've got an idea," said Dwight. He rolled his chair toward the worried-looking Grady and said in an encouraging voice, "Let's just pretend for a minute that the business is really going to go great guns. Assume the best. Now, could you live with an overall 100 percent long-term increase in volume, Grady? I mean long-term, like starting in a few months and going on forever."

"Sure," said Grady. "Even when I look into forever, I don't see volume doing much more than doubling."

"Good," said Dwight, laughing jovially at what Ed considered a rather dry joke. "Because I have a plan I like a lot if we're talking about a big long-term volume increase. It would cost some money, but if things get that good we ought to have some money to spend." He paused as if to gauge his audience's response.

"Let's hear it," said Ed. "We're here to look at all the possibilities." Grady nodded and Madeline smiled at Dwight.

"As I mentioned before," Dwight began enthusiastically, "the main thing we do here regarding sauce production is mix and cook the ingredients. Right now we have a conventional cooking setup. The ingredients are put into huge kettles that are set over electric heating elements, a lot like those"—he bowed slightly to Madeline—"on your stove at home. We cook the sauce, then move the kettles of finished sauce on to the bottling area.

"Well, about a year ago, I went to a convention in Japan. Man, oh, man, those orientals can sure make the beer." After a moment of silent appreciation he went on. "This little old convention focused on new manufacturing technology. I saw something there that I've been thinking about ever since. It's a completely different approach to the kind of cooking we do. Well, now, it isn't completely different from the layman's point of view"—he looked at Madeline, who smiled at him encouragingly—"but it is technically very different.

"What they have developed"—he paused again for effect—"is a way of using convection heating on a large scale. Instead of just using kettles, we'd put the ingredients in these great big flat pans. These would proceed on a conveyor belt through a cooking tunnel that's just a stretched-out version of a convection oven. The heat circulates around the pans as they move through the oven. The flat pans mean that more surface area of sauce is exposed to the heat at any one time. Because of these two things, cooking time for the sauce is reduced by 50 percent. On a single shift, without having to spend any more money to run the plant, we could turn out twice as much sauce!" Dwight's chair creaked as he almost bounced with excitement. "Sounds great, doesn't it?"

"Wow," said Grady, sharing Dwight's enthusiasm. "Twice as much right here with the same people. That's amazing!"

"But won't there be a large capital expenditure?" asked Madeline. "I seem to recall from production class that new technology is infamous for its high cost."

"Aha," said Dwight. "I was just hoping you'd ask that question, little lady. You will be amazed to find out that things look better than you might think. May I present you with a few facts?"

"Yes," said Madeline, Ed, and Grady all at once.

"Now I can't promise you these numbers will be perfect," said Dwight modestly. "I gotta tell you that I don't even have me a calculator." He grinned around the group.

"To be honest, Dwight," Ed said, "I believe that all any of us can do is work with the best numbers we have. The calculator doesn't make much difference. In fact, in this business, if you wait for perfect numbers, it's too late to do anything with them anyway."

"That's not what you tell me," murmured Madeline in a somewhat sharp undertone.

"Now, ma'am," said Dwight, who didn't seem to be missing a nuance of Madeline's actions, "you have to remember that old Dwight's been running this plant for fifteen years and for near about fifteen years before that I was doing everything else there is to do what with one factory and another. Ed's just making allowances for an old fool who doesn't know how to use modern technology."

Madeline looked slightly unnerved by the latest of Dwight's folksy speeches but gave him a slight smile nonetheless. Apparently encouraged, he got up, stepped to his desk, and picked up a piece of paper.

"Basically, what I did," Dwight said, as he went back and settled into his chair, "was put together some rough estimates of what we're looking at with the present equipment. I figured out what it costs to run two shifts and what it would cost to run three shifts. These are your current variable manufacturing costs only: labor, benefits, supervision, and the cost of power to keep the plant running. Now let's see." He took a pair of reading glasses out of his shirt pocket and looked down at the page.

"We've got fifty people on the line at one time. Four supervisors when we run one shift. Only two additional supervisors each for a second and third shift. The highest power costs are to run the daytime shift." He looked up to explain. "Power rates go down around here through the early evening and overnight because the power company is trying to keep those generators running all the time.

"Now, when I put all this together"—he pushed the reading glasses up on top of his wiry graying hair—"it gives me a total cost for one shift of $387,000 a year. Two shifts run $699,000 annually. And I think that I could add a third for a total cost of $1,006,000. I can't be sure of that 'cause I've never done it, but it's a pretty good guess, I'd say."

Ed nodded to indicate he was following the numbers as Grady took notes in an apparently minuscule script.

"So looking at all this," Dwight took the glasses off and folded them up, "I'd say that the variable cost of putting on a third shift is $1,006,000 minus $699,999 or $307,000 a year. Of course, we might have, as I said earlier, some heavy maintenance or repair costs if we added this shift. Or in the worst case of equipment failure, we might even have to stop the production run, meaning we'd be paying for a third shift but not getting as much out of them as we want. I don't even *have* numbers for those little problems, though I suppose I could make some up if it's real important to you."

"Let me make sure I got this right," said Grady, pausing in his writing. "As far as you can tell, to add a third shift will cost $307,000 a year. For this amount of money, production can probably be increased by 50 percent. But there are two uncertainties. One is whether the third shift will cost more because of increased maintenance costs. The other is whether we will really increase output by 50 percent because if there are big maintenance problems, productivity declines."

"Yessir," replied Dwight. "Now you want my estimates on the other alternative?"

"Yes," Madeline spoke up. "Now you're going to answer my original question. How much it will cost to convert?"

"Well, ma'am," replied Dwight, smiling at Madeline somewhat playfully, "I'm happy to oblige. Now just remember that we don't have to have a big increase in line operating costs either. That means the total we'd have to spend to change a few things around here and buy the equipment we need is only about $750,000." Madeline raised her eyebrows in apparent disbelief.

"I know it sounds like a bargain," Dwight said, "and I went so far as to have that little old Japanese salesman for the convection system come in and go through the plant with me. He confirmed the price. Guaranteed it for three months, in fact. The only thing I can figure out," he concluded, scratching his head, "is that the Japanese government is subsidizing this industry to get it on its feet and we've got the opportunity here to take advantage of their generosity."

"So you're saying," said Ed thoughtfully, "that we can double capacity permanently for an additional capital expenditure of $750,000 with virtually no increase in line operating costs. Or we can increase capacity by 50 percent for $307,000 a year with no additional investment."

"That's a pretty fair summary," said Dwight. "There are a few other considerations. The new system would have a one-year guarantee so we wouldn't have to pay for maintenance on that part of the plant. It doesn't use any more power than the system we run now, so we don't need to put in anything extra for that. But on the other side, I don't think we could sell the equipment we pull out for anything but scrap iron so we wouldn't make anything much there to offset the purchase price."

"It sounds like you've worked up a pretty strong liking for the second alternative," said Ed. "You'd like to see ConCom spend the money to make this conversion."

"I would, no doubt about it," answered Dwight. "I'm an old-time plant manager. I like to see things that work right, that get the job done. But I try to keep your point of view in mind too. I won't say to do it if you don't think there's a damned good reason to do so." He looked at Ed for a minute, then turned to Madeline. "Excuse my French, ma'am."

"But there *is* a good reason, demand aside," responded Madeline, who had been making some calculations on her note pad, aided by a calculator she'd taken out of her handbag. "Can I tell you what I figured out here, Ed?" Ed nodded. "If we run three shifts and produce 9 million e.u.'s a year, the variable cost to produce each is 11.2 cents. But with the new equipment, we can run two shifts and produce 12 million e.u.'s a year, so the variable cost to produce each is only 5.8 cents. That's an amazing savings!"

"But it's only amazing *good* if we need the capacity and use it," Grady interjected. "It's amazing *bad* if we're dumb enough to spend money to convert our factory capacity to 12 million e.u.'s and then we only sell 6 million e.u.'s a year. Especially since you could say that the factory's capacity now is 9 million e.u.'s because we *could* run three shifts if we had no other choice."

"And remember," Ed added, "that ConCom depreciates new equipment over ten years so each year we'd have to pay off $75,000 in depreciation expense. Your figures work out okay if we are running at a high percent of capacity, but if volume fell off, for example, it would end up costing us *more* to produce a jar of sauce."

"But we're only talking about $750,000 in the first place!" said Madeline almost angrily. "Why should an enormous corporation like ConCom make a fuss about such a relatively small amount of money?"

"Let me answer that, Madeline," said Ed. "It's really a pretty good question. You see, the powers that be never, ever look at any amount of money as a small amount. Every single capital expenditure request has to go through an absolutely appalling number of people, each of whom likes nothing better than to say no to whatever it is.

"They're intent on saving that $750,000 for something really good—some investment that will return 1,000 percent to the corporation or that offers $5 million in tax shelters. Remember, if there's nothing good enough and they don't spend the money, it can show up as an increase in earnings and everybody likes that."

"Ed, are you sure you're not overstating the case?" asked Madeline tartly. "You make it sound like we could never get a capital request approved, no matter what."

"Sometimes I feel that way," said Ed wearily. "If we do decide to go for this, we'll have to work on our demand projections so they look watertight. We all know that projections always have a high degree of uncertainty in them. *They* know exactly the same thing. But we'll have to sweat and slave and make it look inevitable and then go in to one committee after another and say it all over again with the same message of absolute certainty. And even then . . ."

Ed stopped abruptly. "I'm sorry to get off on this particular tangent. Maybe it's just getting late in the day and my batteries are worn down."

"Oh, we can recharge those batteries in no time in New Orleans," said Dwight enthusiastically. "We'll just go out and take a little tour around the plant." He hesitated as he took in Ed's doubtful expression. "Well, maybe you'd recharge better at that place out on the Lake. They start serving about five o'clock. A couple of cold beers, two or three dozen oysters. Boy, oh, boy. You'll never want to go home!"

"That place on the Lake sounds great," conceded Ed. "But only after we finish here. Maybe I can summarize where we are. I feel like we're going around in circles and maybe a brief summary will help move things along."

"Good idea," said Dwight. "Make sure we're all on the same train before it heads out of the station."

"Yes," Ed replied. "We certainly don't want that train to leave before we're all aboard." Dwight chuckled heartily.

"Okay," Ed said, taking a deep breath. "Here's how I see it now. What it all comes down to is whether we really think demand is going to rise permanently. Grady was tentative about his volume projections, but I know he's been thinking it all through since before Italiano advertising went on the air. I agree with him that the best we can say at this time"—now Ed looked at his notes—"is that we must be prepared to handle a 40 percent increase in volume for the next six to twelve months. That means 8.4 million e.u.'s, which could conceivably be covered with a third shift."

"And for the twelve months after that," Grady added, "we should plan for another 20 percent increase, which gives us 10.08 million e.u.'s a year. This could be covered with three shifts working six days a week. Dwight, is that right?"

"Yes," said Dwight after a brief hesitation. "It could be done, but don't forget, it hasn't been done before. When you're dealing with a factory like this one, there's a lot you can't know about till you try it. But of course, if we invest in that new equipment . . ." He looked at Ed for a long meaningful moment, and when it was apparent that Ed understood what he meant, he looked up at a clock on a side wall of the office.

"You know, I've got my own idea about how to get us going here," Dwight continued. "I do think we ought to go out and take a little walk around the plant before it gets much later. I don't want my special friend here"—he gave Madeline a large wink—"to leave without seeing how a real factory works. Besides, whenever I hit a tough problem, I just go on out there and watch the jars come off the line for a little while. It's real soothing if you wear one of those hearing protectors. And I usually find that after a while the answer to whatever's on my mind just comes to me in a flash!"

Ed looked at Grady, who shrugged his shoulders very slightly. "Well," Ed said and looked thoughtful for a moment. Then he began putting his papers back into his briefcase. "We could certainly use a few minutes to let this all sink in. I guess watching the bottles come off the line is as good a way to get some perspective as any. Besides"—he snapped his briefcase shut and stood up decisively—"if all else fails, there's always the red-hot catfish and the ice-cold beer."

Indicate your choice here:

_____ Option 1. Plan to meet all demand increases with additional production from the existing facility.

_____ Option 2. Convert the existing facility to produce sauces using the new Japanese convection technology.

7

Handling the Nubian Network Opportunity

August 22, 1987

It was 2:25 P.M. on what had to be the hottest day of the year. Ed Cunningham tried to get comfortable in a piece of modern sculpture that passed for a chair in George Vulcani's dramatically decorated outer office. George, known for his punctuality, would be out momentarily. Meanwhile, the chair was awful but the perfectly adjusted air conditioning pouring out of the overhead vents almost made up for it.

At 2:31 by Ed's watch, the chairman's door opened and George looked out. As Ed stood up and returned George's handshake and greeting, he found himself excited about the meeting. Although he'd worked with the chairman and his staff often in the year since he became division president, this was one of the few times he'd met with the chairman alone. Usually there were several staff people with George, or Ed was making a presentation along with the other division presidents.

As he followed George into the office, Ed started speculating on exactly what they were going to talk about. George had only said "an interesting possibility for Specialty Foods." Ed hoped "interesting" wasn't a euphemism for "difficult" or just plain "weird." Chairmen could get a little out of touch with the day-to-day realities, and George seemed to try to make up for this by a hands-on involvement that could test the patience of any division president.

George led the way to a pair of easy chairs next to a small writing table. "Let's sit over here. I haven't asked anyone else to join us today because I wanted to talk to you informally, without somebody pushing a lot of facts and figures at us before we have a chance to think about the opportunities here."

Ed felt himself falter slightly as he took a seat. He was just getting Specialty Foods into some kind of reasonable shape as a separate ConCom division and now George was talking about new opportunities. It was flattering to be invited to talk to the chairman like this, but there was an element of risk here too.

George looked at Ed carefully and chuckled. "You look a little concerned, Ed," he said. "You should know me well enough by now not to believe those articles you read in the business magazines. I haven't single-handedly gone out and committed ConCom to pick up a new business in years. Those boys in Mergers and Acquisitions have put me on the straight and narrow. This is just an idea, Ed, just an idea."

Ed made an effort to look relaxed. "Oh, absolutely, I understand, sir—ah, George." Get a grip on yourself, he thought. The man hasn't even *said* anything yet and you're getting worried about Specialty Foods already.

"Let me tell you how this came up," George continued, as he leaned back and crossed his ankles. "As you may know, my wife Geraldine is a professor of organizational behavior at Yale. When we first met a few years ago, she got me interested in some of the less hierarchical approaches to management that were being used in other countries. I read a lot of books about Theory Z and Japanese and Swedish management structure and worker participation. I thought it was interesting but I didn't see ConCom as a company in need of major overhaul. After all, we're not in the internationally competitive businesses like automobiles or computers. We're just making food products and we're mostly competing with other U.S. companies who are doing the same kind of thing.

"Then about a month ago, Geraldine took a trip over to Japan to do some research. She came home very excited about what she'd found. Even in low-tech areas, like those we produce in, there can be large cost savings due to long-term worker productivity increases, reductions in manufacturing errors, and better delivery of the products into the marketplace.

"Being the typical husband, I listened to what she said but I didn't think seriously about it until I happened to pick up the Annual Report of one of our competitors. The whole damned thing was centered on how the company was positioned to move into the twenty-first century because it was changing its organizational structure to be more like the Japanese.

"I knew that this company's stock price had gone up pretty dramatically recently—it has a much better price-earnings ratio right now than we do—but I hadn't been able to figure out why. Well, in the Annual Report the chairman claimed it was because the stockholders had been kept abreast of these organizational changes and they bought into the long-term productivity gain idea and were now willing to pay a premium to be part of a company with such a bright outlook."

George got up and started pacing up and down the office. "You probably know how I feel about our stock price, Ed. I think it's a damned shame. We've been down near the bottom of the heap of food companies for a long, long time and no matter how good we are we can't seem to move up." He stopped suddenly in front of Ed's chair. "So when I see this self-serving letter from the chairman talking about how the participating worker is the happy worker is the productive worker, and how this idea—not earnings yet, just an idea—can increase the stock price, I see red."

George sat back down abruptly and stared across the room. After a moment of silence, Ed felt compelled to respond. "Hmmm," he said thoughtfully.

"Exactly," George said, turning toward Ed. "I'm glad you see it my way. This is a challenge ConCom can't let pass by." George cleared his throat and loosened his tie slightly. "So I went back to Geraldine and got a complete rundown on her research and some of the kinds of things we might do here. All very informal, of course, but it did make some sense. Not going Theory Z or some complete religious conversion—but doing something, an experiment, maybe something involving worker participation or quality circles or something fairly safe like that." He paused and looked at Ed expectantly.

"Yes, absolutely, I see what you mean." Ed nodded. Better to keep agreeing at this stage, at least until he knew what George had in mind for Specialty Foods.

With Ed's affirmation, George resumed enthusiastically. "So imagine how excited I was when I went to a dinner party over the weekend and met Isadora Dunwiddie." He paused meaningfully.

"Isadora Dunwiddie?" echoed Ed. Who the hell is *she*, he thought.

"Isadora Dunwiddie. Yes. The young woman who was written up on the front page of *The Wall Street Journal* a few weeks ago. One of those articles in the middle column. I think the title was 'With a Maa-Maa Here—Or, Goats Can Be Lovable.' "

"Oh, that Isadora," Ed replied, thinking feverishly. "The woman with the, ah—the animals . . ."

"Exactly," George said, leaning forward eagerly. "She has a herd of several hundred Nubian goats. Charming little creatures, with the long droopy ears. She actually had pictures of them in her wallet. Eat mostly fresh alfalfa, I believe, and often bear twins."

He's gone completely off the deep end, Ed found himself thinking. George, Isadora, *The Wall Street Journal.* Goats. They're all crazy.

George appeared to notice the look on Ed's face and to pull himself together. "Well, I'm getting a little far afield," he said, shaking his head. "My family kept goats when we first came to America. I've had a weakness for them ever since.

"The point is, Isadora has quite a productive little company based on her goats. She started with a small herd and got interested in using the milk they produced. She went to France, studied goat cheese production, and came back to set up her own operation. All of her products are fresh milk cheeses, not mold-sprayed, and in the past year her cheese sales have reached about $350,000. She uses milk from her own herd plus what she buys from local farmers. She's been cultivating these outside suppliers because she thinks the business still has the opportunity to double in the next couple of years as she starts selling products outside her immediate geographic area.

"As the business has grown, she's ended up with a good-sized staff. It takes about a dozen people to manage the herd. Cheese manufacture takes another ten. And she's doing all her own sales and distribution, so that's three people."

"This reminds me a lot of some of the Mountain Gourmet manufacturing units," interjected Ed. "The apple products in particular. About the same number of employees, though their sales are only in the $250,000 range. And I haven't seen anything that says they expect to double their business."

George nodded. "There are some similarities, Ed. That's why I thought of Specialty Foods. But what's more important here are the differences. Nubian Network isn't run like anything we've got anywhere in ConCom right now. It's completely different. Isadora has got participative management like you wouldn't believe. You could even say that the company isn't run by Isadora at all. It's run by everyone."

George's voice was enthusiastic. "In some ways it's a lot like People Express Airlines in its heyday. Every employee can do several jobs. The person who milks the goats this week might be delivering the finished products next week and running the cheese-making equipment the week after. Besides that, management decisions are made by a team or committee on which each employee serves at one time or another. Isadora always sits on the team because she's been there since the beginning and she knows the most about what's going on. But everybody else rotates through for three-month staggered terms."

Ed tried to keep his face blank. Goatherds making management decisions? Isadora's company had to be located somewhere on the West Coast.

"Now, this sounds pretty crazy at first, I'll agree," George continued, again noticing Ed's expression. "But Isadora told me about a typical situation where they used this approach that convinced me there's something to it.

"They had a horrendous bottleneck somewhere in cheese production. Isadora was positive they were going to have to make a large capital investment in more cheese-making equipment. Needless to say, cash is tight in a growing operation like this one, so she wasn't too happy about the prospect. Before telling the management committee what she thought, though, she asked all the employees to think about what they saw as the source of the problem and what ideas they had for solving it. They were supposed to pass their ideas along to the current committee members.

"A couple of the goatherds who'd just finished a stint in manufacturing were talking about the problem while they were running the milking machines. All the goats were inside for milking at the same time and they agreed that the milking bottleneck was as bad as the production bottleneck. But instead of just complaining, they started thinking about solutions to *both* problems. Now remember, these are really just a couple of youngsters talking—in their twenties, probably never finished college, much less going to business school. They decided that if the goats could be reprogrammed to be milked at variable hours then milk would be available for cheese production over more hours of the day. The cheese production bottleneck was actually *following* the milking bottleneck: the first processing of the milk all has to take place within a certain time after the milk is produced since this is a fresh milk product.

"They brought their idea to the management committee. One of the committee members that month was a part-timer who was also a veterinary student. She said that she'd read about staggered milking schedules for cows and that it could probably be done for goats too. The bottom line is that it worked: no new equipment, better human productivity in several areas, and the goats don't seem to mind a bit. And it wasn't some expensive consultants who came up with this idea. It was a couple of unskilled employees."

"Interesting," agreed Ed. He was beginning to get interested in this approach after all. "I know from when I worked in Dry Groceries that lots of times the folks out there on the production line are the ones who have the best insight into what's going right and what's going wrong. I guess this kind of participative management, or whatever the experts like Geraldine would call it, is built on that basic idea."

"So you think maybe I'm not so crazy on this subject?" asked George, smiling at Ed.

Ed swallowed. "Not at all—I never thought . . ."

"Goats are a bit unconventional," George continued. "But they're not the main point here, as you can now see."

Ed returned George's smile. "I'll admit, I was a little hesitant. But now I'm getting the picture." There was a moment of silence.

"So what are you proposing for Specialty Foods?" Ed continued. "That Isadora spend some time with us generating ideas? Or Geraldine or someone like her help us set something up?"

"Actually I've got a more dramatic proposal," George said. "It turns out that Isadora is quite interested in selling Nubian Network."

Ed's smile faded. "And you think ConCom might be interested in buying?" he said slowly.

"Of course, it would all depend on the financials, the purchase price, and so on," said George. "I meant it when I said my days of single-handed acquisitions were over. But I don't even want the Mergers and Acquisitions team to take a look at it if I don't have a place to put it."

"You see," George continued, shifting his chair a little closer to Ed, "I've decided to try a little participative management myself and ask you to think through the options with me. We'll be here awhile, I'd guess. How about a cup of coffee or a Coke?"

"Sure, a Coke would be fine," said Ed. This social touch would give him a few minutes to get his thoughts together. He hadn't known what to expect, but then nobody could have anticipated this one. A whole new operation for Specialty Foods, a new management style, a new product line.

George walked over to a cabinet in his office. Behind the wood door was a small refrigerator. He took out two cans of soda. After closing that door, he opened one overhead and took out two glasses and a small tray. "Chairman's perks," he said, carrying everything to where Ed still sat. "I like self-sufficiency. Sometimes I'm here when nobody's around, so I've set things up to operate comfortably on my own." He opened the first can, poured the soda, and handed a glass to Ed before pouring a glass for himself.

"Here's to Nubian Network, whether we go after it or not. A great little organization." Ed held up his glass for a clink with George's and took a quick swallow.

"Okay, I'm ready to go," said Ed, setting down his glass. If need be he'd continue to organize his thoughts as he went along. George seemed reasonable so far. Maybe he did want a brainstorming session, not just a "yessir" approach.

"First," began Ed, "I've read some of those same books you were talking about, and I found the ideas interesting, too. But after so many years working my way up the hierarchy, I guess I wasn't the person who was going to buy in right away to taking it all apart.

"However, I've got to admit that recently some of those thoughts about participative management were coming back into my thinking, too. We had a devil of a time recruiting this spring. A number of our first choices among the MBAs we interviewed either went to smaller companies where they were more involved in the big picture, or went to consulting, where they planned to get enough hands-on training to start their own businesses, or went to companies that are trying some of these kinds of things, like some of the California high-tech organizations.

"So I see the basic attractiveness of moving ConCom into an experiment like this. But the first question I have to ask myself is if Specialty Foods can handle this kind of a thing right now."

Ed stopped and took another sip from his glass. "I've been there about a year now and the division's eighteen months old. We've had a lot of issues to deal with as we've tried to take products that were positioned and marketed differently and pull them together. On the one hand, we've got Italiano, an old product line essentially sold through grocery stores across the country. At the other end of the spectrum, we've got Salsa! Salsa! Salsa!, a brand-new product sold fresh-packed through specialty food stores in the Southwest.

"I've had to try to organize advertising. And a coherent sales structure. And a bunch of people who used to work for a completely different company—the Mountain Gourmet people who came in when we bought Scarborough. I'm doing okay. We've made progress in all these areas. But I don't know if we're ready for one more new organization with one more new way of doing things and products that require yet another kind of selling." Ed shook his head. "It might just be too much too soon."

"I think you've got some good points there, Ed," said George, "but let me turn it around 180 degrees and give you another way of looking at things.

"ConCom is an old company and, despite my despairing about our stock price, a successful company. You've heard the saying, 'Success breeds success.' Well, I'd add to that 'Like breeds like.' We're set in our ways even more than a lot of other organizations, which is one reason we had to take our entries into the gourmet food business and set them up in a separate division, away from the people who already knew how to do everything well. It was pretty clear from how the new Italiano products were evolving that what they knew how to do well didn't happen to be what needed to be done in this situation.

"When I look around ConCom, I see one place where the corporate culture is not completely entrenched. Of course, that's Specialty Foods. Your division hasn't been around long enough to think you know all the answers. If we tried some kind of experiment in participative management—whether it was Isadora's company or not—we might have a fighting chance in your division that we wouldn't have anyplace else.

"And I don't need to add that if it went well in Specialty Foods, I'd have every division president in here begging to try it too." George's eyes sparkled, as he seemed to visualize the procession that would appear at his door. "Whereas the untried is a threat, the successfully tried is tremendously attractive. Especially when those guys who've been division presidents for years see a young whippersnapper like you gathering the laurels." George smiled slightly and shook his head appreciatively. "It would be quite a scene."

"I understand what you're saying," replied Ed, "but I'm still not sure about Specialty Foods as a guinea pig. Just for the sake of discussion, let's talk about how we could best undertake this experiment if we did decide to give it a try. That might help me clarify my thinking. I guess it would be Nubian Network versus building up something from within the division."

George got up again and started walking around the room, picking up odds and ends off tables and shelves and examining each thing briefly.

"That's how I see it," he said thoughtfully. "Let's assume that Nubian Network looks good businesswise. My intuition says this is going to be the case and that this acquisition is a real possibility. If I'm right, my first preference is to pick up the company and to use it as the basis for this experiment because I think this would be the quickest and easiest way to go.

"I see you look skeptical," George continued. "Let me tell you how I've seen these things go before. If you decided to set things up from within, first you'd have to work with some outside consultants—Geraldine types, who, believe me, can eat up your time. They want to talk about everything and then talk about how you *feel* about talking about everything. Then you'd have to spend some more time convincing the employees who were going to be part of the experiment that it was in their best interest. Since we're talking about all levels of employees here, that could involve the unions and get you into renegotiating contracts and so on. And that's the easy part. Because next you'd have to live through your subordinates' resistances and screwing things up because they don't think it will really work and threatening to quit because they were hired to work in a different kind of company doing a different kind of job.

"But you'd miss all that if we just picked up Nubian Network," George continued, perching on the corner of his desk. "They already know how to operate that way. The employees like it or they wouldn't be there at all. You just keep the ball rolling, we observe, cycle some other Specialty Foods types through there, and gradually soften up the rest of your organization for expanding the experiment."

"The way you put it is very convincing, George," Ed replied, "but what still worries me is that I can tell just as good a story from the other side."

"Let's hear it," George said enthusiastically, returning to the chair across from Ed.

"Okay," said Ed. "I see that the very things you worry about as a negative could be a plus. Using an outside consultant would take a long time and could get me deeply involved from the beginning. But that would give both me and the rest of the people who end up being part of the experiment a chance to get used to the idea of a new management approach. We could phase it in, make it fit into our business plan and planning cycle, introduce things a piece at a time, and work through the resistances and questions and fears.

"Besides that, using outside consultants would give us an opportunity to decide just what kind of experiment we should be running here. There are so many alternatives: without trying very hard, we've come up with participative management, quality circles, and Theory Z. And we both alluded to other things they're trying out in Japan and Sweden and even in our competitors' organizations. How can we be so sure that Isadora Dunwiddie's approach would work out best for ConCom and Specialty Foods?

"And a final thing," Ed continued before George could answer. "Any acquisition is hard to integrate into the corporate culture, even if you're putting together two things that are very similar. I see that with the Mountain Gourmet situation. This is something so new and different that the rest of the division might see it as totally alien and so it would be that much more difficult to carry the ideas into the rest of the division."

George looked thoughtful. "You're a mean opponent, Ed," he replied. "You put your arguments very well. In fact, you make me question each of these options, too. Shall we just talk through everything one more time to make sure neither of us has anything major to add?" Ed nodded.

"Okay. First is the question of whether Specialty Foods should take on this experiment at all. I have to rely on your judgment there, although it would be my first choice among the divisions. If you say no, I'll look for another place to try something out.

"If your division is willing to be the site of the experiment, then we get to the question of how to go about it. One option is to acquire Nubian Network, subject, of course, to a clean bill of health on the numbers side. I'll be honest about this—if you don't want

Nubian Network, ConCom doesn't go after it. The products are too far afield to go into any other division.

"The last option is for Specialty Foods to be the scene of the experiment but for us to develop something from within. This could turn out to be better than acquiring Nubian Network—that seems to be your first reaction. Or it could turn out to create more problems than it solves. That's *my* gut feel."

"I don't think I have anything to add to that," replied Ed.

"Then I guess we both get a few days to think about it some more," George said. "I asked Mergers and Acquisitions to start a quick-and-dirty analysis of Nubian Network. We can't honestly make a final decision here until we know if this is one of our alternatives." George stood up.

Ed stood up also and put out his hand. "It's been a pleasure," he said sincerely. "When you said to come in for a little brainstorming, I never expected we'd cover such a range of ideas. For me, today's experiment in participative management has been a plus. In fact, I've enjoyed this so much that it might prejudice my decision about whether Specialty Foods should be the division for your experiment."

George laughed as they walked toward the door. "I'm not sorry to hear that," he said. "You should have the preliminary assessment of Nubian Network by the end of the week. Shall we say we'll meet next Monday to make a decision? I'll have my secretary set it up."

August 24, 1987

On Friday, Ed received a copy of the preliminary report from Mergers and Acquisitions. They felt that Nubian Network was sound, that the asking price was appropriate, and that an acquisition was not contraindicated during the current fiscal year.

Indicate your choice here:

_____ Option 1. Ed recommends that Specialty Foods not serve as the site of the organizational design experiment; con-

sequently, ConCom does not pursue the acquisition of Nubian Network.
_____ Option 2. Ed recommends that ConCom acquire Nubian Network and integrate it into the Specialty Foods Division.
_____ Option 3. Ed recommends that Specialty Foods serve as the site of the organizational design experiment but with a new design rather than through the acquisition of Nubian Network.

8

Balancing Corporate Reporting and Division Spending Needs

September 10, 1987

Ed Cunningham jabbed the Up elevator button impatiently. It was amazing that over here in the exclusive top management area something basic like the elevator never seemed to work right. Ed had been stuck between floors or ridden straight down to the boiler room more times than he cared to remember. Today's situation was even more frustrating: the elevator simply never came. After another vindictive jab, Ed headed for the staircase and a climb of four flights to the top-floor boardroom. As the stairwell door slammed behind him, he was sure he heard the elevator doors creak open.

Several minutes later, he emerged into the fifth-floor hallway only slightly breathless. As he walked past the elevator, the doors slid open, revealing two secretaries who were laughing and chatting without an elevator problem in the world.

At the end of the hall was the board conference room where today's meeting was being held. Ed always felt somewhat inspired by the boardroom with its portraits of ConCom luminaries, past and present, the richly patterned oriental rug that stretched the entire length of the room, and the two dozen leather easy chairs arranged around the generously proportioned walnut conference table. His wife, Claire, called it the worst kind of corporate seduction: the appearance of endless money and power without a smokestack or unionized laborer in sight. She was right. And yet . . .

Three of the other V.P.'s were already gathered at the far end of the conference room. As Ed walked toward them he heard Afolabi Smith's deep, booming voice. "I deal with it by thinking of our little group of corporate V.P.'s as a subcommittee of the U.N. Security Council," he was saying to Joy Okaido and Manfred de Chazan. "Otherwise, I'd have to laugh at us as we gather in these imposing surroundings. We have our black, our oriental, Manfred here, who looks terribly European, and"—he pointed toward the approaching Ed—"our all-Americans." He shrugged. "We're either part of the U.N. or the illogical outcome of the 1970s equal-opportunity laws. I prefer the former explanation."

"Frankly, I simply focus on the view," rejoined Joy. Although she looked like a delicate Japanese flower, Joy had grown up in a working-class section of San Francisco and she usually presented the most practical and down-to-earth management perspective of any of the six V.P.'s.

"And not a bad view, is it?" said Ed as he joined the group.

"We deserve it for what we put up with," said a voice from the door. Sonny Cobb and Ken Winsor walked in. "By the way, what are we putting up with today?" Sonny added, striding across the room like he was back on his hometown football field.

"I heard it had something to do with your division, Sonny." Joy spoke up again. "Sales or earnings, most likely. When Ralph calls us together, it's not usually for an advertising copy review."

Suddenly the door Ed was standing near opened, preventing further speculation. As Ed stepped back from the doorway, Ralph Myerson walked in from his private office, followed by a large, rather ungainly woman Ed had seen only once or twice before.

"Good afternoon," said Ralph formally and walked immediately to the chair at the head of the table. He stood there for a moment, his humorless expression, dark suit, and narrow tie giving him the appearance of a small-town funeral director ready to manage a group of unruly viewers.

As the room fell silent, he took his seat. "Please be seated. Ladies, please take these seats." He gestured to the chairs immediately to his right and left. "Gentlemen . . .

"Thank you for coming," began Ralph as the last chairs scraped. Afolabi's large shoulders were between Ed and Ralph. Ed pushed his chair back slightly, then forward again, trying to get a better perspective on the president. Suddenly he realized that Ralph had fallen silent and, without expression, was watching him shift his chair around.

Ed blushed furiously. "Sir—sorry—okay . . ." God, the man had icy eyes. At that moment, Afolabi moved his chair back to see what Ralph was staring at and Ed's view was cleared. Ed quickly put his hands in his lap and tried to sit perfectly still. This seemed to satisfy Ralph, who resumed.

"Let me introduce Dora Pluckett," he said, turning to the woman on his right very slightly. "She is the top analyst in the Corporate Planning Department and she has been responsible for putting your earnings projections together."

Dora nodded to the group and smiled comfortably. At least she looked like a normal human being, thought Ed, whereas Ralph Myerson clearly was not. Ed focused his full attention back to Ralph guiltily. It was bad enough to look foolish once without asking for a repeat.

"We have a rather unusual problem that Dora has identified," Ralph was saying. "By the third quarter of most fiscal years, I would have invited you here to see if we could identify opportunities to raise your divisions' earnings for the year. However, this year you have already identified significant earnings expectations. Therefore, I will not be asking for the generation of more money." He looked at each of the V.P.'s in turn, pausing, Ed felt, rather longer as his eyes met Ed's. "Rather," Ralph finally went on, "I wish to hear suggestions of how to reduce the earnings number you will report at the end of the year. We will be looking for a total earnings reduction in the range of $8 million."

There was a momentary buzz among the V.P.'s, which was quickly suppressed as Ralph looked up and down the table again. *Reduce earnings!* This was certainly not what Ed had expected and, from the headshaking, smiles, and seat-shifting around the table, it appeared that he was not alone in his surprise.

"I have asked Dora to prepare an explanation of the situation, anticipating that you would all find this unusual. However, allow me to point out that Consolidated Commodities has been in this position before. It is simply your relative *youth*"—Ralph paused over the last word as if it left a bitter taste in his mouth—"that prevents you from being familiar with this type of problem."

"George and I faced a similar problem only a few years ago," said Dora Pluckett chattily. "For several years running in the late seventies. Although I suppose that wasn't really so recent. Time flies when you're having fun!" She laughed heartily at her own joke. Clearly Dora Pluckett did not share Ed's nervousness around Ralph Myerson, but for the life of him Ed didn't see how anyone could ever warm up around such a seeming stoic.

"As you'll see, it is quite simple," continued Dora. "Probably this type of thing comes up more often than you'd expect and other companies handle it internally—just as we plan to.

"As you all are well aware"—she smiled around the table companionably—"our primary mission as a publicly held corporation is to return reasonable earnings to our shareholders. ConCom, like its sister corporations, has a range of alternatives when it comes to how these earnings should be managed.

"At one extreme, we could pay out all earnings to our shareholders in the form of dividends. This would generate a lot of income for the shareholders and that might make some of them very happy. However, there are two negatives to this approach. First, the shareholders would have to pay income tax on the money we paid out. We could give them a dollar today, but after taxes they would have less than a dollar to spend or to reinvest.

"Furthermore, if we paid out all of our earnings, ConCom would be left with no money to invest in our future operations. This might be all right for the short term or if we didn't intend to keep running the business indefinitely, but over the long term it would put the corporation in a very undesirable position."

Dora paused and turned to Ralph Myerson, apparently to check on how she was doing. He nodded minimally and she continued.

"At the other extreme, we could reinvest all the earnings into ConCom and not pay out anything in the form of dividends. This is the situation you often find in start-up or rapidly growing companies where management believes they can generate much higher earnings in the future if they continue to grow now. Rather than paying out earnings and then having to borrow to finance growth, they simply use earnings to build the business.

"In this situation, shareholders don't get any money today but they get to maintain their holdings in what will supposedly be a bigger and better corporation in the future. It's a kind of forced investment, really. If you are a shareholder in our company, you'll keep investing in our company. If you don't like this plan, sell the stock and stop being one of our shareholders."

Ed noticed that Manfred was nodding thoughtfully as Dora spoke. Trying to make a good impression on Ralph probably. There was certainly nothing new in what Dora was saying.

"This leads us to the stock trading implications of earnings. People buy stocks with different goals in mind. Either they want to generate present income, in which case they'd buy stocks that have large current earnings streams and that pay out a lot of those earnings. Or they want to push income into the future, rather than realizing it right now. In that case, they'd buy stocks that don't pay dividends but rather reinvest earnings. Some people put all their money into one of these two types of stock, while lots of other people want some of each kind of stock and so have a mixed portfolio.

"Now with ConCom, we like to think we have the best of both possible investment opportunities." Dora looked at Ralph again. He responded by slowly lowering and raising his eyelids.

Dora continued, obviously pleased. "We have a payout ratio of approximately 25 percent. For every dollar of earnings, we pay the shareholders $.25 and we reinvest $.75. We've maintained this basic ratio for years, with slight adjustments one way or the other.

"Not only have we been consistent in this respect, but also we have maintained a smooth earnings increase over the years. Why don't you each take one of these charts so you can see exactly what I mean?" Dora handed some papers to Joy and Ken, who were sitting nearest her. They each took a sheet and passed on the other pages.

Chart 1

	Fully Diluted Earnings	Payout Ratio	Dividends
1979	$2.49	.24	$.60
1980	2.69	.24	.65
1981	2.95	.24	.71
1982	3.15	.25	.79
1983	3.37	.25	.84
1984	3.59	.25	.90
1985	3.95	.26	1.03
1986	4.39	.26	1.14

"As this chart shows, earnings over the past eight years have gone up an average of 8 percent a year, with a high of 11 percent and a low of 6.5 percent. With the minor adjustments in the payout ratio, we've been able to keep the dividends increasing from $.60 in 1979 to $1.14 per share in 1986. If we went back even twenty-five years, you'd see pretty much the same thing."

"There's more to this story, Dora," said Sonny Cobb, looking up from his copy of the chart somewhat impatiently. "Let's stop talking theory here and get to the real world. All this earnings and dividends stuff is only important because of what it does to the stock price, right?"

Dora laughed her hearty laugh again, but Ralph Myerson looked more humorless than ever. Sonny, as usual, was undaunted. "Come on, come on, let's hear it," he prompted.

"Yes, you're completely right," Dora continued. "It's one thing to talk financial theory. In fact, you can argue for days about what shareholders want and about the value of current after-tax dollars versus the possibility of future before-tax dollars. But it finally all comes down to what an individual investor is willing to pay for a share of ConCom. And that is, of course, our stock price."

Dora picked up another stack of papers next to her. "Let's look at this chart. It shows our stock price and price-earnings ratio for the same period of time." She passed out the papers.

Chart 2

	Fully Diluted Earnings	% Change	Price-Earnings Ratio	Stock Price
1979	$2.49	—	10-12	24⅞–29⅞
1980	2.69	8.2	11-14	29¾–34¾
1981	2.95	9.7	14-16	41¼–47¼
1982	3.15	6.8	10-12	31½–37¾
1983	3.37	7.0	8-11	27–37⅛
1984	3.59	6.5	7-9	25⅛–35⅞
1985	3.95	10.0	12-14	43½–55¼
1986	4.39	11.0	12-15	52⅝–65⅞

"As this chart shows, our stock price has not followed as neat a pattern as our earnings. Even taking into account the ups and downs of the Dow-Jones averages, our stock has displayed volatility. Especially look at 1982 through 1984 when earnings grew, but at a lower rate than formerly. During these times our price-earnings ratios dropped from as high as 16 times earnings in 1981 to a low of 7 in 1984. That implies strongly that when we don't do what the market wants and expects—when our earnings stream is interrupted or irregular—the stock price reflects that problem."

"And that is what we wish to avoid over the next few years: a run-up of the price as we had in 1981 followed by a sharp decline." Ralph Myerson's somewhat thin voice overrode Dora's last few words and she stopped speaking, looking again at the president.

"Thank you, Dora," he said dismissively. "Let us continue right to the issue at hand. Two of you gentlemen have turned in quite high earnings projections for the year. Now that we have eight months of actual data, the year's earnings are quite likely to be at or near your projections. Dora and her staff have reviewed your projections and we have all agreed that your numbers look quite sound.

"The bottom line"—Ralph appeared to savor the phrase—"yes, the bottom line is that no matter how we look at things, when all the numbers are netted together, there is an overwhelming likelihood that earnings will increase over 13 percent this year, compared to a target increase of 11 percent. This, of course, is a higher rate of increase than Consolidated Commodities has experienced for some time and a rate that I believe could not be sustained."

This time even the president's cooling presence could not keep down the excitement among the vice-presidents. Ed, who had vowed to maintain an extremely low profile for the rest of the meeting, heard himself whistle appreciatively, but luckily his reaction was drowned out by the others' comments and exclamations.

Ralph ignored the brief fervor. "In order for each of you to understand the problem fully, I have asked Afolabi and Sutton to identify their areas which will generate significant incremental earnings this year."

Ed looked up and down the table. Who on earth was Sutton? Across the table Sonny busily began taking papers out of his briefcase. Could Sonny's given name be Sutton? If so, had Ralph Myerson dug this personal information out during a private raid on Sonny's employment file? At this point, Sonny spoke up, confirming his other identity but leaving Ed as puzzled as ever by Ralph Myerson.

"Shall I begin?" Sonny asked, looking at Ralph and then at Afolabi.

"Certainly," said Ralph. Afolabi nodded.

"Well, let's see," Sonny said, hunching forward slightly over his papers as if he were trying to read his own notes. "It was really that end run that did it. We were facing a fourth down situation and suddenly I just decided to go for it!" On this upbeat comment, he looked up and suddenly seemed to recall where he was. He leaned back in his chair and smiled engagingly around the table.

"Well, it's 'Bears Watching' that we have to thank. Most of the Grain Products Area volume comes from breakfast cereal sales. While some of the other big producers rely almost exclusively on their tried-and-true brands—cornflakes, raisin cereals, and so on—ConCom has always had an unusually strong position in the cereals that have a shorter life cycle, what you might be so rude as to call the 'fad' cereals.

"Over the years, we've had dozens of cereals that built on an external stimulant such as cartoon characters, hot children's toys, even current events like the milestones in the space program. But we kept looking for something a little different that would give us more of a unique position. Then the packaging people came up with Bears Watching."

Suddenly Sonny ducked down under the conference table, only to appear seconds later with a box in each hand. The boxes were quite unlike anything Ed had ever seen before. Rather than being rectangular, they were shaped like the simplified outline of a teddy bear. Each was imprinted with a picture: one was an antique Teddy Roosevelt–style bear complete with a pince-nez. The other was a charmingly coy bear with a pink-and-white-gingham-patterned tummy.

"As you can see," Sonny said, looking appreciatively and somewhat wonderingly at the two boxes, "this product introduced a completely different factor into the fad cereal market. Suddenly it wasn't just that there was a new cereal inside—though the cereal itself is quite tasty and, of course, shaped like teddy bears. Suddenly a box of cereal was more than a box of cereal—it was a toy, a storage box, a collector's item.

"I was so excited about this that we skipped our usual test-market phase and rolled the product out immediately. The results have been phenomenal. We've captured as much as 5 percent of the cereal market in certain areas and no less than 2 percent in any region. This compares to what we usually consider a good performance of 1 to 2 percent average penetration. We've never had a cereal that managed to get over 3 percent of the market before."

Sonny paused and shook his head, obviously still amazed by his product's success. Before he could regroup to continue his presentation, Ralph Myerson spoke.

"Thank you, Sutton." Sonny opened his mouth to respond, but Ralph was speaking sharply. "Of course, we do not assume that even such a success as Bears Watching will continue indefinitely." Sonny closed his mouth and, for once, remained silent, his usual enthusiasm quelled by Ralph's firmness.

"Consequently," Ralph said, "this product gives earnings a large boost during this fiscal year, but we clearly cannot rely on the product to grow beyond its present volume. In fact, the product's life cycle probably does not extend beyond the third or, at most, the fourth quarter of next year."

Ed thought for a moment that Sonny was going to challenge Ralph's statement, but Sonny appeared to think better of it. Rather, he slumped back in his chair and a wistful look crossed his face as he turned the gingham bear box around and around in front of him. Ed could almost hear him thinking of what a loss it would be when those few quarters passed and Bears Watching was only history.

"Afolabi, please present your situation." Ralph was moving right along. No regrets on his part—just the numbers, please.

Afolabi did not pause to look at his notes as Sonny had but launched immediately into his well-organized presentation. Ed was struck again by Afolabi's self-confidence and real sense of presence. He had once heard that Afolabi had developed his leadership style as a black activist during the early 1960s when he marched through the South with Dr. Martin Luther King. The rumor had it that Afolabi had then been known as "Willy" but that he had changed to an African name as part of his acknowledgment of his ethnic heritage. Sutton and Willy rather than Sonny and Afolabi. . . .

Meanwhile, Afolabi was talking about microwave ovens and the *New England Journal of Medicine*. Ed felt that he must have just missed something important.

"Apparently the original research was highly statistically inaccurate. A faulty computer program at the medical school, according to the researchers. Pure fraud, according to the skeptics. At any rate, when the second article ran in the *New England Journal* in January, it spawned a series of articles in the popular press that completely exonerated the microwave oven. There seems to be absolutely no scientific proof that foods heated in microwave ovens provide an intestinal environment that promotes growth of precancerous cells or that hosts parasitic development.

"As these articles have appeared, sales of microwave ovens have rebounded exponentially and volume on the microwave products of the Frozen and Refrigerated Area have also risen sharply. We had the production capacity to support this, but all the incremental sales are going straight to increased volume projections for the year for my area." Afolabi concluded his presentation smartly, depriving Ralph of the opportunity to cut him off.

"Thank you," said Ralph immediately. "And there you have it, ladies and gentlemen. You are all quite in agreement as to the issues here?" Everyone around the table nodded. "Then let us discuss solutions. Dora?"

"You'll all be glad to know," said Dora, smiling happily, "that the solutions available to us are quite simple. You see, it's all quite straightforward once you get used to the idea. After all, we're only talking about $8 million." She picked up yet another stack of papers and passed them to Ken and Joy.

"I've made a list of possibilities that are relevant to any of your businesses. What I suggest is that we review each briefly to make sure that you understand its thrust and that you then spend a day or two determining which option is most appropriate in your particular situation."

"We will then meet with each of you separately to hear your suggestions and work out a unified approach," added Ralph, looking at each V.P. in turn. Obviously everyone was going to have to like at least one of Dora's suggestions or Ralph was going to choose one for him or her.

Ed looked down at his copy of Dora's work sheet as she continued.

"First, we have a very simple option. Expenses that you expect to incur in the first quarter of fiscal 1988 can be incurred in the last quarter of fiscal 1987. For example, if you were planning to shoot commercials in January, produce them in December instead. Or if you were going to do some market research, move it up by a month or two."

"That might be harder than it sounds," said Joy. "Those commercials that I was going to film in January aren't even written yet."

"What you must think of here," Dora answered smoothly, "is the spirit of this spending rather than the letter of spending. If you are quite sure that the commercial will be written and actually filmed in January, you could have the agency bill you for estimated production costs in December and pay the bill before the end of the year."

"Are you sure I can do that?" asked Joy, sounding puzzled. "I thought that on our accounting system, even an expense that we prepaid in cash, like the insurance premiums on a manufacturing facility, had to be recognized on the accounting records a little bit at a time, spread across the months when the expense would be used up, so to speak."

"That's right." Sonny spoke up. "My accounting people are very clear on that. We have an accrual method of accounting, so what's important isn't when the cash is paid out, but when the benefit of the service accrues to the corporation."

"You've identified an interesting issue here, Joy," said Dora, smiling again and completely ignoring Sonny. Ed noticed that Ralph was sitting in absolute silence, looking wholly detached from the discussion.

Dora continued. "Part of your responsibilities as head of your area is to inform the accounting staff as to when the benefits of expenditures take place. Let's return to the advertising example. If you tell the accounting people that you are planning to benefit from the commercial during the current period and if the records from the advertising agency show billing during the current period, it is unlikely that any accountant is going to ask to be shown the actual commercial."

There was a momentary silence as the group realized the full impact of what Dora had just said. Then Sonny spoke up again. "Let me get this straight, Dora. I know and the agency knows that the commercial is not being filmed right now. But the accounting people only know what the paper work shows, and if I sign off on it, that makes it true for them."

"You understand the point quite well," replied Dora. Ralph remained silent.

"So you want me to tell them we've done something that we haven't done," added Sonny bluntly.

"I think we could express it a little more tactfully, Sonny," Dora went on. "We don't tell them an untruth. We simply allow them to reach their own conclusions and we don't dissuade them from these conclusions during the fourth quarter."

There was quiet throughout the room for a few moments. Then Ken Winsor spoke up. "Sort of a case of what they don't know won't hurt them." He nodded in support of his own idea. "Sounds okay to me. After all, accounting is there to serve management, not vice versa."

"I suppose it is the most practical approach," Joy said, looking at Ken thoughtfully. "You'd feel okay about it?"

"Sure," said Ken. "I've worked creatively with the accounting team before. But usually we were on the opposite tack: getting the advertising agency to delay billings, for example, rather than speed them up."

At the head of the table Ralph finally spoke. "I believe you gentlemen and the lady have a clear understanding of the principles of which Dora is speaking. Shall we have her continue with her other suggestions?"

Everyone nodded except Sonny. "I'm not sure I agree with Dora's approach," Sonny said slowly, "but I'm willing to hear more." He leaned back in his chair as if to show how unconcerned he was, but Ed noticed that he was drumming his fingertips repeatedly on the chair arm. "Maybe I'll like some of the other ideas better," Sonny added, looking hard at Ralph.

"I'm certain you will find the overall approach acceptable by the end of today's meeting, Sutton," said Ralph, looking fixedly at Sonny. Sonny broke Ralph's stare by looking straight across the table at Ed, who shrugged slightly.

"Let me continue." Dora spoke up. "Some of these other suggestions are, in fact, more commonplace.

"One option that is really quite simple is to increase expenditures for your area, with the increases taking place in the fourth quarter.

What manager has not wished he or she had more money to support advertising or promotion, for example? This would not be pulling spending forward, but rather increasing this year's budget on a one-time basis."

"This sounds great." Joy spoke up enthusiastically. "I'd love to do something like run an extra set of coupons on my fruit candy sheets for the Thanksgiving or Christmas holidays. That ought to give my volume projections a little boost." Suddenly she paused and put her hand over her mouth. "But how will that help things?" she went on, apparently impatient with herself. "We're trying to manage volume down, not up!"

"Obviously, the timing is very important here," said Dora supportively. "You've got the right idea already, Joy. Running the coupons before Christmas or even in the week between Christmas and New Year's would be ideal. Then retail sales would be increased during the next fiscal year."

"Wait a minute, Dora," intervened Sonny. He looked and sounded highly skeptical. "You know as well as we do that it's not retail sales that we're concerned with, it's wholesale sales. If I'm going to be running coupons at the end of December, I'll have my sales force out there a month or six weeks beforehand encouraging the grocery chains to stock up on the product before the coupon ever runs. Then they'll have enough volume on hand to meet increased demand."

"I believe," Ralph Myerson broke in stonily, "that you are missing Dora's point about timing, Sutton. Please make an attempt to think through your responses more carefully before you comment on these suggestions. What we are asking for is a spirit of open-mindedness and cooperation, not a detailed critique of each possibility."

"What you're asking for is manipulation of numbers!" said Sonny, his voice reverberating down the table.

"Oh, come on, Sonny," Ken Winsor broke in from his spot next to Dora. "What are you getting so excited about? Dora's not suggesting that we throw the game. Just that we use a little brains in place of nothing but brawn out there."

For a moment Ed thought Sonny was going to leap across the

table and throttle Ken. Sonny's usually open and friendly face was darkened by anger and his finger drumming had accelerated. After a brief struggle with himself, Sonny apparently regained his self-control. He crossed his arms brusquely across his chest and pushed his chair back from the table.

"Please, don't let me interrupt the creativity," he said sarcastically. "From here on out I'm just an impartial observer. Please—go on."

Dora looked at Sonny for a long moment, then rearranged her notes, apparently stalling for time until Ralph Myerson let her know what should happen next. "Please, Dora," he said after a moment.

"As I was saying," Dora began, speaking more quickly, "timing is the important thing here. We all know that shipments can be delayed unexpectedly and that retailers do not always receive goods on the schedule they had originally anticipated." Dora glanced at Sonny nervously and then rushed on.

"So it will be important to manage shipments to move volume forward into the oncoming fiscal year whenever possible." Sonny said "Hummph" noisily but did not speak otherwise.

"There are a few other possibilities I should mention," Dora went on, "and I'm sure you'll be able to think of others. Perhaps you have been considering a price increase that you think could have a temporary negative impact on volume. This would be the ideal time to take it, if you think that the net volume losses will offset the gains in profit contributions from higher sales prices. Things like that." Dora's voice trailed off and she again ruffled through her notes, this time more uncertainly. Finally she glanced at Ralph, somewhat beseechingly, Ed thought.

Ralph slowly looked at each person seated around the table. Although he was silent, he was clearly regaining control of the meeting. Ed felt himself flush again as Ralph's gaze fell on him. Finally, his visual survey complete, Ralph spoke. Although not hurried, his voice was forceful, almost strident.

"While we have been meeting, my secretary has contacted each of your offices and scheduled individual follow-up meetings for you with myself and Dora. If it was necessary to rearrange your schedule, your secretary was instructed to do so. I look forward to seeing you as scheduled, beginning tomorrow afternoon." He pushed his chair back firmly and stood up. Quickly, Ed rose, as did the others.

Ralph walked toward his office door but had only taken a few steps when he turned back to the group and looked directly at Sonny. "I will be seeing you first, Sutton," he said. "I'm sure you will be prompt." He turned again and continued into his office, trailed by Dora, who looked over her shoulder at the last minute and grimaced at the group in what appeared to be an attempt to smile again.

The moment the door to Ralph's office closed, Sonny spoke. "I'm getting out of here. I don't care for the cooperative and creative atmosphere," he said with heavy irony. "Anybody care to join me?"

"Sure," said Joy ingenuously. "I've got a pile of work on my desk and this meeting isn't going to lessen it." Ed and the others stood in somewhat uncomfortable silence as Sonny and Joy left the conference room by the other door.

"Well, really, it doesn't bother me a bit." Ken Winsor finally spoke up. "I heard from some of the older staff people that during the seventies they ended up burying money almost every quarter and that nobody ever raised a stink about it. I think what Dora said was right. Everybody does it. They just don't talk about it."

"I'm not so sure," said Ed thoughtfully.

"I wish there was a better way, something more subtle," Afolabi added.

"Well, of course we don't have much time to think up too many different solutions," Manfred de Chazan said. "What they're asking isn't really so bad, do you think?" Afolabi didn't answer but shrugged his shoulders as he walked into the hall.

As Ed waited for the elevator with the other three men, they were all silent, apparently lost in thought. For once the elevator arrived quickly. They got in, rode down together, and only broke the silence for quick good-byes before each turned toward a different wing of the building.

Once he'd left the others, Ed began walking hurriedly toward his office. This was such an unexpected turn of events that he wanted to sit down, think about it all in a quiet atmosphere, and play around with a few numbers before he reached any conclusions.

He ducked into his office before anyone had a chance to notice that he was back, closed the door, and walked to the long windows behind his desk to look out over the rolling grass behind the headquarters building.

Whether he had originally planned it or not, Ralph now apparently had decided to work on each of the six V.P.'s on a one-to-one basis. This meant that there wouldn't be another opportunity for one person's concerns to infect the others. Also, Ed thought uncomfortably, it would give Ralph a chance to bring the full force of his personality to bear on each V.P. Ralph could be hard to resist.

And, of course, by having the V.P.'s come in so soon, there was little opportunity for them to get together to compare notes or to plan a palace revolt. Every one of them—even Sonny—would already be back in his or her office, frantically crunching numbers, looking for the best way to bury money without creating problems for the long run.

Ed gazed fixedly through the window, one part of his mind admiring the distant stand of huge trees that ringed the ConCom property, the other assailed by a nagging thought just out of reach. Problems in the long run . . .

Suddenly Ed knew what was bothering him. If he did succeed in fixing this year's problems, pushing volume into the first quarter of next year, for example, what did that imply for the second or third quarter? When volume looked like it was going to drop in the later quarters, could he really go back to Ralph and say that it was just because of the games he'd been playing in the first quarter? If one could judge from Ralph's behavior today and Dora's masked but still evident uneasiness about the process, Ralph would probably have completely "forgotten" about the present corporate demands by next March or April.

Ed turned from the window, walked over to his desk, and dropped into his chair. This was the classic management squeeze. He had to be part of the team and get rid of some inconvenient money. But ultimately if there was a problem he'd be completely on his own. The other V.P.'s, Ralph, Dora—nobody would bail him out.

And what about the worst case, if the external auditors identified a violation of generally accepted accounting principles and refused to give a clean bill of health to Specialty Foods' financial statements? Would Ralph ever say Ed was just doing his job, that Ralph had asked for a little creative accounting? Never. In fact, he'd throw Ed to the lions just to show how clean his hands were.

Okay, thought Ed, that's the situation. Now I'd better come up with a damned good solution that protects me as well as gives Ralph what he wants. Ed took a pad of paper out of one drawer, a calculator out of another, and a loose-leaf folder with the current business plan from a credenza next to his desk. Now he was ready to work.

First, Dora had come up with a number of suggestions. She had undoubtedly discussed these with Ralph, so if Ed followed one of them, it would increase the likelihood that Ralph would accept his first proposal. Ed made a list.

1. Prepay expenses that will actually be incurred in the next fiscal year.
2. Increase spending on a one-time basis. Probably in some area of advertising or promotion.
3. Delay shipment of product into the first quarter of next year.
4. Take a price increase that you were thinking about taking anyway.

Ed read over his list a couple of times, then added a fifth option.

5. Beg off. Convince Ralph that Specialty Foods is too new and too vulnerable to get involved in his games. And too small to have a corporate bottom-line impact anyway.

Ed reread his expanded list. They were all possibilities at first glance, except number 4. There was no area where he'd planned to take a price increase. Besides, given the division's reorganization problems, particularly with the sales force, there was no such thing as a "safe" price increase right now. He crossed number 4 off the list.

Prepay expenses was the first thing to consider. Ed thought briefly about Virgil Wolfe, the top accounting man in the Specialty Foods

Division. Virgil didn't miss many tricks and it was essential, as Dora had described things, that Virgil not identify the fact that the expense would not actually be incurred at the time it showed up on the books.

Ed felt a strong distaste welling up for the process he was considering setting in motion. Becoming president of Specialty Foods had given him a great opportunity to try out his philosophy of good management: teamwork and a collegial atmosphere. He'd especially emphasized this in working with the staff people, who in most divisions ended up feeling like second-class citizens. In fact, it was only a few weeks ago that Virgil had told Ed how happy his staff seemed to be now that they were relatively insulated from the harshness of the other ConCom divisions.

Ed pushed his thoughts of Virgil aside. He hadn't decided to *do* anything yet—he was just reviewing possibilities. However, it would clearly be foolish, given the closeness he and Virgil had developed, to try to do anything blatant, like pay for a series of Italiano commercials that were going to be shot in January or February. He'd need to have the spending apply to something less obvious. Ed thumbed through the business plan notebook, thinking about each of the Specialty Foods products.

As he turned to the section on Salsa! Salsa! Salsa! he suddenly knew exactly what to do. Salsa! was still being sold at retail more or less as an afterthought by the Institutional Foods people. Consequently, its packaging was also an afterthought. It kept the product fresh, it told you what it was, but it didn't help to sell what was inside. The product cried out for good packaging, but Ed had been putting off a redesign because it would be expensive.

Now suddenly he had money and he'd been told to spend it. He could commission the design now, prepaying the design company and artists' fees. Usually, the prototype package would be made in-house, but he could probably also get the design company to handle this and add it to their invoice, which he would pay in advance. Maybe he could even have the designers commission the production of the first run of new packages. Of course, having packages made by outsiders instead of by ConCom would cost more money overall, but that wasn't such a big issue under these circumstances.

Ed started making a few calculations. The design process would cost about $50,000, including artists' fees. A package prototype usually ran about $1,500 inside, so say it would be $3,000 outside. And a run of packages could really add up—assume they'd keep the basic structure of a plastic container with printed labels. They ran about $.06 each in-house, maybe $.075 outside. If they bought 500,000 that would use up another $37,500. So total expenditures would be $90,000.

It wasn't much money, Ed thought, with $8 million to dispose of. Of course, Specialty Foods only accounted for 1 percent of sales of the entire Dry Groceries area, so maybe coming up with a solution to 1 percent of the problem wasn't totally unrealistic. If it wasn't enough, Ralph would certainly let him know!

Ed felt momentarily pleased with himself for having such a good idea to deal with Ralph's problem, but almost at once he realized that he'd been thinking in terms of *using up* money. This was not, he told himself somewhat miserably, the way a manager was supposed to think. You didn't use up money like it was a loaf of bread that was going to get stale. You *invested* money wisely.

But this was a good investment in the long run, he answered back to himself. And, equally important, it was in an area that Virgil Wolfe wouldn't be too interested in. Maybe he'd end up not having to lie about it at all; it would just slip by, undiscussed and undetected.

Ed quickly put a checkmark next to number 1 on his original list. Yes, this was a viable alternative. More cheerfully, he turned to number 2.

"2. Increase spending on a one-time basis." This had some obvious advantages over the prior suggestion. For one thing he'd be spending the money in a way that Virgil would fully approve of. Besides that, as Dora had pointed out, there were always places where the money could be used wisely.

Obviously, the logical starting place for spending more money was Italiano. This was where most of the money for recurring expenses, such as advertising and promotion, went anyway. The most obvious choice, increased advertising for the Italiano umbrella campaign, was probably not a good idea, however. As soon as

Italiano advertising had gone back on the air earlier in the year, sales had begun rising. It would be too hard to hold down retailers' demand for more volume if Ed increased advertising. And, of course, in order for this plan to work, the spending had to result in delayed volume increases or else earnings would simply go up more, making the problem worse instead of better.

What other spending could Specialty Foods put behind Italiano? Ed opened another drawer and took out a file labeled ITALIANO MEMOS. He looked through several papers until he came to a memo from Grady Jennings, entitled "Long-term Spending Possibilities." Yes, there was what he'd been thinking of. He skimmed down the page.

> **Suggestions for Supporting Gourmet Segment of Line**
> —*Supplementary print advertising in local upscale magazines, such as city monthlies*
> —*Recipe contest with local competitions building to national competition; famous Italian chef as judge, trip to Italy as prize*
> —*Couponing for individual products in line*

Ed smiled to himself. The last suggestion would work very well in this case. The gourmet products had never been promoted, though coupons for the secondary products including spaghetti and pizza sauces were used all the time. The gourmet line was performing very unevenly. Those items that were ending up primarily in supermarkets—the olives, olive oil, grated cheese—were building volume nicely. But the more esoteric and sophisticated items such as sun-dried tomatoes—those sold in gourmet shops—were still struggling.

Putting aside the pressure of having to spend money, did it make sense to offer coupons on these products? Ed thought back over a presentation on ConCom's promotional activities that he'd attended several months before. One thing they'd pointed out was that the person who redeemed coupons was not the impoverished mother of eight. Rather, it was the upper-middle-class lady who was a more sophisticated shopper and who had learned just how much she could save by using coupons.

That was the same lady who was Italiano's target. It made sense strategically, then. Furthermore, the retailers already had the product on their shelves because it wasn't moving as fast as everyone would like. So Ed could fudge the question of selling the product in advance of the coupon. Rather, he could let the sales force know that the coupon was going to run and they could tell the retailers that they were going to clean off their shelves. After the coupon boosted demand, they could go in during the first quarter of the next year and refill the shelves, hopefully on the promise of future couponing support.

This looked pretty good, all in all. Now how much would it cost?

Ed decided that on an experiment like this, where anything might happen, he'd limit the coupon target to 1 million people and he'd offer it to be used on either of the sun-dried tomato products, those in oil or the plain dried tomatoes. He'd have to have the coupon worth at least $.25; otherwise nobody would bother to cut it out. The value could be as high as $.50. But if they started off at that level, they'd be locked into $.50 forever. Better to start low, with the possibility of going up. Besides, most of the products only sold for between $.98 and $1.49, so $.25 would present a sizable savings.

Ed took another file out of the drawer in his desk and thumbed through some dog-eared sheets of paper. Here it was—the corporate coupon-redemption statistics. This was an old copy, left over from when he was responsible for couponing as part of his group product manager job. But the numbers tended to remain more or less constant over the years. He looked down the list: $.25 coupons tended to redeem at 5 to 7 percent. Since these products were not well established, he'd take the lower rate.

He figured 1 million coupons times the 5 percent redemption rate meant 50,000 coupons redeemed. The cost to Specialty Foods was $.25 each plus $.075 for handling to the retail grocer, or a total of $.325 each. Total costs, therefore, would be $16,250.

Then there was the cost of placing the coupon. Ed decided he'd have to have Madeline check to make sure he was right, but he seemed to remember that to distribute 1 million coupons via the four-color supplements that went into Sunday newspapers would cost about $25,000, plus another $35,000 for production costs. This would bring the total cost of the couponing to $76,250.

Ed checked off Dora's second option. This was acceptable, too. Then he started thinking about her third idea: delay shipments into the first quarter of next year.

Initially, Ed decided, he didn't like this alternative as well as the two he'd just reviewed. First of all, it wouldn't be doing anything positive for the business, like a new package or a round of coupons would do. Second, it had the potential to do real harm. If product shipments were delayed, the retailers could run out of product on their shelves. Not only would the lost sales never be made up; Specialty Foods might even lose shelf space if the delays were long enough. Ed knew from experience that the sales force would have a hell of a time convincing the retailers to give them back the space that some other manufacturer had already gobbled up.

On the other hand, Ed began to realize, this was the kind of thing that would never land him in real trouble with Virgil Wolfe or anybody else. All the planning to delay shipments could be done verbally with Ozzie Harris, the director of shipping for the Specialty Foods products. Ozzie was a remarkably taciturn individual, seemingly worn down by years of dealing with impassioned Italiano exporters, frenzied American product managers, and stubborn factory foremen who refused to speed up or slow down their production lines. If Ed told Ozzie to sit on a few shipments of one of their products, Ozzie probably wouldn't even ask why.

Ed leaned back in his chair and swiveled slowly from side to side. He began mentally reviewing the Specialty Foods line again. What product could he hold back with the least impact on long-term sales? Something seasonal, perhaps. No, that didn't make sense. If demand was seasonal and you missed it, you were dead. If it wasn't the right season for demand, you wouldn't be shipping product anyway.

What about something whose *production* was seasonal? Ed thought carefully about some of the smaller product lines in Specialty Foods: raspberry jam? Already out the door. Dried apples? Too little volume. Maple syrup?

That was it! Maple syrup.

Maple syrup was a notoriously temperamental product in terms of timing of production and distribution. No one, but no one, could control the start and finish of the maple sap flow. If winter shipments were delayed, all he had to do was blame Mother Nature.

Furthermore, the demand for maple syrup was pretty much always there. When he'd gone through the files ConCom inherited when it bought out Scarborough Foods, Ed had found some market research data on the Mountain Gourmet products. It wasn't very sophisticated, but at least it was research. Apparently, hardly any consumer ever let his (or her) supply of maple syrup run out completely. If he was getting low, he'd go buy more. If it wasn't on the shelves, he'd go back in a few weeks and try again. In other words, the dedicated maple syrup user had already adjusted to the vagaries of maple syrup production and acted accordingly. So withholding shipments would ultimately have little or no effect on total sales.

This was a terrific option, Ed decided. Now what would this mean in terms of delayed earnings?

Ed turned to the section of his notebook that covered Mountain Gourmet products. There were projected sales of maple syrup, broken down into monthly segments.

Month	$ million Sales
January	.1
February	.2
March	.9
April	1.1
May	1.2
June	1.1
July	—
August	—
September	—
October	.3
November	.4
December	.3
TOTAL	5.6

NOTE: Maple syrup production takes place primarily during the early spring months, late February through April. A secondary season is in the autumn, late September through early November.

It couldn't be better, Ed thought. If he held back all shipments this fall, that was $1 million in sales. Profit contribution in the maple product ran—he turned to the next page to check—about 52 percent, so this would be a reduction of $520,000. Of this maybe 40 to 50 percent fell through to the bottom line of profit per se. That would be a final number of between $208,000 and $260,000. This would take care of 3 percent of the $8 million. That ought to make Ralph Myerson very happy.

Ed checked off the third alternative, put down his pen, and thought back over his calculations so far. They all looked good, especially the third. Of course, if he did delay shipping the maple syrup, this would reduce the total sales and earnings for Specialty Foods for the year. Since total division sales were forecast at $25 to $30 million, a reduction of sales by $1 million—4 percent of total volume—was meaningful.

Actually, a reduction of that magnitude was extremely meaningful. Maybe too meaningful. After all, he was trying to build a successful division here. Lots of people were getting paid based on how the division did, not the least of whom was Ed Cunningham. If one of Ed's subordinates had suddenly come into his office and told him to expect a 4 percent shortfall on the annual sales projections this late in the year, he would have hit the ceiling. Now he was going to do it to himself, and just because he was intimidated by Ralph Myerson.

Ed poised his pen over his page of notes. Then decisively he wrote a large question mark next to his checkmark of number 3, delaying shipments.

Again Ed sat back in his chair. He looked at his watch. He'd been in here for over two hours, playing around with these ideas and these numbers. It was amazing that nobody had come looking for him during such a long stretch of time. Probably it was because they knew he'd been meeting with Ralph. Damn it, *everybody* was intimidated by Ralph. Rather than coming to see how he'd done in the meeting, they were all lying low, even Ellie Vogel. Ralph wants a new sacrificial lamb? Thank goodness it's old Ed and not me.

Ed felt himself getting steamed up. He started thinking about the meeting itself, especially about Sonny's concerns and how Ralph had treated them. Sonny was usually enthusiastic but mild-mannered. Yet as soon as he disagreed with Ralph, Ralph came down on him in what could only be described as a humiliating and vindictive manner.

Well, Ed Cunningham could stand up to that kind of pressure. Ed picked up his pen again and drew several dark lines under his number 5, "beg off." After all, Specialty Foods was a brand-new division. It was a minuscule part of Consolidated Commodities and it was ridiculous to expect the division to play a significant role in the kind of manipulation Ralph Myerson was endorsing, even demanding. Ed was coming in pretty close to his profit projections. Let the big players come up with the big solutions.

Ed put his pen down and stood up. Enough of this. He was going to start going around in circles. It was definitely time to get out of the office, to go talk to some human beings, return a few phone calls, look at the afternoon mail, act normal.

He left his office and walked down the hall to his secretary's desk. She looked up from her typewriter. "Why, Mr. Cunningham, I was getting a little worried about you," she said in her most motherly manner. "You've been gone an awfully long time. In fact, a couple of hours ago I was talking to Mr. Myerson's secretary about another meeting with him and she said the meeting you were in would be breaking up any minute."

Ed laughed, his tension falling away suddenly. "He didn't eat me alive this time, Ellie," he said. "I've been hiding out in my office working on a little problem he dumped in my lap. I had to get some things figured out before my next meeting with him. By the way," he said in a casual tone, "what slot did I draw?"

Ellie opened the large calendar book on her desk. "I guess you didn't have to be in such a hurry," she said, looking down the page carefully. "You don't have to report in until 4:00 P.M. the day after tomorrow. In fact, Mr. Myerson's secretary said you were getting the last appointment in this set of meetings."

Ed let his breath out slowly. "To tell you the truth," he said to Ellie, "I'm just as glad I got some of the preparation behind me. Now I can get on with some other things. I'm just off for a cup of coffee. Come into my office when I get back and let me know what I missed this afternoon."

"My pleasure," said Ellie. "About five minutes?"

"Perfect," said Ed, setting off down the hall toward the coffee machine. As he walked along, he thought about the implications of getting the last meeting slot. By the time he got to Ed, Ralph would have gotten his pound of flesh from everybody else and there would probably be little or nothing he'd absolutely have to have from Specialty Foods. Oh, he'd take it gladly, even if it was the million-dollar maple syrup delay. But Ed could probably even get away with choosing his last option—with saying he didn't want to play in this particular game.

Of course, what this might do to his career was an open question. But at least he wasn't first, so he was not in the same no-win situation as poor old Sutton.

As a matter of fact, he'd go over those alternatives again after he finished catching up with Ellie. Since he had the last meeting with Ralph, some of the heat was off and he was beginning to see that this was really quite an interesting little business problem ConCom was facing.

Indicate your choice here:

_____ Option 1. Prepay Salsa! packaging development and manufacturing expenses.
_____ Option 2. Run coupon on sun-dried tomatoes in Sunday supplements.
_____ Option 3. Delay shipments of maple syrup.
_____ Option 4. Do not offer an area for earnings reduction in the Specialty Foods Division.

9

Closing the Apple Products Production Facility

October 6, 1987

As the Green Mountain Airlines plane banked over the Lebanon, New Hampshire, airport, Ed Cunningham lost himself in the beauty of the vibrant autumn colors spread out beneath him. The plane dropped into a landing pattern that led deeper and deeper into a valley between two imposing mountains. Ed could almost see individual leaves of gold, vermilion, and rust flash by. Suddenly there was a bump as the plane hit the landing strip. Regretfully Ed stuffed a sheath of papers back into his briefcase, snapped it shut, and straightened his tie. Although he felt refreshed by the two hours of escape the flight had provided, he hadn't lost the basic feeling of anxiety he'd been carrying with him ever since the possibility of closing the Chelsea, Vermont, plant had arisen several months before.

From the time that Mountain Gourmet had been transferred into the Specialty Foods Division the previous year, Ed knew there were some issues about the Apple Products facility that would have to be resolved sooner or later. However, the major product lines of Mountain Gourmet, maple products and the jams and jellies, had kept him from focusing on Apple Products. As long as volume in these two areas was steady or growing, Mountain Gourmet could meet its modest sales and earnings objectives. It was really a question of keeping the most important things rolling during a time when each month seemed to bring about the addition of another product or product line for Specialty Foods to handle.

As Ed unfastened his seat belt and joined the other passengers getting off the plane, he remembered exactly when Apple Products had become a crisis. It hadn't been gradual: one day the patient had a headache; the next day the patient was in the intensive care unit. The focal point had been around the beginning of August when the first ripe McIntosh apples began coming in. The Mountain Gourmet group product manager had burst into his office, his red hair practically standing on end, his face flushed.

"Ed, Ed, Ed!" he kept repeating as he rushed across the room and around Ed's desk to grab his shoulder. "There's been a terrible accident up in Chelsea. We've got to do something about it right away."

"All right, Win, I'm sure we can take care of it," Ed replied, standing up and clasping the other man's arm in return. "Catch your breath and fill me in. Here, sit down, sit down. I can't do anything until I know exactly what's going on."

Ed pushed Winship Elsworth III into the closest chair. It never failed, he thought to himself. These stuffy WASP types who acted as if they wouldn't be fazed by World War III ended up falling apart the fastest the minute things got rough.

"One of the cider mill operators slipped on some apple pulp and hit his head on the overhead controls," Win began, running his hands through his hair distractedly. "He fell unconscious onto the conveyor line and went through the apple press. Oh, God, it was awful! Nobody even knew he was there until he came out the other side. By that time, his leg was fractured. He was all bruised up. And he'd regained enough consciousness to start screaming curses at the workers at that end of the operation."

Win paused dramatically. "And—you're not going to believe this—he's eighty years old."

"Will he live?" Ed asked anxiously.

"Oh, he's going to be okay," Win conceded almost grudgingly. "But," he rushed on, "the OSHA inspectors are all over the place, the cider press seems to be beyond repair, and three of the ladies who work in the bottling room are threatening to quit because of the vile things he was shouting at them."

This *is* serious, Ed remembered thinking. It was too bad about the old man, but that wasn't the big problem. It was the Occupational Safety and Health people who were the real issue. When they got there, things could go downhill in a hurry. Little facilities like the cider mill that made do with outdated equipment could suddenly be called on to invest hundreds of thousands of dollars in safety programs. Sometimes the costs of the required changes were much greater than the factory's entire sales, much less its profits or capital expenditure budgets.

Over the next couple of days, Ed had managed to gather enough information to get a clearer picture of what was going on. First, he'd received, via Federal Express, a copy of the *Valley News* dated the day of the accident. On the front page of the newspaper, an afternoon local, was a splashy article that apparently had been inserted on a stop-press basis immediately after the accident took place. CHELSEA SENIOR CITIZEN SERIOUSLY INJURED IN FREAK INDUSTRIAL ACCIDENT, screamed the headline, which extended across the top of the edition.

> Chelsea, Vermont. August 5. Joseph O'Malley, aged 79, was seriously injured here today when an apple press that he was operating apparently ran amuck and crushed his body. O'Malley, a long-time employee of the Apple Products Co-op, was operating the press when part of the equipment was jarred loose, striking him on the head. The blow knocked him unconscious and he collapsed onto the conveyor belt carrying apples into the huge industrial-sized press.
> The press, which apparently has no safety sensing device, continued to operate as usual, pressing his unconscious body for a period of several minutes, before the conveyor belt moved him from under the press and into the pulp disposal area.
> Eyewitnesses said that O'Malley was alive as he was ejected from the press and several other employees pulled his bruised and broken form from the belt. O'Malley regained consciousness and immediately began complaining of intense pain in his legs and chest.
> "The man is almost eighty years old," said Oliver Ramsey, an Emergency Medical Technician who arrived at the scene of the grisly accident as part

of the mobile rescue team. "In a person that old the bones are brittle, the heart muscle is weakened, and even the mental functioning is fragile. We took him into the Emergency Trauma Center and we're just hoping for the best. He seems like a wonderful old man, but at his age, anything could be wrong."

Ed had not been cheered by this article, but over the next few days it appeared that Mr. O'Malley had suffered a broken leg and had no other serious injuries. His progress was reported by follow-up articles, but when Ed received copies of the newspapers in which they appeared, he found they were all small articles located in the section of the paper following the want ads.

While news of Mr. O'Malley trickled in, other information on Apple Products had come in from Madeline, who had investigated the situation in one of the analytic frenzies at which she excelled.

The Apple Products facility was located in a tiny town in central Vermont called Chelsea. It was about an hour's drive north of the Lebanon, New Hampshire, airport and an hour south of the Vermont capital, Montpelier, far from the glamour of the Vermont ski slopes and tourist industry. Central Vermont was dairy farming country primarily, but there were also thousands of apple trees there.

These trees were not located in large neat orchards consisting of a few hybridized apple species, like those found throughout upstate New York and Washington State. Rather, these trees were both cultivated and wild, with an abundance of antique species as well as the commonplace McIntosh and Delicious. Some were in small orchards adjoining cow pastures; others were on the edges of forests or in farmers' front yards. The trees represented an enormous variety of apples. In fact, the International Green Earth Foundation, which lobbied to preserve heritage and antique plants against the inroads of commercialization and hybridization, had chosen the apple trees of central Vermont for its 1966 "Hope for Tomorrow" award.

It had been the diversity of apple types that had led to the development of the cider mill and related production facilities during the 1960s. A local dairy farmer's activist wife had set up an apple co-op in Chelsea so other local people could bring their apples, whether wild or cultivated, to be pressed into cider. For so many pounds of apples, you got so much cider free. If you didn't want the cider, the mill paid you. If you didn't have apples but wanted cider, you paid the mill. It had all been financed by a modest grant from the state Agricultural Extension Office, which was looking, at the time, for ways to generate production of new agricultural products.

Gradually the cider had become known throughout New England as tourists stopped at the mill and sampled the cider. Because everybody brought in different apples, the taste of the cider could vary from day to day. But it was never bland and its local character appealed to the Woodstock generation as they traipsed through New England looking for their roots.

In the early 1970s, the mill joined the evolving Mountain Gourmet co-op. By that time, apples were pouring in from all over Vermont as more people got word of how they could earn a little extra cash from the apples that previously they'd raked up and fed to their pigs. The founder, who still ran the mill, needed a bigger market for the increased cider production and the co-op provided it.

Throughout the 1970s, the mill made a lot of money, all of which was put back into the facilities. The primary outcome was a very large cider mill that had evolved from bits and pieces of equipment purchased over the years. Backing up the cider mill were a large vacuum-storage facility, a pulp machine that processed apples so they could be made into apple butter and applesauce, and a simple apple-drying operation. As part of the co-op arrangement, the apple pulp was shipped by refrigerated truck down to White River Junction, Vermont, where another co-op member had a jam and jelly processing plant.

This was the Apple Products setup when Scarborough Foods acquired the co-op in 1981; it was basically unchanged when ConCom bought out Scarborough in 1986.

Apple Products now had thirteen full-time and seven seasonal employees. The Vermont apple season itself lasted about three months, from August through October. During this time there were two people who handled all the apple intake. People still brought in their own apples, but the volume was very high; in fact, some farmers had planted apple trees over the years because they knew they'd find an ongoing market for the apples in Chelsea.

Some of the apples were used during this time and others were put into storage. The storage facility was a large concrete-block building consisting of a series of storage rooms. As each room was filled, it was closed off and a special machine was used to remove the oxygen from the air inside the room, creating a vacuum. In that vacuum, apples did not decay as quickly as they did outside. Consequently, they could be kept for as long as six months and still be suitable for processing. This storage technique had enabled Apple Products to produce for ten months a year rather than only the three or four months when newly harvested apples were available.

For the year-round production, there were five people who ran the cider mill itself, three people in the bottling and shipping operation, one in warehousing, and one in trucking. In addition, the pulping machine was run year-round by another employee and there were two people who worked all year in the office.

Besides the two seasonal employees who handled apple intake, there were five ladies who handled the seasonal apple-drying operation. Because the apples were dried in a special way, using no chemicals or preservatives, this operation was very labor-intensive. The apples were even peeled by hand to prevent bruising. The finished dried apples were sold primarily through health-food stores and were rather expensive. Consequently, demand had never reached the point where the apple-drying operation needed to be run year-round. In addition, there was some question whether apples that had been vacuum-stored could be dried satisfactorily using the Apple Products technique. At any rate, this continued to be a seasonal operation, running for four months a year.

All twenty of the regular Apple Products employees were from the town of Chelsea or the immediately surrounding area. Most of them had worked for Apple Products since the 1970s. The man who'd been injured in the cider mill accident had been running the cider mill itself since the mid-sixties, when he'd taken over the job after he retired from the local post office. He was now close to eighty but his age had never seemed to be a problem before the accident.

The last full-time employee was the manager of Apple Products. Caleb Ross was a man in his mid-thirties who had gotten a degree in agriculture from Cornell and then bought a small dairy farm outside of Chelsea. He'd gotten interested in Apple Products when he took in his apples to be pressed for cider, and a few years before had come on full-time as manager while his wife ran their dairy farm.

Ed's mental review faded as he realized he'd just walked across the tarmac and through the airport, picked up his bag, and gone out to the front of the airport building without noticing one thing he was doing. He looked carefully at the suitcase he was holding. Yes, he had managed to pick up the right bag. But he'd have to keep his thoughts a little more focused during his visit here. He had a lot to figure out in the next day or so. Now where could Caleb Ross be? Ellie hadn't set up a car rental because Caleb had insisted that he wanted to pick Ed up himself.

The road in front of the airport was deserted. All the other passengers on Ed's plane seemed to have disappeared. Suddenly a green pickup truck came racing up the hill and ground to a halt in front of Ed. There appeared to be something written on the door of the truck but it was blurred by a heavy coating of dust. Could this be . . . ?

"Mr. Cunningham?" The driver of the truck was leaning across the cab. His face was shadowed by the bill of a green baseball hat but his voice was friendly. "Mr. Cunningham, it's me, Caleb Ross." The driver leaned across and opened the door of the pickup. "Just throw your bag in the back there and hop in."

Somewhat reluctantly, Ed wedged his suitcase into what looked like a bunch of feed sacks. He climbed into the cab of the truck and put out his hand. "Ed Cunningham. Glad to meet you. I guess my plane got in a little early."

"Nope, I'm just a little late," Caleb said matter-of-factly. "There's a lot of worry up in Chelsea and I was just trying to put a few minds at ease. I told them all that Consolidated Commodities hadn't made up its mind yet on exactly what to do with us, so there was no sense pestering you when you got here. Everybody should just cooperate, answer your questions, and I was sure you'd do the best you could."

Ed nodded; he couldn't think of anything to add to Caleb's assessment of the reason for his trip. Those poor people at the facility were right to be worried: they could all be out of a job as a result of his visit and they probably didn't have a farm and a college degree to fall back on as Caleb did.

Ed's silence didn't seem to bother Caleb as he guided them up a few miles of interstate highway and then over a series of winding Vermont roads. Caleb pointed out the highest mountain in the region, the locations of some of the other local businesses, and where the best fishing was as they drove along the White River. Most of the time, however, he was silent also.

Between landmarks, Ed started thinking back over his preparation for this trip. When he'd been sitting in Fairfield County going through the numbers, he had managed to be analytical only by not thinking too much about the people whose lives were the reality behind his figures. He'd gone so far as to decide not to visit Chelsea to meet the people at all. However, Irma Saloman, the executive vice-president of Corporate Relations, had insisted that he make this trip.

Irma had turned up at Ed's door one day about a week after the accident and invited herself in to hear about how Ed planned to handle the situation over the long term. When he explained that he was going to make this purely a business decision, Irma had protested.

"Let's say you people do decide to close down this operation entirely," she argued. "If nobody from ConCom's even been up there, it's going to look very, very bad. The heartless corporation takes over this helpless little agrarian operation and *Bang!*"—she slammed her carefully manicured hand down on Ed's desk so hard he jumped—"kills it dead.

"After some of the other problems we've had," she continued, folding her hands primly in her lap, "such as alleged pollution and sticky labor negotiations, we just can't leave ourselves too open on this one, Ed."

After they talked it through, Ed had decided that she was probably right. So here he was, in the local version of the company limousine, meandering over winding Vermont highways, unable to enjoy the magnificent scenery or refreshing autumn snap in the air as he went to decide the fate of twenty people and perhaps a whole town.

Caleb turned the pickup into a dusty area in front of a group of rusty ramshackle buildings. "Well, here's the best sight of today: Apple Products," he said proudly. "This front part might not look like much, but it all works." He paused and went on in a less exuberant voice. "Well, it all used to work. Of course since the accident, the mill itself's been shut down."

He turned off the ignition but didn't make a move to get out of the truck. "We've managed to keep all the regular employees on, at least part-time, by not hiring our two seasonal people to handle apple intake and instead splitting that job up between the people who usually run the mill. Except for Joe, of course. I managed to talk him into staying home since the accident. He can manage real well on his post office retirement check. And for a long time I thought he was working just out of mule stubbornness, just to prove to somebody he wasn't too old to work."

The door of the front building opened and a middle-aged man in a flannel shirt looked out, saw the truck, and nodded. "Guess they're getting nervous, waiting for you to come in," said Caleb.

"And I'm getting a little nervous myself," said Ed, opening his door. The sooner they started, the sooner he'd have the additional information he needed so he could get this thing decided once and for all.

The next day and a half went by rapidly. Every employee of Apple Products wanted a chance to talk to Ed and to convince him that Apple Products should be kept open. Although no one told him about the hardship closing the facility would work for himself or herself, many of them told Ed how hard it would be for one of the other employees. One of the younger men had come up with the worst story.

"I'll manage okay," he'd confided to Ed after showing him around the apple storage rooms, "but somebody like that little old Liza Farns is going to have a real problem. Ever since her husband took bad sick with the leukemia, he can't work a bit. And she was already expecting with their third. Her mother's taking care of the children now, but she's a widow herself, so they all are depending on Liza to bring in some money. I've heard her mother's keeping a little truck garden on the side, but with winter coming on I guess that won't be bringing much."

By seven o'clock the next evening, Ed was exhausted. He'd seen everyone and learned all he could. He planned to take an 8:00 A.M. flight the next morning. For now, it was wonderful just to be back at his Lebanon motel, to be out of Chelsea, away from the well-meaning Apple Products employees.

As Ed took off his jacket and tie, he thought guiltily about how much of the basic rethinking of Apple Products he'd managed to put off until now. Madeline had assembled all the numbers, had gotten input from the division's financial analyst, and Ed had just stuck it in his briefcase, postponing until after his trip the hard look at what was probably inevitable.

Tonight he had to sit down and get through it all, even if all the facts were going to lead him to recommend closing the facility. As he settled down in the one comfortable chair his motel room offered, he decided that after he did his unappealing homework, he'd reward himself with a call home to Claire.

Ed spent the next two hours sorting out the information he'd gathered and added it to what he had brought with him. He decided to make some informal notes that he could use later in putting together his formal recommendation to the chairman.

BASIC DECISION
—*Invest in the facility, especially the cider mill*
or
—*Shut down the whole operation*

ECONOMIC CONSIDERATIONS RE CAPITAL INVESTMENT

1. Apple Products has been profitable up to this year. There is every reason to believe that normal operations would provide a continuing operating profit. In 1986, sales were $271,450. Operating expenses were $206,530. Operating profit, therefore, was $64,920 or almost 24 percent of sales. NOTE: Operating profit in other Specialty Foods areas runs around 40 percent of sales, so even though Apple Products is making money, it is making less than other product lines.

2. A large capital investment would be required to continue operation of the cider mill. The mill has a number of major safety violations that it would be extremely expensive to correct. It would be more economical to scrap the existing equipment and buy all new equipment. This would cost approximately $450,000 to provide the same capacity the old mill had.

3. Substantial additional capacity could be added or other equipment could be purchased that would enable Apple Products to reduce the number of employees relative to the output of the mill. This would reduce operating expenses. However, this equipment would be completely different from what Apple Products now has. Rather than pressing raw apples, it would involve chopping the apples, heating them to maximize juice extraction, and then straining the resultant juice. The final product wouldn't be true cider; it would be blander with no pulp, more like commercial apple juice.

4. The current corporate guideline for target return on investment is 17 percent. Small equipment purchases (such as this) are evaluated on a five-year time frame. However,

> *the additional capital investment of $450,000 would not bring about the required revenue increase of $76,500 per year and could generate little labor savings without having a negative impact on product quality. Therefore, the proposal to buy new equipment for Apple Products would not meet this target.*

Ed sighed. He'd hoped to uncover something during his visit that he could use to indicate that this capital investment was a reasonable one for ConCom. But making this investment in Apple Products wasn't going to improve its earnings on cider one bit. Of course, investing in the heat-processing equipment would add capacity, perhaps to the point where the equipment purchase would meet the capital-investment objectives. Briefly Ed toyed with the idea of changing the type of equipment used for making cider. No, he thought, it just wouldn't work. The cider was the heart of Apple Products and the equipment was key to the cider. It would lose its varietal nature and end up just being something you'd buy in a grocery store. In the end, changing equipment would not present a volume opportunity for Specialty Foods because they'd be making a product they couldn't sell through the specialty foods outlets anyway.

If the cider mill was not saved, what would be the financial implications for ConCom? Perhaps he could make a case for the capital investment as a way of preventing other losses.

Ed took out some information Madeline had given him on the asset base of Apple Products. If the assets were not fully depreciated, then closing the facility would result in writing off assets. This might be undesirable to the corporation if other assets were being written off this year. He might be able to make a case on this basis.

"The Apple Products group is working off an extremely low asset base," Madeline had written. "All assets were fully depreciated at the time ConCom took over the group with the exception of the apple storage facility, which was completed in 1984. Its cost was $275,000 to be depreciated over seven years using the straight-line method. Therefore annual depreciation is $39,286, for accumulated depreciation to this point of $117,857. The remaining asset base is $157,143."

Well, so much for that idea, thought Ed. Nobody would balk at writing off $157,000. If only there had been a bigger building or all the equipment wasn't so old or Apple Products had its own orchards with tractors and mowers or whatever orchards needed. Madeline had listed the assets that were fully depreciated below her note. Even the pickup truck Caleb Ross drove was so old it was considered valueless by corporate standards. Yes, as things stood, the financial analyst types would clearly choose not to make the capital investment but to write off the assets.

What would be the implications for the company in terms of the other apple products? The pulp operation could easily be transferred to the jam and jelly plant. They could probably even move the same machine down there. The jam and jelly facility had its own storage space and some could probably be adapted to handle the relatively small quantity of apples used in the pulp-based products.

The apple-drying operation could also be moved, although it produced so little revenue that it probably wasn't worth moving—only about $10,000 in annual sales. Clearly not worth saving, from the financial point of view.

Ed put down his pen. His trip had been a failure, a waste of time. He couldn't find a way of keeping the facility open from the point of view of dollars-and-cents returns. If he hadn't come up here, he could have reached that same conclusion.

But now he'd met all the people involved and they had become individuals in his mind. When he made his proposal to shut down the facility, everybody else would be seeing a neat business proposal, but he'd be seeing faces, employees' houses that needed paint and repairs, the bedraggled Chelsea village green. Caleb had told him that the thirteen people who worked full-time for Apple Products constituted 5 percent of the entire Chelsea work force. God, it was a single-handed recession he was going to induce.

Get a grip on yourself, Cunningham, he told himself harshly. If you wanted to save the world you could have joined the Peace Corps. This is big business and you've worked hard to get where you are. You can't suddenly change everything now.

Wearily Ed picked up the phone. Maybe he'd give Claire a call even if he hadn't quite laid this decision to rest. He dialed his home number; the phone rang several times and then Claire answered.

"Hi, honey, it's me," Ed began. "I sure as hell wish you were here with me."

"Hi yourself," Claire answered. "We all miss you a lot. Has the trip been worthwhile? You sound like things aren't going as well as you hoped."

Ed sighed again. "The trip's been a disaster. This place reminds me of something out of a news documentary on rural poverty." Ed picked up his pen from the desk and started clicking the point in and out. "And all this trip's done is make it abundantly clear that I'm about to make things up here a whole lot worse. I'm about to put twenty people out of work and there's no way to make the numbers show that this isn't the only option."

"That sounds awful," Claire replied. "I suppose you have to look at it from the numbers point of view?"

"That's certainly how ConCom will look at it," Ed said dejectedly.

"I guess that's how they make so much money." There was a moment of silence. "Is there some way you could do something with those people that wouldn't require an investment by ConCom? Maybe you could help them find other jobs or help them take over the operation of the Apple Products setup themselves or something like that?"

"That's a very nice idea, Claire," said Ed somewhat impatiently, "but Specialty Foods isn't a social service agency. I've got a business to run."

Claire didn't answer.

"It's not such a bad idea in theory," Ed finally conceded. "Usually, we could assign people to another part of the operation, but when you take out apple cider there isn't much of an operation left. Or you could send people to a plant that ConCom operates elsewhere. But all these people grew up in Chelsea and most of them farm on the side, so they're completely immobile. Or if they were executive types you can out-place them. But these poor people make less than $10,000 a year. Do you realize that one out-placement fee is about twice that?" Ed could hear his voice rising in frustration.

"Ed, Ed." Claire was getting calmer as Ed got more excited. "Please, I'm on *your* side."

"I'm sorry," Ed answered, "but I've been going around in mental circles for two days now. None of the things I know how to do will work in this situation."

"Let me try out another perspective," said Claire. "Now don't jump all over me. Just give it a chance."

Ed took a deep breath. "Okay, go ahead."

"You're a human being with feelings about these people and their problems but you're also a ConCom employee. You have an obligation to think about the company, your career there, and these employees all in a kind of equation. Unless you can find a way of balancing out all three things, you're not going to be happy with any choice you make."

"That's a good point," Ed said. "I'm juggling so many things that I can't tell where I'm going."

"Yes. But I think that all in all it comes down to choosing between two things." Claire sounded more self-assured as she went on. "First, you can go in and make the clean, clear-cut business-motivated decision. ConCom closes the facility. You and that PR woman—"

"Irma Saloman."

"Right—Irma—you work out a plan to handle the press, to phase out things so your action is not so harsh. You offer the people other jobs; maybe some will take them. You relocate the manager. You do the best you can with a sad situation and come out of it looking like a firm, strong, but thoughtful corporate player."

"And number two?" asked Ed.

"Second, you take the conscientious liberal approach. You go in and ask the corporation to defer making a final business decision for, say, three months. Then you work like crazy with the Apple Products manager and the Chelsea mayor and the Vermont Office of Economic Development and anybody else you can find to try to get something going for those twenty people. If you succeed, you feel good and you've done good. But if you fail, you've cost ConCom unnecessary money and you look like a fuzzy-brained do-gooder who can't face up to the hard decisions."

Ed took another deep breath. "No wonder this has been so painful," he said. "But the way you put it is probably pretty accurate."

"Thanks," replied Claire, laughing.

"You're welcome," Ed continued seriously. "Just let me go through it again. The first choice is low risk but low reward. There probably won't be a big problem if Irma and I work things out tactfully. We shut the facility down and in a year nobody around ConCom remembers it ever existed.

"The second choice is high risk and uncertain reward. If I succeed in getting something going for these people, ConCom might consider that a plus. We like to talk about our social responsibility. On the other hand, if I go in with what is basically a proposal to do nothing, it could reflect very badly on me. The only way I could cover myself would be to set a limit on the delay. Even then, top management might see it as a way of trying to get out of making a difficult decision. And waffling on decision-making is one of the cardinal sins at ConCom."

"So you've said many times," said Claire supportively.

"And let's say they're willing to wait and I can't pull off something for those people in Chelsea." Ed seemed almost to be talking to himself. "Then I've wasted corporate funds, postponed the inevitable, and made a fool of myself. To say nothing of adding a lot of responsibilities to what is already about a one-hundred-hour-a-week job."

"A hundred and ten hours, I'd say," Claire amended lightly. Then she continued in a more serious tone. "But now that you've stated the problem so well, I'm curious. What *are* you going to recommend?"

Indicate your choice here:

_____ Option 1. Close the Apple Products facility immediately, writing off the storage facility and offering continued employment to any employee who is willing to relocate to another ConCom facility.

_____ Option 2. Continue to operate the Apple Products facility until and only until December 31, 1987. During the three-month transition period, look for alternatives to ConCom's continued operation of the facility.

10

Choosing a New Group Product Manager

November 16, 1987

Ed Cunningham glanced at his watch and fought down the desire to squeeze in one more phone call before Martha Bleecker, Specialty Foods' Human Resources liaison, turned up at his office. Instead, he decided, he'd take a minute to retrieve his jacket from its usual spot behind the door, straighten his tie, and neaten up his desk.

Even while he was putting on his jacket, Ed had to laugh at himself. Martha, though certainly not much older than he was, had a schoolmarmish air that caused him to be on his "company behavior." In some ways, it wasn't surprising that Martha had never risen higher in the ranks than her current staff position: she was a real rules person rather than someone with the kind of freewheeling problem-solving orientation that Ed felt made a good general manager.

As Ed headed back toward his desk, there was a knock at the door and Martha walked in, followed by a rather rotund young man. In her navy blue suit, white silk blouse, and small floppy bow tie, Martha looked exactly like an illustration from one of the more conservative (and now apparently outdated) handbooks on dressing for success.

The young man was another story. He, too, wore a navy blue suit and a white silk shirt, though his shirt was open at the neck. But despite his rounded form and the fact that his clothes rather eerily replicated Martha's, he did not look in any way soft or ef-

183

feminate. In fact, there was something tough and aggressive in his appearance, perhaps heightened by the fact that while Martha had highlighted her outfit with conservative gold earrings, the young man had chosen two extremely large and flashy pinky rings.

"Good afternoon, Ed," said Martha, shaking Ed's hand with a practiced firm clasp. "Please let me introduce Sal Alfredo. He is the representative from Safety Systems, Inc., a personnel screening service in Miami, that the Human Resources Department has retained."

Sal's handshake reinforced Ed's impression of Sal as something of a tough guy. If his grasp was any indication, Ed thought, what looked round in his business suit probably looked like Arnold Schwarzenegger at the gym. It wasn't so much that Sal *squeezed* Ed's hand; it was more that Sal managed to give the impression of intense coiled physical strength without having to squeeze anything at all. Altogether a somewhat rough customer, thought Ed, surreptitiously wiggling his now free fingers. Definitely one of those people I'd rather have on my side than on someone else's.

Ed gestured toward the two chairs opposite his desk. "Sit down, please," he said, as he walked around to his own chair. "I'm glad we could get to this meeting before the Thanksgiving holiday," he said to Martha. "Especially since we're being joined by an out-of-towner." He smiled slightly at Sal.

"The holiday's no problem for Safety Systems, Inc.," Sal answered unbidden. "We believe that our clients need safety three hundred sixty-five days a year, twenty-four hours a day, and we provide it. Our computers, our sensors, our evaluators are on duty year-round, Mr. Cunningham, and we want all of our clients to know it."

"Computers and sensors?" asked Ed in surprise. "What exactly does your company do? I just assumed since you were working with Human Resources that you were some kind of executive recruiters."

"Oh, Safety Systems is much more than that," said Martha seriously. "We are talking about the 1980s, Ed. We don't just hire people because they are part of the social success network, because they know someone and come highly recommended. *That* is the road to white-collar crime, to seeing your employees sell corporate secrets and reveal inside information to reporters. Consolidated Commodities' Human Resources Department has chosen a much better road: we are moving into reliance on scientific data, computerized assessment of factual information, and new ways of evaluating individuals' integrity."

"Hmmmm. Very interesting," said Ed. What in heaven's name could they mean by new ways of evaluating individuals' integrity and not relying on the success network? No more recruiting luncheons? No more quiet phone calls from friendly headhunters? No more screening interviews conducted over an informal golf game with a mutual friend?

Almost as if he had read Ed's mind, Sal spoke up. "Many people like yourself, Mr. Cunningham," he said sincerely, "only know one way of doing things. You end up hiring people who seem like you, so you assume they are trustworthy. They went to the same schools, belong to the same clubs, know the same people. But we at Safety Systems, Inc., know only too well that the people you can trust least are often those you feel most comfortable with. Look at your insider trading scandals on Wall Street. Look at your fall of the Penn Square Bank, which almost took Continental Illinois down with it. Look"—he paused dramatically—"at your Richard Nixon!"

"Richard Nixon?" Ed said somewhat incredulously. True, he had turned out to be less honest than one would have liked, but what did that have to do with ConCom's hiring policies?

"Richard Nixon simply illustrates," said Martha decisively, "that even the most prestigious positions are vulnerable to abuse by the person who holds that position. Sal's firm has a truly impressive list of people in whom others placed their faith, who had impeccable credentials and faultless contacts, but who turned out to be rotten—to the core. This"—she paused meaningfully—"is what the Human Resources Department wishes to avoid and this is why we have entered into a very costly and yet well-worthwhile arrangement with Sal's company."

"Well," said Ed. Perhaps this all had meaning for Specialty Foods; perhaps not. At any rate, right now he was more interested in the business he had to conduct with Martha. "Perhaps we can discuss this further as we talk about what I had to cover with you today, Martha."

"Certainly, Ed," said Martha politely. "I believe you said you want to discuss setting up a new position in the division?"

"Yes," Ed said, rearranging himself more comfortably in his desk chair. "Specialty Foods is such a new division that it has taken me the better part of my first year as president to decide exactly what middle management positions we need around here. As our businesses grow and develop, we'll want to do a major organizational redesign. But right now, I've got a burning need to add a person within the existing structure.

"Because Specialty Foods is such a small division, I've got a lot of people reporting directly to me who'd come in farther down the chain of command under other circumstances. I've got people in various levels of Accounting and Finance and Production, plus a whole bunch of Marketing people. It's the latter group that I've been thinking about reorganizing."

Martha nodded and Ed continued. "Right now, I've got one person who holds the title of 'Group Product Manager.' That's Grady Jennings. He is responsible for the entire line of Italiano products, with sales somewhere in the $25 million-per-year range. He's got tomatoes, various prepared sauces, and some gourmet products that are picking up steam.

"Then I've got a bunch of other product groups that have come to Specialty Foods from one place and another. There's a large group of varied products sold under the Mountain Gourmet name. There are some imported products called Good Taste. Then I've got one odd duck, a fresh refrigerated product called Salsa! Salsa! Salsa!, which is a kind of a Tex-Mex table sauce.

"Obviously, this group of products is tremendously varied. But, even though they're not under one name or even in one category, they have certain problems and needs in common. Consequently, what I want to do is create another Group Product Manager position in the division and have that person take responsibility for this whole array of products. He or she would, of course, report directly to me, and the people in charge of the various products groups in these different lines would report to the new grouper. I've put together a job description. Shall I run through it briefly?"

"Yes," said Martha. "Of course the job description is the starting place, so I'm glad you've got this already taken care of."

"Happy to oblige," said Ed. "I've got a couple of copies here. You can read through it with me."

> *Job description:*
> *Group Product Manager, Specialty Products*
> *Open 1/1/88*
> *Responsible for strategic product development and policy implementation for all products in the Specialty Foods Division that are marketed primarily or exclusively through specialty food retailers.*
> *These include: Apple Products line, Good Taste line, Salsa! Salsa! Salsa!*
> *Specific responsibilities include:*
>   *—Annual marketing plan development*
>   *—Annual volume and earnings projections*
>   *—Realization of volume and earnings projections and marketing strategy as determined by above plans*
>   *—Implementation of plans, including:*
>   *—Advertising management*
>   *—Promotion management*
>   *—Packaging management*
>   *—Product development*
>   *—Coordination with:*
>   *—Sales*
>   *—Production*
>   *—Other line services, including importing*
>   *—Advertising agency*
>   *—Corporate staff, including legal and consumer affairs*

Ed paused. Martha nodded, then asked assertively, "Is there anything in your overall personnel plan to allow for this, Ed? You know, it is very important that division presidents adhere to their advance personnel planning."

Ed laughed. "And you know that it is a foolish division president who doesn't build a little slack into his personnel plan. As a matter of fact, when I came over to start Specialty Foods I wasn't sure how fast we'd grow during the first year, so just to be on the safe side, I put in *two* additional group product manager jobs."

Martha pursed her lips. "These plans are supposed to be quite precise, Ed," she said disapprovingly.

"Don't worry, Martha," Ed answered easily. "I usually wouldn't take such liberties with the planning process but this was an entirely new division."

"Well, I suppose . . ." Martha relaxed slightly. "So if this position is already in your personnel plan, I see no reason why it should not be filled at your earliest possible convenience."

"Great," said Ed. "I've even got a couple of people in mind, and when I mentioned it to them, they both said they were interested."

At this point, Sal Alfredo roused himself. During the preceding discussion, Sal had sat silently in his chair next to Martha's, his eyes moving from Ed to Martha, and back again, a stern look on his face. Although he had not actually looked at Sal as he talked to Martha, Ed had felt a kind of judgmental force reaching him from Sal's side of the desk.

"This is exactly what Safety Systems is talking about," said Sal somewhat peevishly. "Exactly."

"What do you mean?" Ed asked good-naturedly. "Do you focus on vetting personnel plans to make sure managers like myself aren't engaging in any illicit padding?"

"I'm afraid this is not a matter for joking, with all respect, Mr. Cunningham." Although his words were polite, there was a slightly threatening quality to Sal's voice. "It was exactly this kind of thing— 'a couple of people in mind,' " he said in a surprisingly good imitation of Ed's voice, "that gave us the Teapot Dome Scandal, the Dreyfus Affair, and Watergate."

Amazement delayed Ed's response to this sweeping accusation. He found his mind racing through his high-school history courses:

what in heaven's name could Teapot Dome, Dreyfus, and Watergate have in common? And how ever could they possibly have a damned thing to do with the Specialty Foods Division?

"Perhaps I should explain, Ed," said Martha, apparently noting Ed's raised eyebrows. "As we mentioned earlier, when positions are filled from a preselected group of people—acquaintances, friends, current employees—this greatly increases the likelihood that certain weaknesses or shortcomings of the person being considered for a position will be overlooked.

"For example, it is unlikely that you would review the original résumé or job application of an employee whom you wished to promote from within. And yet, that employee might have been here for many years. Perhaps when they were hired, screening techniques were inadequate. We have found—shockingly—that there were actually cases in Consolidated Commodities where one or more references were not checked at all, where transcripts were not requested from colleges, where previous employment histories were not even verified in writing!"

"But, Martha," Ed said, "if an employee has been here for years, isn't his performance on the job the thing that we're mostly interested in? If the guy was lying about his education or work experience, we'd have seen that he couldn't do what he was supposed to be able to do. If he was a cheat or a liar or a thief, he would have revealed this in his behavior over the years of his employment."

Before Martha could answer, Sal spoke up again. "It's exactly a gentleman like yourself, Mr. Cunningham, who would have such a naïve belief." He looked at Ed pityingly. "And it's a company made up of such gentlemen"—now he turned to Martha—"that badly needs the services of Safety Systems, Inc."

Martha nodded and Sal went on. "Have you read any books by John le Carré, Mr. Cunningham?" Now Ed nodded. "You remember how they uncover moles who've been at the highest levels of the intelligence services for years and years? How these men were trained since childhood to be sent out and infiltrate democracies and undermine their futures?" Ed nodded again, though somewhat tentatively. "Well, there you are!" concluded Sal with a small smile of self-satisfaction. "That's exactly what Safety Systems is talking about."

"But, Sal," Ed said, frustration creeping into his voice, "we are not talking about Her Majesty's Secret Service. We are talking about an American corporation."

"But it's not that simple anymore." Martha now spoke, concern filling her voice. "We've got product secrets, confidential financial data, internal assessments of possible responses to government directives. These are the 1980s, Ed, and we all have to face up to that!"

Ed opened his mouth to reply to this comparison, then quickly closed it again. They'd been talking about this foolishness for almost half an hour, the clock on his desk told him. He'd never convince these two that they were going off the deep end and they'd never convince him that he shouldn't trust the people he knew he could trust. It was time to change the subject, and change it once and for all.

"Well, I'll give some thought to what you've said," Ed finally replied. "Meanwhile, could we get back to my group product manager position?"

"Certainly, Ed," said Martha, again returning to her polite tone. "I simply invited Sal to attend this meeting with me so that when we began discussing how we would screen people for any new positions you would understand why Human Resources has changed its policies."

"Why don't you tell me about the changes, Martha?" Ed said resignedly. "Then I'll do my best to work within the system."

"There are two main things you need to be aware of, Ed," Martha said, while Sal went back to his silent observations. "Neither calls for additional actions on your part: both will be handled by Human Resources. But both have major implications for your choice of candidates available for the position."

"Go on," said Ed. If he didn't have to do anything, how bad could it be?

"First, each person under consideration will be thoroughly investigated in terms of education, work experience, and personal character," said Martha with a kind of stilted enthusiasm filling her voice. "We will contact relevant background sources by phone, by mail, and by personal interview."

"You mean somebody goes to their house and talks to the neighbors?" said Ed jokingly.

Neither Martha nor Sal smiled.

"You *do* mean that somebody goes to their house and talks to the neighbors," said Ed. Good lord.

"In addition," Martha continued, "each potential hiree will take a battery of tests designed to determine his or her honesty and personal integrity. These tests have been developed by Safety Systems and are being used in a number of other large companies. They appear to be very accurate in assessing character and in picking out rotten apples before they can infect the organization." This mixed metaphor seemed to satisfy Martha and she looked at Sal, apparently for his approval. However, he frowned back.

"Safety Systems, Inc., recommends enhancing the power of these tests with polygraph screening," Sal said accusingly, "but I haven't been able to convince ConCom to use them."

"*I* certainly think they're a good idea, Sal," Martha said quickly. "But the lawyers had some questions. . . ."

"We also recommend regular urinalysis to uncover drug use, chromosome work-ups to see if you've got any of those guys with the extra chromosome—the ones that make you violent, you know?—and for the top jobs, we like to see three-day stress tests."

"Three-day stress tests?" asked Ed. He'd heard of these other awful invasions of privacy, but this one was new.

"Something special Safety Systems, Inc., has developed," replied Sal proudly. "The person under consideration goes on a three-day retreat, kind of. They're on a highly restricted diet—basically spring water and vitamin pills—put into total isolation, and they aren't allowed any outside stimulation along the lines of books or television. Oh, and they've only got the clothes they arrive in. I'll tell you"—he paused, as if struck anew by the wonder of this screening technique—"it really separates the men from the boys."

"You mean people being considered for top jobs are actually willing to be subjected to this kind of"—Ed swallowed the word that came to mind first—"foolishness?"

Sal looked hurt. "We're talking about $500,000-a-year jobs, Mr. Cunningham." He looked at Ed meaningfully. "They do it or they lose it. When Safety Systems, Inc., comes in, it's just that simple."

Ed shuddered. Thank God somebody in Human Resources was drawing the line somewhere.

"So with these new plans in place, what do I need to do, Martha, to get my search underway?" Ed asked, even more determined to bring the discussion to a close.

"Oh, nothing, really, Ed," said Martha, to Ed's surprise. "Just give me the names of the people you're considering and while you're doing whatever you want to do in terms of interviews, we'll be conducting the investigation and arranging for the independent evaluation. When everything is completed—surprisingly it only takes two to three weeks—you and I meet again and put our data and your data together. We agree on a person and you extend the invitation."

"*We* agree? Are you telling me in a roundabout way that I don't get to decide for myself whom I hire?" Ed asked impatiently.

"Not at all," intervened Sal soothingly. "Safety Systems, Inc., doesn't consult with any company that plans to reduce its manager's autonomy. Martha just means that she will help you interpret the data that Safety Systems, Inc., makes available."

Only partially mollified, Ed again decided to let this all go for now and worry about it when the time came.

"I've got two names for you right now, Martha," Ed said. "One is Grady Jennings, who's the grouper on Italiano. The other is Winship Elsworth, who's a product manager on Apple Products."

"Grady Jennings and Winship Elsworth, both from this division." Martha nodded and appeared to make a mental note of the names. "Just let me know if you add a candidate. Also, of course, there is the possibility that when Human Resources reviews the job description, we will send over one or more candidates for your consideration."

"Of course," said Ed. "We'll keep in touch, Martha, and try to get this decision made before the end of the year. Let's see. Nothing else on my side, so I guess that's about it." Martha nodded her affirmation and Ed stood up. Martha stood up also, leaned over Ed's desk, and repeated her firm handshake. Sal followed and repeated his nonsqueeze. "My pleasure, Mr. Cunningham. Safety Systems, Inc., looks forward to being of service to you."

As his two guests left the room, Ed found himself trying to visualize the "retreat" where Safety Systems sent the poor devils who were slugging it out for the $500,000-a-year jobs. What was the world coming to? What were managers like himself thinking of when they went along with it? Although realistically, maybe Safety Systems, at least as it was involved with ConCom, wasn't worth making a fuss about.

The next day, his musings about Safety Systems temporarily shelved, Ed decided to get on with his own part of the search for a new group product manager. He asked his secretary Ellie to contact the Human Resources people and get copies of the original résumés Grady Jennings and Win Elsworth had used when they applied to ConCom. Neither man had originally come into Ed's former division, and he was interested in finding out more about the backgrounds that Safety Systems would be investigating so carefully.

After lunch, Ellie brought in the two men's Human Resources folders and Ed started reviewing them with interest.

First, he decided, he'd take a look at Grady Jennings' records. Grady was his first choice for this job. Grady was experienced as a group product manager and this would be a big advantage in trying to form a cohesive whole out of the widely diversified products that would fall under the new grouper's authority. Besides that, Grady was solid, reliable, and seemed to have both good sense and the ability to conceptualize marketing direction. In fact, if Grady was working for somebody else in another division, Ed would make every effort to get him to take the job. But, of course, since Grady was already working for Ed, giving him this job would be playing musical chairs, because Ed would then be faced with the prospect of finding a person to take the job that he was moving Grady out of. An important consideration.

Ed picked up Grady's résumé and read through it carefully.

RÉSUMÉ OF GRADY JENNINGS
301 Cotton Mather Hall
Northeastern University
Boston, Massachusetts
(617) 555-9987

Job objective:	Marketing position leading to general management responsibilities

Previous Employment

Summer 1980	Assistant to the President, Shawmut Bank, Boston, Massachusetts. Conducted market study for new branch locations
1976–1979	Held a number of positions at Shawmut Bank, including Teller (1976); Head Teller, Milk St. Branch (1977–78); Management Training Program Participant (1978); Assistant to Vice-President, Marketing (1979)
Summers 1970–1976	Counselor, Camp Mohican, Bath, Maine. Worked with preadolescent boys in camp for inner-city children
Part-time 1972–1976	Retail sales, Filene's and Jordan Marsh Department Stores, Boston and suburbs

Education

1979–1981	Northeastern Business School, Boston, Massachusetts. MBA with Honors. Concentration in Marketing
1972–1976	Boston University, Boston, Massachusetts. B.A., History, Magna cum Laude

Personal History
  Grew up, oldest of six children, in Watertown, Massachusetts. Financed own college and graduate school education. Hobbies include camping. References available on request.

Interesting, Ed thought. The poor but bright boy putting himself through school. Watertown—one of those somewhat gritty Boston suburbs where gentrification didn't take place until long after Grady had moved out. And Grady hadn't quite managed to make the leap all the way out, to some Ivy League school. Instead it was reliable but unglamorous Boston University and Northeastern Business School. But of course with honors. Again, the poor but bright boy.

Ed reread Grady's work history. Shawmut Bank was probably pretty sorry to lose him, thought Ed. That summer job as assistant to the president meant they were trying to entice him back to the fold and let him know he had a shot at the upper levels. But somebody from ConCom had apparently convinced him he was better off getting out of Boston and honing his marketing skills in product management.

Ed glanced at the next sheet in Grady's personnel file. It simply listed his positions at ConCom by date. He'd come in as usual, at the assistant product manager level. Had moved smartly ahead to associate in eighteen months, to product manager in another eighteen months. Two years there, then into the Italiano group product manager job in 1985.

Grady was now probably about—Ed looked back at the résumé briefly—thirty-two or thirty-three years old. He was probably thinking about how soon he'd move beyond grouper, though he was certainly young enough not to feel that things were passing him by. Though, of course, moving to what Ed was calling mentally the Specialty Products position would basically be a lateral move. It would be a plus to Ed to have him there, but Grady might see it as a negative signal.

Ed decided that if Grady was his first choice, he'd simply have to talk this all over with him. Meanwhile, he'd take a look at Win's résumé.

Ed opened the second file on his desk. On top was the résumé of Winship Elsworth III. Unlike Grady's résumé, which was printed on regular typewriter-weight paper, Win's résumé looked like an invitation to the White House. It was printed on a heavy cream-colored stock in a slightly, but tastefully, italicized typeface. Even after several years in the grungy files of the Human Resources Department, this piece of paper carried weight and authority.

Curriculum Vitae
Winship Elsworth III
Penthouse A
556 Park Avenue
New York, New York
(212) 555-7211

Career objective:	Dynamic management position with significant growth opportunity in Fortune 500 corporation

Education:

1980–1982	Graduate School of Business Administration, Harvard University, Cambridge, Massachusetts. Master's in Business Administration with a concentration in Business History
1976–1980	Harvard College, Cambridge, Massachusetts. Bachelor of Arts, Asian Studies
1972–1976	Phillips Exeter Academy, Exeter, New Hampshire
1964–1972	Horace Mann, Riverdale, New York

Employment:

Summer 1981	Boston Consulting Group, Boston, Massachusetts. Management consultant specializing in international marketing strategy issues, primarily with clients in the Far East
Summers 1979, 1980	Far East Investors, Incorporated, New York, New York. Summer internships specializing in financial development opportunities in the Far East, particularly in lesser-developed nations
Personal	Grew up, an only child, in New York City and Marblehead, Massachusetts. Have traveled extensively, including throughout Asia. Hobbies include travel, polo, racquet sports, and oenology. Fluent in Mandarin.

Amazing, thought Ed. Reading Win's résumé was like walking into another world. For God's sake, he had put down his grammar school. Though, of course, it was certainly prestigious. As was every other school he'd attended, his address, his summer jobs—even his hobbies.

Although, except for the paper, Win's and Grady's résumés looked more or less alike, it would be hard to conceive of two more different stories. Grady was the poor boy hoisting himself out of his blue-collar world by his bootstraps, while Win was the rich kid walking right into privilege and gracious living. Fleetingly Ed wondered if Far East Investors, Inc., was the family business. It was possible: maybe he'd look it up in Standard and Poor's. And "specializing in financial development opportunities in . . . lesser-developed nations" sounded suspiciously like moving businesses into countries where peasants ran sewing machines for $.50 a day while companies like Far East Investors got rich.

Don't be so prejudiced just because the guy grew up with a silver spoon in his mouth, Ed admonished himself. You're just looking for things to confirm your somewhat superficial opinion that Win is nothing but a pampered, well-connected, upper-class twit. Just because he lost his cool over the problem at the Apple Products cider facility doesn't mean he wouldn't be able to handle a group product manager position. Although, Ed noticed, looking back through the résumé, unlike Grady, Win mentioned no academic honors and little evidence of drive beyond the prestigious summer job he'd held during business school.

Ed put the résumé back in the file folder and looked at Win's employment history at ConCom. This was interesting, he thought. Whereas the norm—from the Human Resources Department's point of view, the *rule*—was that no one could be promoted to product manager in under three years, Win had gotten there in only a little over two. Either this meant that his previous boss had thought he was a very high performer or, Ed thought cynically, Win was very well connected somewhere at ConCom as well as everywhere else.

Ed closed Win's folder, stacked the two folders in his OUT basket, and took the afternoon mail out of the IN basket. On the top was an envelope from AAM&N, which apparently had come up on the morning "wagon," advertising agency jargon for the delivery service AAM&N used for communicating with its biggest clients. Above the agency address in the upper left-hand corner were the initials "SAS." Ed picked up the letter enthusiastically. It was from Sandra Sullivan, the account manager on Italiano, his favorite AAM&N employee.

Inside were two sheets of paper. The first was a handwritten note on AAM&N stationery.

>Dear Ed:
>
>I heard from the grapevine that you were looking for a new Group Product Manager for Specialty Foods. Are you sitting down? I'd like you to consider me for the job. Yes, I realize that I'm on the other side of the business right now, but they do teach us a few management skills here at AAM&N.
>
>Seriously, my résumé is enclosed. I've been thinking for some time that a logical career move for me is to get more operating experience and I believe that a position in your division would be extremely valuable in that respect. I also, by the way, think that I could do a good job for you.
>
>I hope to hear from you soon.
>
>>Best wishes,
>>Sandra

This is a pleasant surprise, thought Ed, leaning back in his desk chair thoughtfully. All of a sudden here's another candidate and this one wouldn't require hiring anybody to take her place. If she has the right credentials, of course. Ed realized with some surprise that he didn't really know *what* Sandra's background was. He turned to the second sheet of paper.

>Sandra A. Sullivan
>Apt. 6H
>456 West End Avenue
>New York, NY 10024
>(212) 999-9900

Job objective   Marketing position in medium or large corporation that provides opportunities for hands-on, day-to-day marketing management as well as for growth into general management responsibilities.

Employment history

1982– present	AAM&N Advertising, Inc. New York, New York
1985–87	Account manager. Responsibilities include development, with client, of strategic advertising objectives and coordination of creative and media planning and development. Advertising budgets for clients range from $1.1 to $17.9 million. Client products include line of mainstream Italian food products, line of wine coolers, two children's breakfast cereals.
1984–85	Assistant account manager. Responsible for coordination of all creative activities in both advertising and promotion areas for multiproduct snack food group. Client budget: $22.6 million.
1982–84	Media buyer, spot markets throughout the United States.
1978–1981	Kansas City Independent Schools, Kansas City, Missouri. Elementary school teacher.

Education

1981–1982	M.A., Management, Simmons College, Boston, Massachusetts. Focused on advertising and promotion area, with thesis on advertising to children.
1974–1978	B.A., University of Montana, Missoula, Montana. Major in Early Childhood Education, Minor in Psychology.

Definitely promising, thought Ed. This wasn't the glamour résumé of someone like Win Elsworth, but it was solid. Besides, there were some advantages to hiring someone who was already on her second career. Sandra was probably eagerly trying to make up for her late start in business. This meant she'd be one of those willing employees who'd make an extra effort and put in the time required to get a grip on something like this new grouper job.

Ed, feeling quite pleased with things, opened the top drawer of his desk and took out a pad headed FROM THE DESK OF EDWARD J. CUNNINGHAM.

Dear Sandra:

Although surprised, I was delighted to receive your résumé. Please give Ellie Vogel a call to set up a time when we can meet for an informal interview. If you're still interested after you hear more about the job, the next step will be some screening ConCom is now doing through the Human Resources Department. I look forward to hearing from you.

> Best,
> Ed

Ed stuck the note in an envelope, addressed it to Sandra, and tossed it into his OUT box. Things were looking good, he thought in satisfaction. Three candidates, all interested, all with adequate or even more than adequate credentials. Now all he really had to do was sit back and wait to hear from Martha Bleecker after Safety Systems had done whatever it was they had been authorized to do.

During the next two weeks, Ed met with Sandra, but otherwise put the grouper choice on a back burner. Then, just as he was thinking about following up with Martha, a large manilla envelope arrived from her in the inner-office mail with her return address.

Eagerly, Ed opened the envelope. He felt a carefully controlled wave of optimism. He had a hard choice to make here and maybe there was actually going to be something useful in these reports.

His optimism was short-lived. Inside the large envelope there were three sheets of paper—nothing more. Ed looked at the first one. Maybe these were just preliminary reports.

> **Report on Sandra Sullivan**
> **Confidential**
>
> *All previous education and work experiences verified. All check out as per report of subject.*
>
> *Character interviews:*
>
> *Investigation into background of subject yielded information that subject has strong background in domestic arts, interest in children and in small animals. Active participation in community up to and including present time. Regular church attendance. Appears to be happily married, though no children.*

> *Psychological assessment:*
> *Subject appears normal, with internally consistent values and standards. Only significant deviation: high scores relative to female norm on aggression scale.*

Good lord, thought Ed. This was it? He'd been waiting for three weeks to find out that Sandra Sullivan liked small animals but was an abnormally aggressive female? Sighing, Ed picked up the second sheet of paper. Maybe Safety Systems did better on men.

> **Report on Winship Elsworth III**
> **Confidential**
> *All previous education and work experiences verified. All check out as per report of subject.*
> *Character interviews:*
> *Subject comes from socially prominent family and has displayed no dissonance between personal interests and those appropriate to social class and background. From an early age, displayed strong interest in business and commerce, apparently operating an import-export business during prep school. Subject displayed structured altruism, as appropriate to social standing, donating profits of business to Alumni Association of said school.*
> *Psychological assessment:*
> *General internal consistency in values and attitudes. Some conflicts between entrepreneurial tendencies and desire to be a team player.*

Well, this report, while as astonishingly brief, at least made a little more sense. Ed looked back over the sheet again. It did look as if the evaluator was rather too taken with Win's social standing to be completely objective. But the psychological assessment was interesting. So far, Ed thought, he'd never tapped into Win's entrepreneurial tendencies. Maybe if Ed gave him the wide range of products that would fall under the new group product manager's control, one or more of them would challenge that entrepreneurial interest and Win would really make something happen with it.

Somewhat more comfortable now with the Safety Systems approach, Ed started reading the last of the three sheets, the report on his favorite candidate, Grady Jennings.

> **Report on Grady Jennings**
> **Confidential**
>
> All previous education and work experiences verified. All check out as per report of subject.
>
> Character interviews:
>
> Subject appears to have strong interest in helping others, especially those less fortunate than himself, since an early age. Active in youth groups, scouting, and church groups, including (during adolescence) a Youth for Evangelism program. Strong identification with "big brother" role, both with siblings and with other children. Movement in early maturity into social action, including some ultra-liberal activities.
>
> Psychological assessment:
>
> Although generally normal in terms of overall functioning, subject displays severe conflict between desire to help others and desire to help self. Altruistic tendencies are not well integrated at this time. Potential for reduced functioning levels if resolution is not reached.
>
> Warning: *This employee may present risks to the employer.*

Ed dropped the sheet of paper impatiently. What was all this garbage, anyway? Restless, he got up and walked to the windows on the far side of the room that looked out over a small fountain beside the ConCom headquarters. Not well integrated? Grady Jennings was one of the most put-together people he knew. He didn't seem to suffer from the minor but annoying faults of so many of Ed's other subordinates: he always got things done on time, he was conscientious, he looked out for the people who worked for him, even going so far at times as to let them off the hook or cover for them when Ed would have been more harsh.

Although, Ed thought, as he turned back from the window,

maybe that was what they were talking about. Covering for people, looking out for them, being the big brother, taking care of people who perhaps shouldn't be taken care of.

Ed went back to his desk and picked up the report on Grady again. He reread it slowly, with a more open mind. Hmmm—ultra-liberal activities. Ed seemed to remember that Grady's wife was still involved with something like that—executive director of some far-out antinuclear group. Grady had once complained that she was never home, saying she split her time between lobbying in Washington and marching around trying to keep nuclear power plants from opening.

And then, Ed mused, there were the evangelistic religious activities. Everybody knew those guys were a little nuts, knocking on doors of people who didn't want to talk to them, stopping people in the street to give them pamphlets about the end of the world.

Suddenly Ed hit his fist on his desk loudly. What in the world was he thinking of? This stupid report was talking about something that Grady did—if Grady had, in fact, even done it—when he was in *grade* school. Nowhere in the report did anyone say how they had gotten information, if it was verified. They didn't tell what tests they had given the "subjects"—victims might be a better word—nor who had evaluated the results.

Impatiently, Ed picked up the phone. He'd just have a word with Martha Bleecker about the kind of slander his candidates were being subjected to. Women who were too aggressive, men who were too altruistic! This kind of "report" was so filled with innuendo that it was only worthy of the McCarthy era, not of modern management in the 1980s.

Finally, after three or four rings, Martha answered. "Martha Bleecker here. Can I help you?"

"You certainly can, Martha," began Ed, aggravation coloring his tone. "I've just gotten these so-called reports from Safety Systems, and I want to tell you, I think they leave something to be desired."

"I'm sorry you feel that way, Ed," said Martha tightly. "What exactly do you feel is lacking?"

"Any explanation of the scientific basis of the charges—yes, I'd say charges isn't too strong a word—made in these reports."

"Ed, Ed," said Martha in a conciliatory tone. "Of course I can see how you'd have such questions. I had them myself. It wasn't until I flew down to Miami and met with the people from Safety Systems that I understood exactly what they were doing. Do you realize that the president and founder of Safety Systems, Dr. Karl Saffron, has two Ph.D.'s? First he has a Ph.D. in Clinical Psychology from a university in Vienna and then on top of that he had a Ph.D. in Criminology from NYU! Besides that, the man had spent over twenty years perfecting the tests he uses and had books, simply books, of data indicating the accuracy of his work!"

"Look, Martha," broke in Ed as Martha stopped for breath, "I don't care how many damned degrees the man has. I have some big questions about these reports. The important thing I want to know is what kind of obligation I have to accept these findings and act according to Safety Systems' recommendations."

"As I said in our meeting, Ed," Martha answered, sounding tense again, "the decision of whom to hire in a situation like this is ultimately up to you. But I should mention that if, after we talk, you decide to offer the position to someone whom I feel we cannot support, I will be obligated to report our difference of opinion to Harold Harrison."

"And then exactly what is he going to do, if I may be so rude as to ask?" Ed responded.

"I can't say for sure," said Martha snippishly, "because so far no one has taken the kind of action you suggest. But I must say that as vice-president for Human Resources, Harold is quite committed to the Safety Systems approach. In fact, I don't think I would be revealing any secrets if I told you that Harold has committed over $1 million to our contract with Safety Systems, Inc."

"One million dollars?" Ed felt his heart drift down toward his stomach. If Harold had spent $1 million, he must really mean it. Old Harold was known as the cheapest cheapskate in Consolidated Commodities. In fact, Ed had heard that the secretaries in his division were still using electric typewriters instead of word processors because Harold was too tight to spring for the hardware.

"But of course, we can't be sure about Harold's response, can we?" said Martha, somewhat smug now.

This promised to go nowhere, thought Ed. "Look, Martha, I just got these reports and I've got to say they were not at all what I expected. I think what I want to do is take a couple of days to go over them, review my candidates' résumés and work histories myself, and maybe even talk to each person again. Let's say I'll get back to you when I've decided exactly what I want to do. We can work out our differences—if we've still got any—then."

"I'll look forward to hearing from you, Ed," said Martha, now sounding rather tired of the conversation as well. "Have a nice day."

Ed hung up the phone and returned to his fountain view. After hearing about Harold Harrison's investment, it was tempting to keep the reportedly questionable Grady where he was until things blew over. It was hard to decide if there was enough to be gained in terms of business development to justify locking horns with Harold. Besides, it was rather a shame to put Italiano in the hands of someone new just when volume was starting to take off after several years in the doldrums.

If he decided to leave Grady where he was and hire Win, of course, he'd certainly be on the side of the angels as far as the Human Resources people were concerned. Except for the time when he completely lost his head over the Apple Products accident, Win had seemed like a reasonably promising employee. And it would be much easier to replace Win on Apple Products than to replace Grady on Italiano.

On the other hand, he could leave both Grady and Win where they were and bring in Sandra. That would have the advantage of adding a strong player to the management team while leaving Win and Grady in charge of big pieces of the division's product line. Sandra would have time to learn the ropes, which might take a while since she'd be completely new to product management. But with Win and Grady in place, Ed would have time to help her. He could promote Grady when they reorganized, give a more seasoned Win the Italiano line then, and everyone would be happy.

Was this all just a way of side-stepping the major issue? Ed asked himself sternly, turning from the window. Maybe he should offer Grady the job just to show Harold that he wasn't going to buckle under to any pseudoscientific system as interpreted by a reformed thug from south Florida. Maybe standing up to Safety Systems, Inc., was where his real responsibility as leader of the Special Foods Division lay.

Indicate your choice here:

_____ Option 1. Compromise. Try to satisfy the needs of Specialty Foods and the Human Resources Department by offering the position to Win Elsworth.

_____ Option 2. Strike a blow for aggressive women and gain a new member of the management team by offering the position to Sandra Sullivan.

_____ Option 3. Offer Grady the position, having fielded the objections of Harold Harrison and the Human Resources Department.

How It All Turned Out

How to Use This Chapter

Now that you've spent a year with Ed Cunningham as he grappled with the decisions facing the Specialty Foods Division, it's time to see how everything worked out. This chapter will tell you what happened next and more.

Before you start reading, you might find it helpful to refresh your memory of Ed's options and your choices by glancing back at Chapters 3 through 10. Then you'll be ready to go.

First, we'll give you "the big picture" on each chapter. By this we mean the broad management overview that a seasoned executive could bring to a specific management situation. Specifically we'll discuss the key decision factors and the management issues central to the decision-making. Here you'll have the advantage over Ed: he had to settle on one choice and could only make an educated guess about why things worked out the way they did or how they could have been different.

Second, for each option in each chapter, you'll get a complete picture of what would have happened if Ed had chosen that option and only that option. The numbers will be there, the management impact, and even the personal career implications for Ed.

And third, we'll give you a way to put your year together and figure out how your individual performance rated. In each chapter, each option will be scored in terms of how well that option fit into the overall needs of Specialty Foods, Consolidated Commodities,

Inc., and Ed Cunningham, senior vice-president. A few options will rate a perfect "10." Others will receive lesser scores, ranging from 9 down to 1. By adding up your total scores for the year, you'll be able to see if you would have been next in line for Ralph Myerson's job or ended up as just another pretty face in the headhunter's roster of "available" managers.

THE SOLUTIONS
Chapter 3: Choosing an Advertising Campaign for Italiano

The Big Picture

In the Italiano advertising decision there were three make-or-break factors. Ed, Grady, and the advertising team identified two of these factors but didn't go very far in their thinking about the third.

The first key factor was how good each campaign actually was in terms of persuasiveness, recall, and sending the right message to consumers. Second was how much money was left after testing and commercial production to spend on advertising itself. Third was how soon all the testing and subsequent decision-making could be finished so the advertising could go on the air.

In this situation, it was impossible to predict in advance exactly how important each of these three factors would be relative to the other two. However, there were two things Ed needed to do to maximize the likelihood that things would turn out well for the year: one was to think long and hard about the advertising campaign he chose, using the input of the various experts available. The fact that Ed, Grady, and Josh each had a different "gut feel" about which campaign was superior was a kind of red flag: there must be some uncertainty here or everybody would have been more likely to come out in the same place.

The other thing Ed needed to do was to move things ahead as

rapidly as possible. Italiano clearly needed advertising support: historical data indicated that when advertising was reduced or withdrawn, volume dropped. Volume losses could never be construed as a desirable course of events.

How Each Option Turned Out

OPTION 1

Ed and Grady agreed to follow Grady's recommendation and run a disaster test on Grady's choice, the map campaign using the photomatic format. When the results of the "overnights" came in, it turned out that the test had paid off: the map campaign *was* a disaster.

The report was as follows:

> *Unaided recall (percent of people who could volunteer information on the commercial without prompting):*
>   8 vs. target of 15.
> *Aided recall (percent of people who could remember the commercial with prompting):*
>   15 vs. target of 26.

Those who remembered the commercial recalled its message well. Viewers were able to name the brand correctly, identify two or more products in the line, and remember that the products were imported and were of high quality. This was a plus, but it didn't make up for the fact that there simply weren't enough people who could remember the commercial at all, even the morning after they saw it.

When Ed and Grady saw the results of the test, they decided they'd have to go with one of the other campaigns. They thought about testing the other two but decided that it would take too long and cost too much money. They went back to Ed's first choice, the brother and sister campaign. Three commercials were produced at a cost of $250,000.

The ads went on air as soon as the first commercial was completed, toward the end of March. By this time, Italiano sales had declined to an annualized level of $24.6 million.

The campaign ran all year with the other two commercials alternating with the first. The total media expenditures were $1,733,000. By the end of December, the advertising looked effective. Sales had rebuilt to an annualized level of $30.01 million. This was a gain of 22 percent, which Ed expected to continue through 1988. Off the December 31 base, this would lead to 1988 sales of $36.6 million.

OPTION 2

Ed and Grady agreed to disaster-test Ed's first campaign choice, the brother and sister campaign, using the animatic format. The campaign passed the ComCon hurdle rates with results on the "overnights" as follows:

> *Unaided recall (percent of people who could volunteer information on the commercial without prompting):*
> 16 vs. target of 15.
> *Aided recall (percent of people who could remember the commercial with prompting):*
> 25 vs. target of 26.

The people who remembered the commercial had a good recall of most of the important messages. Many people commented on the personalities of the characters and their interaction. Most people had good recall of the Italiano name but there was some confusion regarding what products were in the line. Very few viewers mentioned that the products were imported, but almost everyone had a strong impression of a variety of good-tasting products.

Because Ed and Grady were satisfied with the results of their test, they moved quickly to get the advertising shot and on the air. AAM&N produced three commercials at a cost of $250,000 and advertising began in mid-March. After testing and production, the remaining media budget was $1,735,500.

By the time advertising went on the air, Italiano sales had declined to an annualized rate of $24.7 million. After the advertising ran throughout 1987, sales had rebuilt by 22 percent to an annualized rate of $30.13 million. Ed expected the rate of increase would continue through 1988, resulting in a sales projection of $37.7 million.

OPTION 3

Ed and Grady were convinced by Josh D'Arcy that the most promising advertising campaign was the celebrity campaign. They authorized a test of the campaign using a livamatic with the actual celebrity. The total cost of the test was $22,500 plus $10,000 for the celebrity. The commercial test was delayed for several weeks because the agency did some pretesting to decide who would be the best celebrity to use for the campaign.

When the test results did come back, they were as follows:

> *Unaided recall (percent of people who could volunteer information on the commercial without prompting):*
> *19 vs. target of 15.*
> *Aided recall (percent of people who could remember the commercial with prompting):*
> *30 vs. target of 26.*

The message recall was excellent. There was very high recall of the celebrity's identity and association of him with the Italiano brand name. Most viewers were able to identify two products in the line and some could identify as many as five. There was also high playback of the facts that the products were good-tasting and imported.

Ed and Grady were very excited about the results of the test. Not only did the commercial test well, but also they both agreed that the star chosen was someone they liked a lot and would enjoy working with. They urged the agency to get the first commercial shot and on the air at once.

But the celebrity played hard to get when he heard how well the campaign tested. Finally, after a lot of negotiating, his fee was set at $25,000 per commercial. These negotiations postponed the start of shooting the commercials and advertising did not go on the air until April 1, when the first commercial was completed.

By that time, Italiano sales had dropped to an annualized rate of $24 million. Ed felt that they would need every bit of the $1,642,500 remaining in the advertising budget to rebuild volume.

Ed was somewhat surprised, therefore, when sales reached an annualized rate of $31.44 by the end of the year. This was a rate of increase of 31 percent. Ed calculated that if the sales grew in 1988 at the same rate, volume would reach over $41 million by the end of that year.

OPTION 4

Ed and Grady decided to take the conservative route and test all three campaigns using livamatics. As Ed finally said, after they'd discussed the pros and cons for an hour, "When you come right down to it, it's only money."

The total testing cost was quite a bit of money: $67,000 plus $10,000 for the celebrity. Because they were testing three different campaigns and because the agency did some pretesting before choosing a specific celebrity, the test results were not available until the middle of March.

When the test results finally arrived, Grady, Ed, and the agency team all heaved a sigh of relief that they had decided to run the tests. There were major differences in the scores of the three campaigns. Furthermore, the campaign with the best scores also looked much better on message takeaway.

Overall, the Italian map campaign scored worst, failing to meet the ConCom hurdle rates. The brother and sister campaign scored significantly better, passing the hurdle rate, but only barely. In contrast, the celebrity campaign scored substantially above the hurdle rates and message recall was excellent. (See the above sections for specific scores.)

Ed authorized the agency to make the celebrity a very attractive offer right from the beginning because he was certain that investing in that particular actor would pay off. For a fee of $25,000 per commercial, the celebrity agreed to begin filming immediately. The agency put everything on top speed and the first commercial went on the air two weeks after the test results were in, debuting at the end of March. By that time Italiano sales were down to $24.6 million at an annualized rate.

Almost immediately, sales started bouncing back up. Ed decided that the celebrity campaign had the potential to build volume in a big way and that he had the test numbers to back up his hunch. When the division presidents met in late March to go over budget projections, he made a very convincing case for making further media investments in the celebrity campaign. Because ConCom was doing well for the quarter, some extra funds were available and Specialty Foods received an allocation of $500,000. This increased the Italiano media budget for the year to $2,098,000.

The campaign and media levels proved to be quite effective. By the end of the year, Italiano sales had risen 36 percent to an annualized rate of $33.46 million. Ed projected that at this rate of increase, sales in 1988 would top $45 million, making it very easy for the Specialty Foods Division to more than better its $50 million-a-year sales objective.

OPTION 5

After much soul searching, Ed and Grady decided not to test any of the campaign ideas but to follow Ed's instincts and go with the brother and sister campaign. Needless to say, this decision cost them nothing in out-of-pocket expenses.

The first commercial in the campaign was shot right away. Advertising went on the air four weeks after the meeting—a new record for AAM&N production! Over the next few weeks, two more commercials were made.

The total cost of producing the three brother and sister commercials was $250,000, leaving $1,750,000 in the media budget. When the commercials began airing, Italiano sales volume had declined to $25 million annualized. Volume began rebuilding and by the end of the year had reached $30.75 million annualized. This was a net gain of 23 percent for the year.

Although Ed was pleased with the results, he kept having a nagging feeling that maybe one of the other campaigns would have been better and that testing would have ended up paying for itself.

In the end, however, he decided the campaign wasn't bad and he would continue it into 1988. After all, if the rate of sales increases continued, volume would reach a very respectable $37.8 million.

The Scores

Option 1. Test only Italian map and act on the results.

Grady's choice left a lot to be desired but at least the mistake was discovered in time. Decisions were made on a timely basis and the sales gain for the year was quite respectable.

Net score: 4

Option 2. Test only brother and sister and act on the results.

Following Ed's judgment was a better idea than following Grady's. Again, things moved along and the results for the year weren't bad. But of course they could have been much better, especially in the long run.

Net score: 5

Option 3. Test only the celebrity campaign and act on the results.

Josh D'Arcy was vindicated. The campaign was great. But the fact that only one campaign was tested meant that it was impossible to assess completely how good it was and to move things along to capitalize on this information. Consequently, volume declined substantially before the campaign began and Ed didn't have the ammunition to ask for extra media money to make up for the losses.

Net score: 6

Option 4. Test everything.

This option was costly in the short term but really paid off, even in terms of the Year 1 results. By Year 2, this campaign could make a big difference to Italiano. Besides, Ed gets points for "doing it right"—but only since right paid off.

Net score: 10

Option 5. Don't test anything. Follow Ed's instincts.

This option worked out okay but it was needlessly high risk. In this particular case, Ed made a reasonable choice, but despite his years of marketing expertise, there was no guarantee that he would be right. Too many factors can intervene when a manager relies on "mother-in-law research"—when he asks his mother-in-law (or wife or best friend or even himself) what she thinks and then makes a big commitment based on the results.

Net score: 3

Chapter 4: Choosing a Sales Force Organization

The Big Picture

The most important thing Ed had to do in grappling with the Specialty Foods sales force decision was to make a choice that was good for the division over the long haul despite many pressures to put short-term objectives first.

In any large corporation like Consolidated Commodities, there is tremendous pressure on managers at Ed's level to deliver short-term volume and profit. Quarter after quarter, Ed would have a set of numbers to which he had committed himself—usually with grave doubts—and he would have to find a way to "make the numbers." Managers and even whole corporations have experienced dramatic setbacks when they repeatedly met these short-term objectives at the expense of long-term business building.

Viewed from the perspective of short-term/long-term trade-offs, Ed's two major choices are fairly easy to assess. The best short-term option was to use Marvin Gross to build sales quickly. Ed hypothesized, reasonably enough, that Marvin could probably build volume enough in Year 1 to pay for his services and still return a high profit to the division. However, longer term—even as early as Year 2 and surely by Year 3—this option locks ConCom into a needlessly expensive arrangement.

The two other options, which look less desirable short-term, both focused on building an in-house sales force. These had the potential to cost ConCom money in Year 1 because sales and profits would not be as high as they would have been with Marvin Gross. However, by Year 2 or Year 3, the less expensive in-house sales force would be building sales volume and a permanent cost savings would be in place.

It is worth noting that Ed had the advantage of making the sales force decision in the start-up year for Specialty Foods. For probably the only time in the life of the division, nobody—not even George Vulcani—could say for sure what the sales and earnings of the division would be. This relatively freewheeling and open situation gave Ed the perfect opportunity to bite the bullet and accept lower numbers while he built up the long-term potential of the sales force. Once a set of expectations developed, after the sales results for Year 1 came in, Ed would never have the same chance to hold earnings down while the in-house sales force got on its feet.

Ed had one other important issue to deal with here. He needed to spend enough time to come up with a strong sales force arrangement while giving himself time to determine the strategic and operating direction of the entire Specialty Foods Division. If the Marvin Gross alternative was ruled out because of the long-term profit implications, then Ed had to decide if he could afford the time needed to back up Billy, who was actually relatively inexperienced in the specialty foods area. The best way Ed could look at the more expensive alternative of hiring Sarah Spotsworth was to think about how much it would cost the division for him to neglect his other responsibilities so he could provide the help he could otherwise buy from Sarah. From this point of view, Sarah, even at twice the cost, was a bargain.

How Each Option Turned Out

OPTION 1

Ed decided to set up an in-house sales force using internal resources exclusively. Billy Burke rose to the occasion and did an excellent organizational job. By the end of the year he had twenty salesmen who were able to make regular calls on about 50 percent of the potential retail customers for Specialty Foods products. These salesmen were a mix of veterans from Dry Groceries, salesmen who were raided from other specialty food sales forces, and neophytes who were recruited out of college. This sales force cost Specialty Foods $1,294,000 annualized: $124,000 for Billy; $240,000 for three supervisors; and $930,000 for twenty salesmen.

Because the sales force was not fully developed, the Italiano line continued to be sold to large grocery-store chains by the Dry Groceries sales force. Stewart Spencer and Ed worked out a deal wherein Specialty Foods paid 10 percent of sales for this service. Since about $20 million of the line was sold through these outlets, this cost Specialty Foods $2 million annualized. Ed planned to phase this arrangement out during the next year with appropriate cost savings.

The only big problem Ed encountered was in warehousing and distribution to support the in-house sales force. Despite his best efforts, it was not easy to bring about changes in the ConCom approach. When Ed met in November with the executive vice-president who handled these services for the whole corporation, he replied to Ed's recitation of woes by saying, "My distribution philosophy is simple: a jar is a jar is a jar." Special warehousing and shipping services ended up costing Specialty Foods twice as much as Ed had estimated, or close to 6 percent of sales.

Ed managed to get total Specialty Foods sales for the year up to only $38,112,945. He had two main problems in building volume. First, the sales force was not able to grow quickly enough to give access to all retailers. Second, Specialty Foods was not able to expand the number of products available from Good Taste, because Ed decided that warehousing and distribution problems had to be cleared up before additional imported products were added to the line.

When Ed looked back on the year, he found, therefore, sales of $38,112,945, selling expense of $3,294,000, shipping and warehousing expense plus importing expense of $2,304,000. Using his rough Cost of Goods Sold estimate of 60 percent, he calculated that the profit contribution for the division was 40 percent of $38 million, or $15.2 million minus the above expenses of $5.6 million, for a bottom line of $9.6 million, or 25.3 percent of sales.

Ed was very pleased with the sales effort and believed that he would be able to straighten out the shipping and warehousing problems over the next year. His only regret, however, was that doing so much within the division without any outside help had been an enormous drain on his time. Not only had he ended up working horrendous hours, but he felt that some of the long-term planning issues he should have been looking at had become low priority. He was afraid that if the remaining distribution and salesforce issues weren't resolved soon, the division would end up suffering over the next two to five years.

OPTION 2

Ed decided to go with an in-house sales force headed by Billy Burke plus management consulting from Sarah Spotsworth and her team. Sarah provided extensive support to Billy Burke and Ed as they set up the in-house sales force and worked out the distribution and warehousing problems. By the end of the year the sales force was up to thirty salesmen. Sarah was able to help Billy deploy these salesmen for maximum client contact, including using five salesmen to take over national selling to large grocery chains. These salesmen were able to handle the full Italiano line plus presenting gourmet products to the buyers.

With Ed's blessing, Sarah also convinced Billy to go to a very intensive supervision setup, hiring all six supervisors who were in the original in-house sales budget, even though the sales force itself was not fully staffed. The thirty salesmen, with this level of supervision, were so successful that by the end of the year Billy thought the original estimates of sixty-five in the sales force might be too high, though he wasn't sure yet. All in all, Billy and Sarah estimated that the salesmen were reaching 85 percent of potential retail clients.

Total costs for the in-house sales effort included $124,000 for Billy, $480,000 for the six supervisors, and $1,395,000 for the thirty salesmen (all figures annualized).

In September, Sarah asked Ed to assign a high-level division staff person to work out warehousing and shipping for the division. By the end of the year, Dave Morrison was just beginning to get problems worked out. Because it took so long to address this problem, warehousing and shipping costs were above Ed's estimates by about 50 percent, ending up at 4.4 percent of sales. Importing charges also went up as more products in the Good Taste line were imported. Total importing charges for the year were $500,000. Sarah and Dave believed that these could be managed down in the years to come.

Because the sales force was reaching so many clients and because additional products were coming in from the Good Taste line, annualized sales were close to Specialty Foods' $50 million target. Total sales were $47,560,000.

At the end of the year, Ed worked out the financial picture for Specialty Foods. Using his rough Cost of Goods Sold estimate of 60 percent, the $47,560,000 in sales had generated 40 percent in profit contribution, or $19 million. Total sales expense was $2 million. Warehousing and shipping was $2.1 million plus $500,000 for importing. This left $14.4 million, or 30.3 percent of sales for profit contribution.

Sarah Spotsworth's total charges for the year were somewhat above Ed's estimate, totaling $102,950. Ed was very pleased with the sales numbers, however, and was amazed at what his staff had been able to accomplish in dealing with some very serious warehousing and distribution issues. Furthermore, Sarah and her staff had been able to provide enough support that Ed found he had been able to focus more on long-term strategic issues that he felt were important in determining the ultimate direction of the division.

OPTION 3

Ed decided that Specialty Foods needed the momentum and expertise that would come from using an established specialty food agency. He retained Marvin Gross and his organization to handle all importing, warehousing, distribution, and selling for the Specialty Foods Division. Marvin worked closely with Ed, and among other achievements, he was able to get the full line of Good Taste products imported into the United States by the end of the year.

The Gross organization was phenomenally successful in selling to specialty food retailers. There were some problems in transferring the segments of the Italiano line that were sold to national grocery chains, but in terms of volume these were offset by increases in the Italiano product sales outside of these channels.

As promised, Marvin's total charges were 14 percent of sales. He was successful in bettering Ed's sales target slightly, with annualized sales reaching the $51.2 million level. His fee, therefore, was $7,168,000. The only additional selling expense was Billy's salary and travel budget, totaling $124,000, as Billy maintained his position as coordinator with the outside sales agent.

When Ed computed the cost and benefits of his chosen sales structure at the end of the year, he used the rough Cost of Goods Sold estimate of 60 percent. Consequently, the sales of $51.2 million generated a profit contribution of $20.5 million. Subtracting Marvin's and Billy's expenses left a final profit contribution of $13.2 million, or 25.76 percent of sales.

At the end of the year, Ed was delighted that the target sales volume for the division had been exceeded. He knew this would go a long way toward justifying top management's decision to establish a separate division for Specialty Foods. However, he felt that his success had been built on a short-term solution to his problems and he was seriously considering beginning to set up an in-house sales force during the next year.

When he had very tentatively broached this subject with Marvin, however, Marvin had said that the 14 percent commission rate he gave Specialty Foods was dependent on an exclusive selling relationship and that this exclusivity ruled out competition from an in-house sales force. As a result of this discussion, Ed was considering another meeting with Henri Margolis to see what commission he could negotiate with Henri.

He was concerned, however, that moving to another broker would have a negative impact on the part of the business that would continue to be brokered, since Henri was less familiar with the product line than Marvin. This would compound possible volume losses due to the inexperience of the fledging in-house sales force as it came on-line.

At times Ed felt that there wasn't a good solution to the problems he was experiencing and that he should have faced up to the problems of establishing an in-house sales force. Now top management had the idea that Specialty Foods was out of the woods and could be counted on to meet higher and higher volume objectives over the next several years.

The Scores

Option 1. Set up an in-house sales force with no outside help.

This scores well on long-term thinking but not so well on short-term gains, with sales of only $38.11 million and profit contribution of $9.6 million, or 25.3 percent of sales. Furthermore, the demands on Ed's time may have negative long-term implications.

Net score: 5

Option 2. Set up an in-house sales force with the support of an outside consultant with expertise in specialty foods.

This was the big winner: Specialty Foods gets its own sales force for the long run, sales are much higher than in Option 1 ($47.56 million), and profits are the highest of any of the three options ($14.4 million, or 30.3 percent of sales).

Net score: 10

Option 3. Turn the entire sales operation over to a specialty foods distribution company.

This looked good short-term: sales were the highest of any option ($51.2 million). However, profits were less than in Option 2 ($13.2 million, or 25.76 percent of sales) because of the high fees. And most serious, Specialty Foods was dependent on expensive outsiders to keep sales up at heavy ongoing costs.

Net score: 2

5: Establishing a Transfer Price for Salsa!

The Big Picture

As in many other situations Ed Cunningham faced throughout his first year as president of the Specialty Foods Division, the Salsa! pricing issue turned out to be more than just a cut-and-dried numbers problem.

There was, of course, a fairly complex numbers issue here. What is a fair price for one division to charge another in a corporation like ConCom? The most useful way of looking at a situation like this is to start by assuming there is no such thing as one "fair price."

For example, even the kinds of numbers that Arnie Clowder would have described as basic divisional overhead were a convention. Undoubtedly part of the "basic division overhead" was Salsa!'s allocation of "basic *corporate* overhead": somewhere, on some line of every product's costs, was money to pay Ralph Myerson's salary. What was the "fair" allocation of this expense to Salsa!? Should Salsa! pay a percent of Ralph's salary based on the percent of total corporate sales Salsa! represented? Or perhaps Salsa! should pay more because its volume was small and it required proportionately more management attention. On the other hand, perhaps Salsa! should pay less, because at least through one channel of distribution, specialty food stores, it was a new product and needed a certain amount of protection during its infancy.

Although there are certain basic accounting guidelines which can serve as a starting place for making internal pricing decisions, for defining various types of overhead, and setting other common charges such as depreciation expenses, within the broad rules there are many ways costs can be recognized and assigned. In a large corporation like ConCom, internal transfer prices are often a combination of accounting conventions and negotiated arrangements between people like Ed and Arnie. For the person who holds profit responsibility for a product, it is always a good idea to ask how costs were assigned. The answer, while not necessarily easy to understand, is essential to grasp if a manager is truly going to have control over his or her products, their costs, and their returns.

Arnie Clowder and his inappropriate behavior may well be, unfortunately, as typical a management problem as are pricing decisions. Particularly in an intensively competitive, rapidly paced organization like ConCom, any personal weaknesses or problems that individual employees have to deal with can be magnified and intensified.

In the past, corporations seemed to deal almost exclusively with the end result of employees' emotional problems. For example, a company might worry about high absenteeism on Monday morning rather than about the fact that people on the production line had problems with alcohol. Then employee assistance programs became fashionable. Employees in need could be identified and channeled into programs that would help them return to being productive members of the corporation.

Unfortunately, some corporations still act as if people in management, especially top management, are somehow not like the rest of humanity, that top managers don't *have* problems or that anybody who is so far gone as to have a *noticeable* problem shouldn't be in top management anyway. Any manager who is faced with a peer's obvious problem, then, needs to think carefully about the corporate climate in which they both find themselves.

There is one further consideration in a case like Arnie's. It is difficult for a layperson to know exactly what is going on when another person begins displaying strong signs of mental distress. If in doubt, a confidential discussion with a mental health professional, either inside or outside the corporation, could serve as a safety net for the innocent bystander like Ed.

How the Options Turned Out

OPTION 1

Ed decided that not only did he have to do something about the pressure Arnie was putting on him to pay more to Food Services for Salsa!, but also he had a moral obligation to ConCom to alert someone to the Food Services issues.

Ed met with George Vulcani later in the week and, after some brief small talk, told George about Arnie's behavior during their meeting and about his follow-up conversation with Bart Small. As Ed talked, he could see that George was not happy about what he had to say.

"After all my years in management," George responded, "I've seen all sorts of strange behavior. Maybe the man had a hangover: those Food Services people have to do a lot of heavy entertaining. Maybe he's getting divorced and his wife moved out last week." Ed remembered that George had been divorced himself a few years ago and reportedly the separation had been prolonged and messy. "Just because someone loses his temper doesn't mean he can't continue to do his job."

George then pointed out that the division had been making money hand over fist for the last fifteen quarters and that their projections showed them continuing to do the same. He went on to say that maybe this Bart person had been raked over the coals by Arnie and had it in for him. When Ed tentatively suggested that George hear Bart's story firsthand, George indicated that he considered it highly inappropriate for the chairman to be listening to unsupported statements by junior assistants.

Ed, unwilling to give up, asked George if perhaps the psychiatrist who ran the Employee Assistance program could talk to Arnie. George answered tersely that that program had been set up to help the kind of employees who were most likely to have personal problems: the secretaries who were single parents, the people in the mail room who got bored and took drugs, the men on the production line who went out with their buddies night after night and developed an alcohol problem.

"Forget this psychology stuff," George finally said. "Now that you are a division president, you've got to learn to work things out with your peers. I can't help you and neither can some shrink. It's up to you, Ed, and I think you can do it. After all," George concluded, "if we don't look out for each other here at the top, who will look out for us?"

Thrown back completely on his own, Ed decided he would approach Arnie in as low-key a manner as possible. He dropped by Arnie's office, hoping that Arnie would feel more at ease on his home territory. Ed pretended that he knew no more about Arnie's proposed price increases than what had appeared in Arnie's memo.

Arnie explained each of the straightforward parts of the price increases (which added up to $.08 of the $.15 increase) in a fairly quiet and reasonable tone. Ed, in turn, was agreeable and conciliatory.

Then Arnie said he wanted Specialty Foods to help pay for some enormous overhead increases he was facing. Ed said calmly that the division couldn't afford to do that.

At Ed's refusal, Arnie began shouting and storming around the room. After a few minutes with no response from Ed, however, again he suddenly seemed to give up. This time he didn't threaten Ed but simply said gruffly that he'd changed his mind and that

Food Services would only charge Specialty Foods the additional $.08.

Although this was more than Ed wanted to pay for Salsa!, he decided it was the best deal he could negotiate with the volatile Arnie. He'd try passing on about half of the increase to the wholesaler; hopefully, the increase would not have a major impact on Salsa!'s volume.

Throughout the rest of the year, Salsa!'s volume rose, reaching an annualized rate of 325,000 pints per year by the end of December. Every time Ed approved internal invoices from Food Services, he asked himself if he had done the right thing for the division by being so conciliatory with Arnie. He also wondered occasionally if Salsa! volume would be building more rapidly if he had not been forced to pass on a price increase.

More important, Ed continued to feel that somehow he'd let ConCom down. He knew that Bart Small's assessment of the situation in Food Services was probably accurate, even if the booming restaurant business in the United States created so much demand for Food Services products that the problems were being masked. But if no one higher up in ConCom was willing to tackle the problems of one top management player who was falling apart, it was hard to figure out what one new division president could have done differently.

OPTION 2

Ed decided that he had to come to terms with Arnie Clowder and his problems and that he should help Arnie do the same. In the next several days after his meeting with Arnie, Ed felt angrier and angrier about how Arnie was planning to take advantage of Specialty Foods and about how Arnie had threatened him. Ed felt that his honor as well as his pride and authority demanded that he confront Arnie and handle the problems himself.

In his calmer moments, Ed also decided that someone who was as volatile as Arnie might actually be helped to see his problems if a peer, whom he had previously seemed to like and respect, stood up to him and pointed out how inappropriate his behavior was.

When Arnie called to set up another meeting, Ed decided that he'd be honest with Arnie and not gloss things over. Arnie came into Ed's office alone, without Bart Small, but with a sheath of papers and a more or less normal demeanor.

Arnie began by explaining to Ed what the various components of the price increase would be. He showed Ed some numbers in the papers he had brought to justify the increases. Then he started talking about how important it was for Specialty Foods to pay the additional $.07 in allocated overhead because overhead had gone up so much.

Without specifically referring to his conversation with Bart, Ed asked Arnie if he had also decided to charge Specialty Foods a higher percent of the total overhead allocation for Salsa! As soon as Arnie heard this question, he started becoming agitated. He began asking Ed if he had talked this all over with Bart Small. Although Ed said absolutely not, Arnie loudly accused Ed of lying and began telling Ed how Bart had it in for him, was photocopying Arnie's confidential papers, listening in on his phone calls, et cetera.

Ed said that maybe the division really did have serious problems and that instead of getting mad at Bart Small, Arnie ought to start facing up to what was going on. At this, Arnie became extremely angry and shouted at Ed that Bart and Ed were out to get him, were slandering his good name, and so on. Finally, Arnie slammed out of the office, still quite out of control.

Ed didn't know what to do. He decided to think things over before taking any more action, but he was forced to think about Arnie again when Bart Small appeared at Ed's office door later in the afternoon. Bart told Ed that Arnie had just fired him, had demanded that he give the keys to his desk and office to Arnie, and had sworn that Bart would never work in the food business again.

Ed told Bart that although he hadn't referred to their conversation, Arnie had jumped to the conclusion that they had talked. The only thing to do now, he suggested, was to go to the head of the Employee Assistance program and try to get some advice.

When Ed and Bart met with Dr. Jerome Wittgarten, they described what had happened with Arnie. Dr. Wittgarten told the two men that in cases like Arnie's, it was almost impossible to get the person who was having problems to confront his pain and inappropriate behavior in a business situation. Rather, it took a personal crisis such as a spouse threatening separation or a dramatic external event such as a traffic accident with a DWI charge to get a person to look at himself and his problems.

He also pointed out that they really didn't even know what was wrong with Arnie. He could have a substance abuse problem or some source of chaos in his personal life. He could even have been told he was dying from cancer and be unable to deal with that knowledge. Finally, Dr. Wittgarten told Bart he was sorry he'd been fired but there was probably nothing he or Bart could do about it. He then told Ed that all Ed could do was to work the business issues out with Arnie the best he could and to leave the behavior issues alone.

Ed decided to take himself out of the Salsa! picture as far as possible. He asked his assistant, Madeline Ballantyne, to work with the production supervisor for Salsa! and from there to negotiate with Arnie, who Ed felt might be less threatened by an attractive woman. After several weeks of meetings, Madeline told Ed that Specialty Foods would be paying $.08 a pint more for Salsa! but that she had managed to get Arnie to drop his demand that Specialty Foods pay a larger percent of the general overhead allocation.

Throughout the rest of the year, Ed continued to wonder if he should have talked to Dr. Wittgarten before he met with Arnie, or if he should have appealed to George Vulcani or Ralph Myerson to intervene in the situation. Ed never seemed to see Arnie at meetings he attended, though occasionally he caught a glimpse of him in the company cafeteria. Because Bart Small was gone, Ed had no way of getting additional insight into the internal workings of Food Services. The division continued to look good on paper; apparently ConCom wasn't hurting too much from Arnie's problems. Ed finally put the whole unpleasant incident out of his mind and got on with the Specialty Foods problems at hand.

OPTION 3

Ed decided that given the information he'd gotten from Bart Small, he felt very uncomfortable about continuing to do business with Food Services. Ed was afraid that even if he could work out some more realistic pricing with Arnie right now, Arnie would be back in the future—in a few months, next year, sometime—with more increases that could be used as part of his cover-up of the internal problems developing in Food Services.

Furthermore, Ed was afraid that if Salsa!'s volume really took off, the internal issues Food Services was facing might make it difficult if not impossible to get more Salsa! quickly from that source.

Taking all this into account, Ed decided to start getting quotes from outside suppliers to make Salsa! He met with Billy Burke's brother Bobby, who was the wholesaler handling the Salsa! line, and asked him to identify regional manufacturers who would be able to serve as replacement producers for Food Services.

Once again, the Burke family network of good old boys came through. Within a week, Bobby called Ed back and told him that he had found two suppliers, one in Arizona and one in Florida, who could produce Salsa! Each would be willing to deliver up to 250,000 pints per year at $.22 per pint, $.03 under what Ed was now paying to Food Services and a full $.18 under Arnie's proposed increased price. They were also both willing to be coproducers, thus giving Ed a guaranteed price of $.22 per pint for up to 500,000 pints per year.

By this time, Arnie had called Ed several times to set up a meeting to discuss the proposed price increase and Ed had managed to put him off. Now, with the competitive numbers in his back pocket and with his proposal to replace Food Services with an outside supplier underway, Ed felt that he was ready to meet with Arnie.

When they met, Ed told Arnie that he was seriously investigating sourcing Salsa! outside of ConCom and told him the price at which outsiders would produce the product. Arnie became very agitated when Ed said he had found outside suppliers. When Ed said he'd filed a formal request to source the product outside ConCom, Arnie moved from agitated to extremely angry. He began storming around the office, yelling at Ed and threatening to take the whole issue to Ralph Myerson. Ed pointed out that Ralph would find out about it anyway, since the request would go to him. Arnie was momentarily stopped by Ed's logic, but still left Ed's office cursing and slamming the door.

The next day, Billy Burke told Ed that he'd heard from his brother Bobby, who said that someone from ConCom had called *him* that morning to tell him not to expect any more shipments of Salsa! He was understandably unhappy about this, since he had a number of clients who received the product on a weekly basis and who would be upset if their shipments were delayed. He'd asked Billy to look into it and now Billy was asking Ed what the story was.

Ed called Arnie, who got on the phone, told him where to go in crude terms, and hung up. Ed then called Bart Small and explained the situation to him. Bart said that apparently Arnie had ordered the line supervisor for Salsa! to stop all runs of pint containers of the product. He said that it was unlikely that the line supervisor would defy Arnie's order because everyone was scared of Arnie's temper, and by the way, what had Ed decided to do to help Arnie get control of himself and of Food Services?

Ed, feeling very small, explained that he didn't feel he could do anything to help Arnie, and that he was looking for outside suppliers of Salsa! Bart said very sadly that he was sorry to hear that and that he'd keep trying to think of something to do himself.

Over the next two weeks, Ed made an effort to get his request for using outside suppliers approved, citing the substantial cost savings he could realize. However, the wheels of ConCom turned at their usual slow speed. Finally, three and a half weeks after his request was filed, Ed was empowered to enter into contracts with the two outside suppliers. They immediately began producing Salsa! and shipping it in their regions.

Since Ed had been unable to convince Arnie to change his mind about supplying product in the interim, sales of Salsa! were interrupted for almost three weeks, during the start of what Bobby Burke had expected to be the high sales season, summer in the Sun Belt.

After product shipments were resumed, Billy Burke came into Ed's office and told him that through the superhuman efforts of his talented brother Bobby, no retail outlets had been lost. However, in order to rebuild sales rapidly, maybe they could pass on the $.03 per pint in production savings all the way to the retailers. Ed agreed to this proposal and by the end of the year, Salsa! sales not only had reached their original goal of 250,000 pints, but had increased to an annualized rate of 450,000 pints per year.

Ed noted through the rest of the year how the Food Services Division appeared to be doing. By December, it looked like the division would post record-breaking volumes. Because he felt that he had somehow let Bart Small down, Ed did not call him to see if the behind-the-scenes picture for Food Services had improved any.

The Scores

Option 1. Do not deal further with Arnie.

Ed fulfilled his sense of moral obligation to ConCom by talking to George Vulcani about Arnie's problems. He also was more or less successful in protecting Specialty Foods from Arnie's demands. The main negative here was that George felt Ed's behavior was unfitting for part of the top management team at ConCom. However, given the fact that George saw Ed as the new kid who needed to be taught more about the rules of the game, this probably had no lasting influence on Ed's career or George's opinion of Ed.

Net score: 7

Option 2. Confront Arnie with his personal and professional problems.

Either because he became emotionally involved in the situation or because he had little experience in dealing with troubled people, Ed was unprepared for Arnie's strong reaction to being confronted with the fact that his division had problems of his making. Ed might have done better to meet with Arnie with others present if he planned to confront him, especially since Arnie had indicated a propensity for violence in Ed's office at the original meeting.

Furthermore, there was the firing of Bart Small, which Ed did not anticipate. Although he tried to protect Bart, there was really no one else who could have tipped Ed off about the internal workings of Foods Services so it was not surprising that Arnie focused on Bart as the source of the information. If Ed had been more insightful or if he had talked to the psychiatrist sooner, he might not have been responsible for Bart losing his job.

Net score: 4

Option 3. Find an outside supplier for Salsa!

Although Ed was faced with having to tell Bart Small that he had decided to do nothing about Arnie, and although Ed continued to have doubts about the future health of Food Services, Ed and his division emerged completely unscathed from the Arnie Clowder crisis. In fact, by going to outside suppliers and passing on the price savings to the end retailers, Ed was actually able to improve the health of the Salsa! business and probably develop a better base for growth in future years.

Net score: 9

6: Planning Italiano Production Systems

The Big Picture

Ed set up a meeting ostensibly to discuss production schedules for the Italiano plant in New Orleans. But the problem Specialty Foods faced was not really a production issue. Rather, it was a broader management problem: how to plan a reasonable course of action when it was impossible to tell exactly what was going to happen in the future.

Madeline's distress at the uncertainty of the situation was certainly understandable. As a new employee at ConCom, she was assuming that if you could put a number on something, it must be real and certain. But in the meeting she found out that Grady wasn't sure of his demand projections, that Dwight wasn't sure how much sauce the factory could produce, and that Ed was forcing everyone to make some kind of decision anyway.

The source of the problem wasn't that Grady hadn't done enough in terms of manipulating numbers. He could have used elaborate regression analyses or other types of computer-enhanced modeling to generate more numbers, but these numbers wouldn't have been any better. In fact, using a computer model in this kind of a situation can produce its own problems, because numbers generated by a computer have an *air* of truth and certainty about them. This can be misleading and can bring managers to make decisions that they feel—wrongly—do not require ongoing reexamination.

Starting with the assumption, then, that there are cases where uncertainty is the rule, how should Ed and his staff have operated to get control of the situation? The most important thing for them to keep in mind was that uncertainty does not equal inactivity. There are actions managers can take to stack the deck in favor of the outcome they believe most likely. In cases of substantial uncertainty, these actions are called for.

In this case, Ed and Grady believed that demand was likely to rise but they felt overwhelmed by their inability to predict the future with certainty. Rather than giving in to their uncertainty, they could have taken steps to increase the probability greatly that demand would in fact increase. For example, they could have developed a backup plan to increase advertising or promotion for the sauces even if this required taking some money from behind other products in the line. They could have started thinking about how they could generate more money for advertising in 1988 to ensure that demand kept growing during that period.

They also could have started doing market research to determine if there were other ways of increasing demand with minimal increases in marketing spending. For example, they might have found that adding a new sauce to the line (a line extension), or changing the advertising or package to emphasize a particularly attractive feature of the product, such as "all natural" or "only imported ingredients," would result in higher sales.

How Each Option Turned Out

OPTION 1

As Ed and the others toured the plant, they decided that they should plan to meet demand increases by adding production from the plant as it now existed. Even after watching the bottles come off the line for some time, they all agreed that it was almost impossible to project volume needs with any greater accuracy at the present time. The main problem was that it was too soon after the reintroduction of advertising to predict what would happen even in the current fiscal year. They concluded that if they couldn't be sure that demand would really increase, it would be a mistake to commit to a $750,000 investment in the plant. In fact, they might be seeing a temporary jump and over time volume could even decline. The additional investment would increase total operating costs by $75,000 a year, the amount of the depreciation expense, and if they ran way under the new capacity, it could actually end up costing more to produce each equivalent unit of sauce. Consequently, they decided to use the current facility and meet demand as best they could.

Assuming that that demand would increase about 40 percent over the next six to nine months and 20 percent during the following year, Dwight reiterated that adding a third shift five days a week would enable them to produce the additional product, even if there were some maintenance problems. (Theoretically, the third shift would increase total output by 50 percent. Since they only needed 40 percent more volume, they felt the margin for error was adequate.)

The next week, Dwight began hiring a third shift. Because of the slump in the oil and gas business, he had little trouble in signing on employees. Furthermore, some current employees volunteered to switch shifts, as did one supervisor, so he was not saddled with a totally green work force.

The plant began running three shifts on August 1, a little over a month after the meeting. During August, everything went well and Dwight breathed a sigh of relief. Then, right after Labor Day, there was a burnout in the heating elements used for two of the giant kettles. This reduced production for several days by 50 percent.

Just when this problem was repaired, bottles suddenly began shattering on the bottling line. The maintenance staff found that the line could run temporarily if bottling speed was cut by 25 percent but that new parts had to be ordered before full speed could be resumed. These parts did not arrive for ten days, so during that period the whole plant had to run at reduced capacity.

Besides plant problems, there were the usual headaches Dwight always encountered. Because all the ingredients Italiano used were imported, there were delays in running the specialty products when the October shipments of mushrooms, herbs, and Italian sausages were held up by storms in the North Atlantic. Also, before Thanksgiving, a midwestern supplier of glass bottles was closed down for several weeks by a union strike, which meant that the Italiano plant was unable to pack the 48-ounce jars for over a month.

Meanwhile, the Italiano advertising campaign was in full swing. In a way, Grady's prediction of a 40 percent increase turned out to be right. It looked like volume for the *year* would be 40 percent higher than the year before. Unfortunately, from a scheduling point of view, all the increased demand was taking place in the last six months of the year because that's when the advertising was running. Consequently, in July through December, monthly demand was more like 80 to 90 percent over that of the same month a year ago.

Between the problems with the equipment and the usual supplier issues, Dwight found that the plant was running further and further behind in production. He decided to run the plant for two shifts on Saturdays to increase output. Plenty of people signed up for the first Saturday, which was in October. But the day dawned unusually beautiful, with clear blue skies and 80-degree temperatures. Only half the anticipated work force arrived. Dwight was able to run the plant, but production was disappointingly low.

The next Saturday, he planned only one shift. This worked out all right, but he could see that even if he kept the plant open for one shift every Saturday, the output would hardly make a difference compared to the enormous demand increases Italiano was experiencing.

Finally, by mid-November, Dwight called Ed and asked for another meeting. At that meeting, the three men reached two conclusions. First, for the short-term, Italiano demand would have to be managed down because production could not be managed up. Ed and Grady decided to reduce the level of advertising drastically for the rest of the year.

This was a hard decision for Ed to make: Italiano was the backbone of the Specialty Foods Division and he had been counting on this segment of the line to ensure that Specialty Foods made its sales target for the year. However, Grady pointed out that absolutely nothing made retailers madder than not being able to supply a product that their shoppers were clamoring for. Better to keep demand down than to antagonize the grocery trade.

Second, Ed and Dwight agreed that the plant should be converted to the convection system Dwight had described in June. Eventually, Italiano spending would be restored and the plant clearly was incapable of ever producing much more than 7 or 8 million e.u.'s per year. New equipment was the only answer.

Over the next few weeks, Ed and Grady prepared their capital request and managed to rush it through the usually endless approval process. However, Dwight found out from George Lu, the equipment salesman, that the convection equipment had started to sell well in the European market and that there was a backlog of orders. It would take six months to get the equipment for the New Orleans plant. He placed the order; the plant continued to produce as much product as possible. The 1988 Italiano advertising plan called for reduced spending through the first six months of the year until the new equipment could be put into place.

OPTION 2

Over their beer and catfish, Ed and the others concluded that although it was impossible to predict Italiano demand so early after the resumption of advertising, Dwight should convert the plant to the convection system as soon as possible. Ed and Grady, in turn, would do the best they could to sell the additional product the plant would be capable of turning out.

The more they talked, the more Grady felt strongly that his predictions of a 40 percent increase in demand made sense and might even be too low. Ed decided that if demand did not increase beyond that amount long-term, he could still make a good case for the changeover because of the substantial reduction in variable manufacturing expenses, which Madeline had identified. This would go a long way toward paying off the additional expenses of $75,000 a year that the division would face as the $750,000 equipment purchase was depreciated over ten years, even if volume remained where it was now.

Ed and Grady prepared a request for capital funds and began pushing it through the approval process as fast as possible. Meanwhile, Dwight contacted George Lu, the equipment salesman who had visited the New Orleans plant. George said that Dwight had called at an opportune moment. The convection system that had been used for demonstration purposes at the trade show was for sale and nobody else in the United States seemed interested. In fact, George's company had planned to ship the whole system to Europe, where several companies had already ordered systems, but it wasn't on the boat yet.

George went on to say that if Dwight could not make a firm commitment to buy the demonstration system right away, George would have to ship the system out. In that case, when Dwight did make a commitment, he'd have to get in line with the Europeans. Then it would take at least six months to get the new equipment.

Dwight called Ed, who said they were still in the midst of the approval process but things looked good. After watching bottles come off the line for a while, Dwight decided to take a chance: he would sign the contract with George and if the purchase was not approved, he'd think of some way of getting out of the contract. It was risky. But by this time, he really wanted that system.

During this time, Grady kept reporting to Ed that Italiano demand was building even better than he had anticipated. Each month he was seeing an increase of 80 to 90 percent over the volume of the same month a year ago. This meant that volume for the full year would be 40 percent ahead of the previous year, even though advertising hadn't gone on the air until well into the fiscal year.

Because he knew the plant would have to be shut down for a week while the new system was installed and because demand was growing so rapidly, Dwight decided to add a third shift on a temporary basis. Numa Patenaude, the plant personnel manager, started hiring people for the third shift, but told them that the job would only last two to three months. Numa was sorry he had to be honest: many potential employees decided not to take such short-term jobs.

But Dwight assured Numa that honesty was the only way to go. Otherwise, there might have been major problems with the union when the shift was discontinued.

In early August the third shift started up. The shift was understaffed and almost all the employees were inexperienced. Productivity was consequently impaired and the shift only produced 60 percent of the volume of each of the other shifts. However, Dwight was at least able to satisfy some of the increased Italiano demand, despite occasional breakdowns and problems with late shipments of raw materials and bottles.

At the end of August, Ed and Dwight got approval for the equipment purchase. This was extremely fortuitous: over the Labor Day weekend, the equipment arrived and Ed authorized payment of the $750,000. Ed never knew how close Dwight had come to having to figure out some way to wiggle out of the contract and to send three railroad cars of equipment, prepaid, on to Europe.

The equipment was installed in early September, with the plant closing for one week. Dwight ran all three shifts for the month of September to compensate for lowered productivity as the employees learned to work with the new equipment.

By mid-October, the new equipment was fully operational. With two shifts, Dwight was able to meet increased Italiano demand. The variable manufacturing costs were indeed reduced, as Madeline had identified, because the plant was running at about 90 percent of capacity. Ed concluded that if the same efficiencies were going to be realized in 1988, the plant would have to continue to run at this level and so he needed a plan to see 10.8 million equivalent units of sauce.

When Ed asked Grady how they could generate this volume, Grady suggested boosting the advertising expenditures for 1988. He pointed out that the extra advertising money could come from the savings in production costs that would be realized if the advertising generated enough demand to keep production high. It sounded a little crazy at first, Grady admitted, but it all made perfectly good sense if you just thought about it one step at a time. Ed finally had to agree and Grady developed an aggressive advertising and volume plan for 1988, which Ed approved.

The Scores

Option 1. Increase production at existing facility.

In this situation, Ed, Grady, and Dwight played into one another's uncertainties about the future of the Italiano sauces. No one was willing to take an aggressive position about the future demand or the future production needs. Grady ignored his gut feel about how fast demand would grow. Dwight put aside his concerns about equipment failure and manpower problems. Consequently, Ed did not develop a proactive strategy but rather reacted to whatever came along.

Although total disasters did not occur, the problems that developed in the plant added up to an inability to increase production meaningfully. Meanwhile, the advertising continued to generate demand, even more than Grady or Ed had anticipated. Finally, Ed paid for his doubts by having to manage demand down. The situation was painful for Ed, who saw the division underperform during his first year as president when, if he had been more decisive, he could have more than met his objectives.

Net score: 3

Option 2. Convert the existing facility to produce sauces using the new Japanese convection technology.

Ed and Grady believed in themselves and in their ability to predict where the Italiano market was going. They were decisive and their approach paid off.

Ed was spared the decision about committing to the equipment order before a formal approval had been made. ConCom would have been in a very difficult position if the capital approval had not gone through when it did and Ed would have been held responsible for Dwight's action. However, as it worked out here, what Ed didn't know didn't hurt him.

Ed did miss one marketing opportunity as the changes took place. He and Grady did not develop ways of building additional volume during 1987 or of ensuring that they would realize the gains Grady predicted. As things turned out, volume rose anyway. But this option would have scored higher if Ed had done more advance planning to provide extra support for the steps he did take.

Net score: 8

7: Handling the Nubian Network Opportunity

The Big Picture

One of the things that makes management jobs exciting but also leads many managers to resort to cigarettes, alcohol, bizarre love affairs, or commitments to running twenty-five-plus miles a week is the element of "You Bet Your Job" that is present in so many management decisions. Every choice, even those that appear routine or simple on the surface, can turn out to provide opportunities for things to go dramatically right or (equally likely) dramatically wrong.

A choice that brings a manager into face-to-face contact with a superior a number of levels above him or, in Ed's case, at the very top of the organization, is especially fraught with both opportunity and peril. It's not surprising that Ed had trouble getting comfortable in George Vulcani's waiting room: he was in what was essentially an uncomfortable and worrisome situation. He was the contestant in a big quiz show and he was playing for big stakes.

In terms of the total ConCom perspective, George was going to get his experiment in participative management, with or without Nubian Network and with or without Specialty Foods and Ed Cunningham. George was committed and he was in a position to get what he wanted.

Consequently, the key management issue here was not what ConCom should do but rather how Ed should play things in order to maximize the likelihood that his career would be enhanced.

There were two things he had to keep in mind. One was how his division would do as the scene of the management experiment and/or as the plug-in spot for Nubian Network. In the discussion between George and Ed, it became apparent that although there were pros and cons to Specialty Foods serving as the experimental division, there was no strong evidence that suggested that the experiment would not be a success. This was not the kind of situation where making a mistake would cost the company millions of dollars that could never be recouped. Rather, it seemed likely that with enough planning, hard work, and commitment on the part of Ed and George, an experiment, including the acquisition of Nubian Network, could be successful.

The second thing Ed had to think about was what impressions George was forming about him and his future "fit" into ConCom. Ed needed to develop as many opportunities to become personally involved with George as possible; he had reached a position in ConCom where the only people who could truly enhance his career were the two men at the very top: George, and Ralph Myerson.

As a manager who'd grown up in the sales/marketing/general management side of ConCom rather than on the finance/accounting side, Ed was more likely to get along well with George. Furthermore, the two men seemed likely to have more in common: they were both married, had houses in the country, and liked sports, whereas Ralph seemed to have little interest in anything outside of the quantifiable. So Ed needed to think carefully about making a good impression on George and enlisting his support for his future career development.

What did George want here? First, he wanted his experiment in general. Second, he wanted Nubian Network in particular. Third, he wanted bold action on the part of the person who'd go along with him in making these desires become a reality. By asking Ed to come in to talk things over with him in the first place, George made it clear that he thought Ed would be his man. If Ed did not take a bold stand, he would force George to rethink his evaluation of Ed—and probably to lessen his opinion of his newest senior vice-president.

How Each Option Turned Out

OPTION 1

Ed decided that Specialty Foods was not the best division for the chairman's experiment to take place. George expressed regret at the time but said he respected Ed's reasoning. In August, he announced that the Institutional Foods Division would be the site of an experiment in participative management. As far as Ed knew from talking with that division's president, an outside consulting team spent a lot of time meeting with him and division personnel and they planned to recommend an outline for partial reorganization shortly after the first of the year.

After their original meeting, Ed did not have a similar meeting with George. George was cordial in situations when he and Ed were in the same meetings, but Ed felt that his opportunity to work very closely with the chairman on an ongoing basis had passed and that another such opportunity was not likely to come along anytime soon.

OPTION 2

Ed decided to support the acquisition of Nubian Network. Because of the personal relationship between the chairman and Isadora Dunwiddie, negotiations for the acquisition proceeded quickly and Ed had an opportunity to spend time with Isadora and to visit her company (which was in fact located on the West Coast, in northern California) even before the acquisition was formalized.

Ed and Isadora found that they worked reasonably well together. By their mutual agreement, an internal consultant from ConCom's Organizational Development area was assigned to help them figure out some of the problems of integration they were likely to encounter. For example, the consultant proposed a plan that had some Specialty Foods employees spend time at Nubian Network but also had Nubian Network employees work in other Specialty Foods Divisions.

The formal acquisition of Nubian Network took place in November. By mid-December, Ed felt that things were going well so far but that he had ended up spending more time working with Isadora than he would have liked. A number of trips to California were particularly taxing, though he was able to schedule some work with the sales force into the same trips.

George Vulcani took a close interest in the acquisition and planning for integration. He and Ed met about once a month to continue their brainstorming sessions.

OPTION 3

Ed decided that Specialty Foods should initiate some kind of experiment in management restructuring. However, he felt that the problems of integrating Nubian Network into the Specialty Foods structure outweighed the benefits of acquiring the organization.

George Vulcani agreed to hire a team of outside consultants to work with Ed in determining what form the experiment should take. The consultants began working in September with a complete assessment of the organizational structure in all the different areas of Specialty Foods. Their first report, which they presented to Ed and to George simultaneously, stated that the division was in disarray because it was composed of components from so many different sources: other companies, other divisions, new products, and so on. They suggested that rather than helping Specialty Foods move into any experimental areas, they work out a plan for reorganizing the division as it now existed along traditional lines.

George and Ed met with the internal Organizational Design staff after the consultants' report. Ed made a case for not following the consultants' recommendations and supported this by showing exactly what progress had been made in the division. He also stated that he thought the relative autonomy of the individual units was important to maintain for the time being and that forced integration would be counterproductive.

After extensive discussion, the rest of the group agreed with him. The outside consultants continued to disagree and told ConCom that they would not work with Specialty Foods unless the division was first reorganized. Consequently, their contract was terminated.

As of mid-December, another organizational design consulting team had just been chosen and Ed was preparing to start all over again with them, providing background information, setting up field visits with the various component groups in Specialty Foods, et cetera. He was not sure how long this would take and what plan for an internal experiment they would come up with, but he doubted that anything substantial would happen before March or April of 1988.

The Scores

Option 1. Do not participate in George's proposed experiment.

Taking the safe way out here was the least desirable alternative. George Vulcani and ConCom still became involved in the participative management experiment, but Ed Cunningham was not a part of it at all. He lost his opportunity to gain a close working relationship with George and didn't appear to make any offsetting gains as a result.

Net score: 1

Option 2. Agree to integrate Nubian Network into the Specialty Foods Division and take an active role in making the acquisition take place.

This option gave Ed an opportunity to work with George Vulcani in a positive way. Because Ed and Isadora did some advance planning for the integration of the acquisition, Specialty Foods' business did not suffer as a result and, perhaps, was enhanced. The only negative was that Ed did have to spend a lot of time on the acquisition, though he managed to integrate his involvement in the project into his work with other Specialty Food businesses.

Net score: 9

Option 3. Serve as the site of a participative management experiment but without the acquisition of Nubian Network.

This compromise alternative had some positive features but also turned out to present some pitfalls. Ed got an opportunity to work closely with George Vulcani, but the use of outside consultants led to two problems. First, there was a lot of poking around into the structure of Specialty Foods itself. As such a new division, Specialty Foods didn't need to have even more questions raised and more attention attracted to its still-evolving internal structure. Second, the consultants used up even more of Ed's time than Isadora would have. Ed could probably have better spent this time doing something—almost anything—else.

Net score: 4

8: Balancing Corporate Reporting and Division Spending Needs

The Big Picture

The immediate decision facing Ed in this chapter was somewhat unusual: the corporation was showing too steep a growth in earnings and the president wanted something done about it. But the bigger decision here is one that comes up uncomfortably often in the life of a top manager. Ed had to meet the needs of the corporation as interpreted by Ralph Myerson while also meeting the needs of the Specialty Foods Division as best known by Ed himself. Because these two sets of needs weren't the same, Ed was, just as he thought, caught in a management squeeze.

How and why does a conflict like this arise? To a certain extent, this situation has to do with the nature of large corporations and how they operate in today's business economy.

A large corporation like Consolidated Commodities is, at first glance, simply a collection of businesses, each of which should strive to do as well as possible in terms of sales and earnings. But when a manager looks more closely at the corporation, he or she can see that there is more here than just a bunch of varying operations operating under a shared corporate umbrella.

On the positive side, the whole of a large corporation can be greater than the sum of its parts. Ideally, businesses are added together in such a way that synergy exists between them. Individual businesses can benefit from economies of scale, learn from one another's mistakes, share staff resources economically, and do business with one another.

Furthermore, the businesses can benefit significantly from shared financial resources. In this case, the component businesses are viewed as a kind of financial portfolio held by the corporation. For example, a company might have one business that was generating a lot of cash, more than it could use effectively, while the corporation also operated another business that was cash hungry. Consequently, the second business could be financed with earnings from the first, with everyone—the two businesses and the corporation itself—ultimately benefiting.

On the negative side, a large corporate entity can become less effective than a series of smaller independent businesses could be. A situation can evolve in which top management is less interested in how well individual businesses are doing today or how well they are preparing for the future. Rather, it becomes obsessed with earnings curves, the perception of the corporation on the part of the financial markets, and ultimately the stock price of corporate shares.

Of course, a certain amount of attention to these issues is vitally important. A large corporation must often go into the open marketplace to borrow money or raise capital through public offerings. A corporation that doesn't look reasonably good to outsiders who control investment dollars could end up in big trouble.

The problem develops when there is a large conflict between the way things *look* and the way things *are*. That is the point of view that Ralph Myerson had apparently developed. And this point of view is exactly what puts the squeeze on the people who have economic, managerial, and moral responsibility for the functioning of the individual businesses, in this case the V.P.'s who were attending the meeting.

Ed was put in a position of having to think carefully through three different factors that come into play in making a decision about how to respond to Ralph. First, there is the question, which Ed addressed head on in his ruminations, of how the action under consideration will affect the business in question. For example, Ed decided that taking a price increase on any of his products was likely to have a negative impact on that product's future, so he ruled this option out completely.

Second, Ed had to think about what he believed was acceptable business practice in the areas he was considering. Ed gave this less direct thought, but clearly was aware that some things were marginally acceptable in terms of how he saw the rules of business.

For example, he expressed distaste for an out-and-out misreporting of fourth-quarter expenditures, as would be necessary if he paid for commercials that were being shot in the next fiscal year. Ed seemed to be somewhat of the "if you don't get caught, you haven't done anything wrong" school of thought. Some of the other V.P.'s, Sonny or Afolabi, seemed to have a stricter set of standards, while Ken and Joy appeared comfortable as long as they were meeting the goals that the man at the top had designated as important.

Third, Ed again faced the problem of what impact the decision he made would have on his career, particulary on his future at ConCom. Although by the end of the chapter, Ed felt that he was somewhat off the hook from a numbers point of view, he had not yet thought about how Ralph Myerson would look at him in the future if he refused to "play." Although he could clearly soften his refusal by how he chose to phrase his bowing out, Ed would have realized that Ralph's treatment of Sonny was not just in response to Sonny's abrasive style in the meeting. Rather, Ralph was quick to show that cooperation and following his direction were extremely important to him and that he was not reluctant to use fairly aggressive tactics to bring errant managers into line.

Because of Ed's management style and his strengths in the corporation, however, George Vulcani's good opinion of Ed would probably always be more important than Ralph Myerson's questions. However, with only two men at the top, Ed was clearly somewhat vulnerable to the loss of support of either of them, especially when there are undoubtedly a number of other competent managers, both at Ed's level and immediately below, who have, at least so far, managed to satisfy the demands of both men.

How Each Option Turned Out

OPTION 1

Ed decided that of the alternatives available to him, commissioning new packaging for Salsa! Salsa! Salsa! would both satisfy the corporate needs Ralph had identified and benefit the division long-term. Although the funds that would be used for this option were not great by ConCom standards, totaling only a maximum of $90,000, Ed found Ralph agreeable to his recommendation. Ed hypothesized that this was because the other division V.P.'s had come up with plans to "bury" much larger sums of money. This was only a hypothesis: not surprisingly, Ralph did not share details of the other plans with Ed.

Immediately after his meeting with Ralph, Ed started looking around for a firm that could handle the package redesign. He got suggestions from other people in the corporation and also contacted one woman he'd worked with before when he was in Grocery Products, but she had sold her firm to a large advertising agency that handled many products that competed with ConCom's. Ed decided that a conflict of interest was inevitable and he wouldn't bother to approach the agency.

Ed also talked to a friend of his wife's who was a graphic designer. While she had some great ideas, he decided he couldn't spend enough money by using her services, especially since she could not help him with getting a package prototype or a first run of packages, which Ed hoped would account for almost half of the prepaid expenses.

After about a month spent on his informal search, Ed felt that his time was running out. He decided to ask the corporate Design Department to help him find a design company, even though he knew that projects involving this staff group often became mired in bureaucracy. Once he started working with this group, his worst fears were realized. They had a number of design firms they worked with and they insisted on having five different companies come in, discuss the project with Ed, submit competitive bids for the project, and so on. Time dragged on and Ed was getting more and more nervous about whether it would be possible to bill any of the $90,000 before the end of the year. After all, he reasoned, if he hadn't even chosen a company, it would be hard to get them to submit an invoice he could pay in advance.

Finally, a few days before Christmas, the onerous choice process was complete and Ed signed a contract with Perfect Packaging, a firm headquartered in San Antonio, Texas. He was pleased with the choice. The company, perhaps because of their location, seemed very comfortable working on a Tex-Mex-type product. And they were small and informal enough that Ed expected to have no problems arranging for early billing.

Perfect Packaging agreed to do exactly what Ed wanted and immediately sent an invoice for $88,562.47 to Specialty Foods. However, perhaps because of the Christmas mail, the invoice did not arrive until December 28. Usually, it took two weeks for Accounting to issue a check after they received an invoice. This would push payment into the next fiscal year, completely defeating Ed's objective of lowering profits in the current fiscal year. Ed had no choice. If the expense was to be paid before the end of the year, Ed would have to ask Virgil Wolfe, head of Specialty Foods' accounting, to rush payment of the invoice through.

Because Ed himself brought the invoice in, Virgil looked it over carefully. Ever the friendly staff member, he started telling Ed all about his holiday plans, and then asked Ed if he could take home some Salsa! in the new containers for a cocktail party he was having on New Year's Eve. Ed's heart sank. He had to say that he didn't have any product in the new containers. Virgil asked why not. Ed admitted that he didn't actually have the new containers on hand yet. Virgil asked if they were already in stock at the factory. Faced with such a direct question, Ed said no, he thought maybe they were in transit someplace—delayed by the Christmas rush.

To Ed's great embarrassment, Virgil assumed that it was ignorance rather than trickery that had led Ed to try to pay for containers he had yet to receive. In his kindest, most professorial tone he explained to Ed why he could not okay the invoice. He asked Ed if the design work and package prototype were completed and offered to get that part of the invoice paid right away, if they were. Seeing all chances for reducing profits slipping away, Ed forced himself to say that yes, that was all done. Virgil signed the request for payment, and finally, barely suppressing a sigh of relief, Ed thanked Virgil for his accounting lesson and help with the invoice and left his office as quickly as possible.

So by the end of the year, Specialty Foods had managed to "preexpense" only $53,000, instead of $88,562.47. Ed decided that given Ralph's original satisfaction with his modest spending plan, the $35,000 probably wouldn't make a bit of difference and that Ralph would probably never notice the change anyway. Really, Ed thought, the only lasting effect of the whole disaster was to put a strain on his relationship with Virgil Wolfe.

OPTION 2

After reviewing the options for reducing Specialty Foods' earnings for the fiscal year, Ed decided that the best way to handle the problem was to try some couponing on the slowest-moving part of the Italiano line, the sun-dried tomato products. Ralph Myerson accepted Ed's recommendation and Ed immediately went to work with Grady Jennings on developing the promotion.

Grady commissioned design of an ad with a coupon to run in four-color Sunday supplements in newspapers reaching a million people. The reach of the coupon was deliberately kept low, primarily because Ed was afraid to be too successful in increasing demand. After all, the products only had limited distribution and they were so unknown to most consumers that it was impossible to predict what impact a coupon might have.

Total costs of production and media placement for the coupon were $59,000. In addition, Grady planned redemption costs of about $16,000. According to the accounting system ConCom used, this $16,000 was put into a reserve fund against which redeemed coupons could be charged over the next year or so as they were sent in by grocers.

Ed's plan was to run the coupon between Thanksgiving and Christmas, to meet increased demand with the product that was already on the retailers' shelves, and to encourage the sales force to restock the shelves *after* the first of the year. In this way, the expense of the coupon would occur in the current fiscal year but the additional profits from increased sales of the products would not occur until the next fiscal year. In fact, Ed was so wedded to this timing that even when Grady told him Specialty Foods would have to pay an additional $10,000 in media costs to run the ad during December, he said to go ahead.

Ed also told Grady not to inform the sales force of the coupon until a few days before it ran. Otherwise, he was afraid that they would use the opportunity to build volume, defeating his plan. However, Grady's assistant Mary Gale misunderstood his instructions and sent a memo to Billy Burke telling him about the coupon before Thanksgiving.

As soon as Billy Burke informed his salespeople of the upcoming coupon, they were thrilled. This was a new sales story on a product that had been driving them all crazy because it was so slow-moving. The salesmen swarmed into the field, telling their retailers the good news.

Unfortunately, all too soon they found out that not all retailers thought the news was good. As it turned out, the sun-dried tomato products had distribution almost exclusively in small specialty stores and in the gourmet sections of department stores. None of these retailers had ever accepted a coupon because no coupons had ever been offered on the products they carried. The gourmet food buyer for Bloomingdale's was so outraged that he would be asked to handle coupons that he called Billy Burke and demanded and got a face-to-face meeting with Ed.

The meeting was a painful one for Ed. The Bloomingdale's buyer was not gentle in informing Ed of Ed's ignorance of the true gourmet food retail environment and Ed had to admit that there was a lot he didn't know. Finally, after an hour of increasingly acrimonious discussion, Ed agreed to try to pull the coupon and let the ad run alone.

It was too late. The inserts had been printed. Billy Burke became hysterical. The retailers would be unhappy. The sales force would be inconsolable. Finally, in desperation, Ed suggested a backup plan: that the salespeople be given extra product to place in grocery stores so that coupons could be redeemed there. The salespeople would get their volume. Bloomingdale's could redirect customers to the local Waldbaum's or Grand Union and everyone would be happy.

Except Ed. Because now it was likely that rather than decreasing profits for the division by increasing expenses but holding demand down, profits would actually rise for the year. Ed believed that the sales force would, in a burst of enthusiasm, sell every sun-dried tomato product Italiano could scrape up, and sell it before the coupon ran. Under Billy Burke's enthusiastic leadership, this is exactly what did happen.

Ed only had two consolations from the whole incident. One was that the amount of money Specialty Foods had planned to "bury" was only about $80,000. Even if every sun-dried tomato was sold, profits couldn't increase by much more than that, so overall the impact of Specialty Foods' fiasco on total corporate earnings would be negligible. The second was that Specialty Foods actually managed to get those blasted sun-dried tomatoes into the hands of consumers. And he knew from a little informal taste-testing he'd done at home with his wife Claire that once you tried the things, you found that they weren't half bad. Maybe now they'd turn out to be a successful product yet.

OPTION 3

After much soul-searching, Ed decided the only option for reducing ConCom earnings that he could live with was to delay the shipments of the fall maple syrup crop that Mountain Gourmet marketed. His plan, which he shared with no one except Ralph, was to work through Ozzie Harris, the head of shipping, to hold shipments until late December.

In October, around the time the first finished maple syrup was supposed to be coming from the small producers into the Mountain Gourmet warehouses, Ed paid Ozzie a visit. He explained that he wanted to build up inventory on the product so that in January he and Ozzie could run some market research: a comparison test of the different shipping alternatives Mountain Gourmet used. Lots of product would be sent out at the same time by different carriers and then the speed of delivery and costs of each could be fairly evaluated against one another.

Ozzie, who'd never been asked to be involved in anything as glamorous as a piece of market research, was delighted to accommodate Ed. After Ed left the warehouse, he felt guilty that it had been so easy to flatter Ozzie into cooperating in what was essentially an underhanded operation.

Over the next six weeks, Mother Nature appeared to be on the same team as Ralph Myerson. Weather in the Northeast, where most of Mountain Gourmet's maple syrup was produced, remained unseasonably warm and the sap runs were delayed substantially. Then when the sap boils began, several of the largest suppliers found that the warm weather had reduced the quality of the sap and that it was taking much more sap to produce a gallon of syrup. Consequently, they informed Mountain Gourmet, their production estimates should be adjusted downward. There wouldn't be as much maple syrup to ship as they had expected.

Ozzie, who had apparently been roused from a career of chronic lethargy by Ed's recruiting him for the bogus market research project, called Ed about once a week to keep him informed on how shipments were coming in. He was worried that they wouldn't have enough product to conduct the test. He was afraid that product would arrive too late to run the test in January. He was worried about one thing after another. Finally, things reached such a point that when Ellie Vogel told Ed that Mr. Harris was on the line again, Ed would simply shut his office door so no one could overhear the strange conversation that would follow and settle down to spend at least thirty minutes reassuring Ozzie that everything would be okay.

By the end of December, no syrup had been shipped. Ed did some calculations and decided that, in fact, about 25 percent less syrup was available than he had anticipated, so shipments would have been reduced by that amount anyway. All in all, he was completely successful in reducing Specialty Foods' profits by over $200,000. Ralph Myerson would be pleased.

Ed also forced himself to figure out how much his subterfuge had cost Billy Burke and Boris DiGiulio, the salesman who was in charge of Mountain Gourmet, in terms of lost commissions for the year. Ed decided that Billy was coming up about $3,000 short and Boris DiGiulio was about $1,000 below the bonus he would have received otherwise. Of course, when sales rose in the next fiscal year, the two men would receive the bonuses. And the bonuses would have been lowered by the crop shortage, anyway.

Really, Ed concluded, he hadn't done the two men any permanent damage. He just hoped they hadn't been planning to use the extra money for their IRAs . . . or Christmas gifts for the kids . . . or Grandma's medical bills. . . .

OPTION 4

Ed found it impossible to make an immediate decision regarding Ralph Myerson's proposals. When he left his office for the meeting, he still hadn't decided which alternative to choose. Every one had some strong negatives. He took all his notes with him and decided to rely on last-minute inspiration.

As soon as he stepped into Ralph's office, Ed could feel himself getting angry at the situation he found himself in. Dora was there with Ralph, smiling her now seemingly preformed smile. Ralph, while not going so far as to smile at Ed, seemed determined to set a pleasant tone for the meeting. But rather than relaxing and enjoying Ralph's good mood, Ed experienced Ralph's pleasantness as a setup for himself and his division.

Still, it was with some surprise that Ed heard himself telling Ralph that he had decided that there was no appropriate means of reducing this year's earnings within his division and that he had no plan to submit for Ralph's approval. As a deep frown darkened Ralph's face, Ed hurried on to explain how Specialty Foods was too small to make any difference anyway and how disruptive it would be for a new division to have last-minute—he swallowed the word "manipulations"—changes in plans.

Ralph again resorted to silence in lieu of a disapproving statement. But Dora spoke up, saying that the other division vice-presidents had come up with plans for enough "prespending" to "fix the little blip" she had identified. Ralph turned his angry look to Dora, who obviously was talking out of turn, then focused back on Ed. Ralph told Ed in no uncertain terms that at this time the point was not to come up with a plan per se, but to indicate his willingness to be part of the team under Ralph's leadership. Ralph went on to say that he had been particularly pleased with Sutton's plan, which had indicated a strong sense of pulling together and of teamwork. After his brief but pointed speech, Ralph told Ed their meeting was at an end and that he planned to seek another opportunity for Ed to demonstrate his ability to engage in teamwork.

When Ed described the scene to his wife Claire, he told her he was glad that he at least seemed to have George Vulcani on his side, because it was clear that he'd never be able to work effectively with Ralph. Despite Claire's reassurances that he had done the right thing by following his conscience, Ed found himself wondering over the next few weeks if he really fit in at ConCom or if his run-in with Ralph Myerson was indicative of a basic "bad fit" between him and the corporation.

The Scores

Option 1. Prepay Salsa! packaging development and manufacturing expenses.

Ed chose the alternative that was most likely to run afoul of corporate accounting practices. In addition, Ed's execution of this alternative was not a complete success. He was unable to "pre-expense" the full amount for which he'd planned. He was forced to bring the whole matter to the attention of Virgil Wolfe, the very thing he had planned to avoid doing at any cost. He strained, from his own point of view, the easygoing relationship with Virgil that he had worked hard to build up. And he ended up feeling that his action was meaningless for ConCom. All in all, this was not the best choice Ed could have made, but at least it satisfied Ralph Myerson's needs to have Ed act as part of the team.

Net score: 3

Option 2. Run coupon on sun-dried tomatoes in Sunday supplements.

Although this option did not end up "burying" profits, at least it had some positive benefits for Specialty Foods. It gave a boost to the sun-dried tomato products. It gave Ed and Grady some valuable information about the different retailers who handled their products and gave them a head start on planning campaigns to benefit non-grocer clients. While Ed was undoubtedly right in thinking that ConCom didn't particularly need Specialty Foods' help in reducing profits anyway, this option did allow Ed to show Ralph Myerson that he was willing to do what Ralph requested as far as was possible in his division.

Net score: 5

Option 3. Delay shipments of maple syrup.

This was the most successful alternative in terms of reducing ConCom's earnings for the year. Because it required the help of an unquestioning ConCom employee, it also carried the lowest risk of creating problems for Ed with the corporate accountants.

Perhaps it was because of the relative success of this option that Ed was left with his feeling of free-floating guilt. All in all, he had probably harmed no one, but his response raises the question of how he will feel the next time a situation like this comes up and if he will be as willing to agree to the kind of "creative accounting" Ralph Myerson may again request.

Net score: 7

Option 4. Do not offer an area for earnings reduction in the Specialty Foods Division.

This option was the most dramatic Ed could have chosen in terms of his emotional involvement in the situation and his future career development at Consolidated Commodities. Ed was obviously correct in thinking that Ralph got the numbers he needed from the other vice-presidents and that Specialty Foods' participation was essentially meaningless from the bottom-line perspective. But once Ed refused to go along with the situation, a lot of the anger, frustration, and even doubt that Ralph Myerson began experiencing at the meeting when Sonny was uncooperative got focused on Ed instead.

Furthermore, it seems that once Ed stopped trying to keep his bad feelings about the situation under control, his discomfort with Ralph Myerson and his management style blossomed into full-fledged career discontent. This could have major implications for Ed long-term, with the ultimate outcome being impossible to predict. Will he stay at ConCom and buckle under? Manage to get fired by Ralph Myerson? Leave ConCom and create a happier and more successful life for himself elsewhere?

Although Ed's actions were positive in terms of their effect on Specialty Foods, the tremendous uncertainty he has introduced into his career and into his position as leader of the division makes this a relatively low-scoring option.

Net score: 5

9. Closing the Apple Products Production Facility

The Big Picture

In this situation, Ed, with the help of his wife Claire, did a very good job of identifying his personal "big picture": the kinds of personal career risks and rewards the situation presented. What he did not see so clearly was exactly what could go wrong in the environmental context in which ConCom operated.

In a large corporation like ConCom, there are good reasons for paying the high salaries of Irma Saloman and her staff. Any big corporation is like a very important person in a very small town. Every action is public knowledge, everybody is eager for an opportunity to second-guess the big-timer. Nobody has much sympathy for the poor little corporation with sales of $5 billion that makes an honest mistake.

Realistically, it is not surprising that Ed could not anticipate the things that might happen when ConCom shut down the Apple Products facility. Irma Saloman and even George Vulcani and Ralph Myerson should have been heavily involved in the decision. They had the benefit of years of experience in dealing with the outside world; this is what Ed lacked.

However, Apple Products was a very small piece of the ConCom action. This led to Ed's being left more or less on his own. This was a case where Ed would have been wise to demand the deeper involvement of other people rather than to think primarily in terms of his own conscience. In the end, as the detailed outcome section indicates, this was not just Ed's problem or just Chelsea, Vermont's problem. It was Consolidated Commodities' problem, and a sticky one at that. Perhaps most important, it was a problem that could and should have been defused, regardless of what Ed initially decided to recommend.

How Each Option Turned Out
OPTION 1

Ed recommended that the facility be closed down effective immediately and top management concurred. The storage facility was written off. The apples that were stored in Chelsea were sold to another company and the pulping machine was moved to White River Junction. No employee of the organization chose to move to the plant there, except Caleb Ross, who accepted a job as assistant plant manager and started to commute from his farm in Chelsea.

Two weeks after Ed made his recommendation, he and Irma scheduled a press conference to be held at the White River Junction plant. Although they only expected reporters from the *Valley News* (the local daily) and the Montpelier paper, Irma felt that a press conference would show ConCom had nothing to hide.

However, the press conference was better attended than Irma expected, with coverage by both of the major papers in Boston. The press conference went all right, although the Boston *Globe* reporter asked some pointed questions of Ed about what alternatives the corporation had considered to closing down the facility, particularly if they had looked into selling the assets to the employees.

In the next Sunday's *Globe*, an article appeared about the decline of the agricultural base of the central New England area. The article focused on the Apple Products story, telling how farmers planted apple trees and now had no place to sell the apples. It also discussed the economic decline of Chelsea, gave the history of Mountain Gourmet, and described how it was originally a people's cooperative.

That Sunday afternoon, Caleb Ross called Ed to tell him that Channel 4 in Boston had sent a TV team up to Chelsea. They had photographed the abandoned facility and then interviewed Joe O'Malley, the elderly man who'd been injured in the cider mill accident. With tears in his eyes, Joe had said that everything was his fault because of his accident. Now he felt like he let the whole town down and his friends were all out of jobs. Caleb called back the next morning to say that the story had run on both the 6:00 and the 11:00 P.M. news.

Ed didn't hear anything else about Chelsea until the annual meeting in January. Apparently the news story had brought ConCom to the attention of SASS (Social Action Securities), a national organization of socially conscious investors headquartered in Boston. The SASS executive director turned up at the annual meeting and monopolized the proceedings with questions about how ConCom treated its agricultural employees. After about the twentieth go-round, George Vulcani lost his temper with the woman and refused to answer any more questions. Although Irma Saloman intervened and managed to smooth things over somewhat, the outburst was reported in the next day's *Wall Street Journal*. Ed thought the article might have contributed to a sell-off of ConCom stock that day, which led to a $2-per-share reduction in the stock price.

OPTION 2

Ed requested that the Apple Products facility remain open, with increased production of dried apples and apple pulp, until the end of the year (approximately eleven weeks). The four employees who usually handled apple intake were assigned to help with pulp and drying. In his request, he estimated that this would cost ConCom $20,000, although Apple Products probably could sell the extra dried apples and the jam and jelly plant had agreed to accept extra pulp.

He also requested that two people be assigned from the corporate staff to help him and Caleb Ross investigate alternatives for the Apple Products employees, such as funding from the state of Vermont for an employee buy-out of the operation. He made it clear that Apple Products did not offer an economically viable investment opportunity to ConCom long-term, but that there could be ways to extricate ConCom without injuring the local economy.

Ralph Myerson, the ConCom president, assigned one person to work on the Apple Products problem until the end of the year.

However, Specialty Foods was charged for her salary and benefits during this time.

The staff person, Gloria Langer, temporarily moved up to Chelsea and she and Caleb began lobbying and making contacts throughout Vermont. Over the next few months, they managed to arrange a grant from the state plus a two-year management support effort that would enable the apple-drying operation to expand to a year-round operation. The business proposition required that ConCom donate the storage facility to be used by the new company. The operation would employ five people full-time. Gloria and Caleb were unable to find anything that would offer employment to the other soon-to-be-terminated employees.

After several meetings with Ralph Myerson, Ed was able to get him to agree to sell the storage facility to the new organization for $1. This transaction took place with a small ceremony in Chelsea, which was covered by the *Valley News*. On December 31, the Apple Products operation was officially closed down as part of Consolidated Commodities.

The Scores

Option 1. Close the Apple Products facility, but offer employment to any employee who is willing to relocate to another ConCom facility.

Ed did his best—for himself and for ConCom as he saw things. But his best wasn't good enough. Not only did ConCom suffer adverse publicity, but it took George Vulcani a long time to forget that the damned Apple Products operation was part of that damned Specialty Foods Division run by that guy he'd originally thought so much of—Ed Cunningham.

Net score: 1

Option 2. Continue to operate the Apple Products facility until December 31, 1987, looking for alternatives to continue operation.

Ed did well—for himself and for ConCom—by doing good. An unpleasant fiasco was avoided, five people kept their jobs, and Ed felt good about how he'd handled things. The only thing that keeps this from getting a perfect 10 is that nobody ever knew how bad things could have been and so they couldn't really appreciate what Ed had accomplished.

Net score: 8

10: Choosing a New Group Product Manager

The Big Picture

It's been said so many times that it's become a cliché: a company is only as good as its employees. And yet, cliché or not, it's still true. The best machines, the most extensive capitalization, the most modern management structures all are ultimately built on people.

In choosing a new group product manager, Ed Cunningham was faced with a very commonplace and ordinary personnel decision. But there are ample opportunities to make costly mistakes even in everyday decisions. Especially in large and complex organizations, it's easy to start thinking that people decisions are too important for people to make. That's when a company like Safety Systems, Inc., can make a sale: with its "scientific" and "objective" techniques, somehow it seems to promise a kind of magic solution to problems like how to predict who will do best in a new position.

That's not to say that Safety Systems had nothing to offer. In this case, the company representative seemed more at home with burglar alarms than with psychological tests. It also appeared that, at least in its approach to Martha Bleecker, it had overpromised what it could deliver. But psychological testing, when well-done and well-interpreted, can be a valuable additional tool for managers to have at their disposal. The key is that testing must enhance informed judgment, not, as Sal Alfredo suggested, replace it.

How the Options Turned Out

OPTION 1

Ed decided that he could probably adequately serve the needs of his division while satisfying the Human Resources Department's need for "scientific objectivity" by offering Win Elsworth the position as group product manager for Specialty Products. Martha Bleecker wholeheartedly supported his choice.

On the Friday after he had received the Safety Systems report, Ed invited Win out to lunch and, over the main course, offered him the position. To Ed's surprise, rather than immediately and enthusiastically accepting the job that he had displayed such interest in a few weeks previously, Win said he would think over the offer. Ed asked him to please make a decision before the Christmas break, which was about ten days away. After seeing Win's hesitation, Ed also asked him to keep the offer completely confidential until he had made his decision.

When Ed returned to his office, he called both Grady and Sandra and told them that he wasn't yet ready to make a final decision on the position but that he would definitely let them know something one way or another before Christmas.

A week went by; Ed saw Win in the hall now and then, but Win just smiled and nodded. Finally, two days before the Christmas break, Win stopped by Ed's office.

After Ed said he had some free time, Win came in and sat down. His relaxed manner and obviously good mood convinced Ed that he was going to say how happy he was to take the job.

"I've got to say how thankful I am for this offer, Ed," began Win. "You see, when I came to ConCom I had one goal in mind. I wanted to see if I could make it on my own, away from the family influence, so to speak. For generations, Elsworths have made fortunes in the Far East and as the oldest son of the oldest son, that option was clearly open to me. But I decided I'd never know if I was only successful because I'd had it all handed to me or if it was because of my own strengths and skills. Now that you've offered me this group product manager position, I know that I can make it on my own!"

Win smiled at Ed broadly. After a minute, Ed prodded, "So you've decided to accept the job."

"Oh, gosh, not at all," said Win to Ed's utter surprise. "Once I knew I could make it here I didn't need to be here anymore. I thought that would be obvious. I've spent the time since our lunch talking to Dad and we've got it all worked out. I'll be heading out to Hong Kong immediately after the Christmas holidays to take over our office there. There's a great future in trading with China out of that office, Ed, and with my background, I'm going to make another fortune for the Elsworths. As a matter of fact, while I'm here, I want to hand you my resignation." He pulled a letter out of his pocket and handed it to Ed.

"It's been real, old boy," Win added as Ed accepted the letter. "Best of luck on your grouper position. Of course, I haven't mentioned anything to anybody." Win laughed easily. "I'm sure some poor guy who has to keep on plugging at ConCom will be delighted to step right into such a plum of a job."

OPTION 2

After thinking carefully about his three candidates and the Human Resources recommendations, Ed decided that he would keep Grady Jennings and Win Elsworth where they were for the time being and hire Sandra Sullivan for the group product manager position. This would give him internal consistency for two big chunks of the business (Italiano and Apple Products), bring in some new management talent, and not alienate the Human Resources Department. Besides, Ed strongly believed that it was important to have women in management positions, because many of the entry-level positions were going to young female MBAs who needed to know that the upper ranks of ConCom were not closed to them.

Ed arranged to meet with Sandra the Friday after he had received the Safety Systems reports. Because he had another meeting in the city that morning, he made reservations for lunch at a cozy French restaurant in Manhattan. Ed wasn't sure how much the people at AAM&N knew about Sandra's plans; he felt that how she left the agency was her business, though he'd certainly discuss it with Jack Bench, her supervisor, after she'd talked to him. Meanwhile, because of his uncertainty, he didn't want to discuss the job offer anyplace where someone from AAM&N or ConCom might overhear the conversation.

Ed arrived at the restaurant first and got the table. Five minutes later a glowing Sandra arrived. Ed thought she must have guessed that he was going to offer her the position and he was glad to see that she was so excited about it.

After they had both ordered, Ed spoke up. "It looks like you might have guessed the good news," he began. "I'd very much like to have you take the position as group product manager for Specialty Products. You could start anytime after the first of the year, depending on when it was convenient to leave AAM&N. The salary, benefits, and responsibilities would be as we discussed." Sandra beamed at Ed. "Of course, you don't have to make up your mind immediately," he added, "though it doesn't look like you're too uncertain."

"Ed, I'm thrilled," said Sandra. She reached across the table and took Ed's hand and gave it a big squeeze. "This is one of the most exciting days of my life," she said. Then she dropped his hand somewhat shyly.

"You mean because of the job?" asked Ed. He'd never seen anyone as excited about an offer. She must have really been eager to make the switch.

"Yes, about the job. And about something else, too," Sandra answered almost coyly. "Though," she added quickly, "of course, this other thing doesn't really have anything to do with my accepting the job or how I'd do it."

"What else is so exciting?" asked Ed sociably. He was thinking maybe she was planning a trip or was going to buy a fur coat or a condominium or something to celebrate her new job.

"You're only the second person to know! Only my husband knews so far," Sandra said playfully.

"Please, I'm dying of curiosity!" replied Ed.

"I just got back from a doctor's appointment," Sandra said, leaning forward confidingly, "and my doctor told me that something I'd hoped and dreamed about for years had finally happened." She lowered her voice dramatically. "I'm pregnant! Isn't it wonderful? And you know what? The doctor even thinks that I might be having twins!"

OPTION 3

After several days of soul-searching, Ed decided that even though the Human Resources Department believed that Grady Jennings was a high-risk employee, Ed could not agree with them. He thought back over Grady's consistent, mature, and sensitive actions as group product manager on Italiano and could find absolutely no evidence of any instability or conflicts that manifested themselves in the work environment.

In fact, Grady had done so well that Ed hesitated to offer him the Specialty Products job because it was technically a lateral move. However, Specialty Foods was not yet ready for a restructuring that might open up a higher position for Grady and Ed wasn't quite altruistic enough to send one of his best managers out of his division. Ed decided he'd offer Grady the job, tell him he would have a shot at a promotion within a year, and then ask Grady's advice in deciding which of the other two candidates would be most appropriate for the Italiano position that Grady would be vacating.

Ed called Martha Bleecker and told her that he had decided to offer Grady the job with a salary increase. As she had promised, Martha reported his plans to her boss Harold Harrison. Rather than offering strong opposition to Ed's plan, Harold was surprisingly conciliatory, leading Ed to wonder if he was less comfortable with the Safety Systems approach than Martha had led Ed to believe. At any rate, Harold said that while he disagreed with Ed's decision, he would not prevent its implementation. He asked Ed to be sure to keep him informed as to how Grady did over the next few months as a kind of informal test of the Safety Systems assessment procedures.

Ed invited Grady to go out to lunch with him, deciding to make the job offer away from the office. On the way to the restaurant, Grady, who was driving, seemed somewhat edgy, honking his horn at a slow car at a green light, muttering under his breath when a car cut in front of him.

When they got to the restaurant and went to their table, Grady seemed even less like himself. He ordered a double vodka martini, even though Ed had ordered Perrier. When the drinks arrived, Grady dispatched his in record time and seemed to be looking longingly into the bottom of the glass, as if wishing it weren't empty.

After the first course arrived, Ed decided it was time to tell Grady about his decision. He had no sooner opened his mouth to begin, however, than Grady, who had been staring morosely into his soup, spoke. "I know why you brought me here, away from the office," Grady said in a flat tone. "You've decided to offer that job to someone else because you're not pleased with how I've been handling things the last few weeks."

"You're mistaken, Grady," Ed began, but Grady seemed not to have heard him.

"I've been trying to do my best but I know my work has been slipping," Grady was saying. "It's because of Marybeth. I know, I know. The true professional doesn't let his personal life intervene in his corporate functioning. But no matter how hard I've tried, I can't keep the two apart."

He looked up at Ed and one tear slid down his cheek.

In alarm, Ed started to interrupt, but Grady was talking on. "We got married when we were so young and both so idealistic and now that has changed for me but it hasn't changed for Marybeth. Each time I've been promoted or gotten a raise, it's just made things that much harder. Marybeth would say she was glad for me but I could tell that my latest success was just another wedge driving us apart."

Grady used his napkin to dab at his eyes.

"Then, when you asked me if I was interested in this position, I went home and told her about it. I don't know exactly why, but this seemed to be the last straw for her. She said that she had wished and hoped that I would outgrow my need for this kind of artificial status-seeking and transfer my skills into some meaningful activity. But now I was giving serious consideration to one more move, and she could see that there'd be another after that and another and they'd go on forever."

Grady stopped and blew his nose hard into his napkin.

"So"—he stopped talking and for a moment Ed thought he was going to run out of the room—"so—she left." Now Grady appeared to be crying in earnest. Meanwhile, the waiter, apparently puzzled as to why the two men had not eaten their soup when he had their entrées waiting in the kitchen, approached the table. Ed waved the waiter away in annoyance. Oh, God, why couldn't Grady have had his nervous breakdown in the *office?*

"I'm terribly sorry to hear that, Grady," Ed said, as soon as the waiter was out of earshot again. "Do you think things are irreversible?"

Grady blew his nose again and appeared to regain some self-control.

"She called me last night," he said, "and told me she still loves me." He swallowed hard and looked at Ed sadly. "She told me she was ready to come back anytime. Anytime at all. All I had to do was call her and tell her I'd handed you my resignation. Once I did that, she'd be back in a minute."

Ed waited again for Grady to go on.

"I just don't know yet what I'm going to do," he finally said. "I think I'll have to take a leave of absence for a month or two until I get this all worked out. My career means everything to me right now, but I don't see how I can make a go of it without Marybeth."

The Scores

Option 1. Balance the needs of Specialty Foods and the Human Resources Department by offering the position to Win Elsworth.

Although Ed decided to ignore his doubts about Win Elsworth and offer him the job as group product manager, Win's inherent self-interest saved Ed from being saddled with a less-than-dedicated employee.

Net score: 6

Option 2. Offer the position to Sandra Sullivan.

Ed will undoubtedly be faced with the temporary loss of his new group product manager as Sandra takes time off to have her child or children. However, there is nothing in Sandra's work history or conversation with Ed to lead him to believe that her reproductive inclinations will permanently affect her ability to handle the job. Ed also will still have Grady and Win to keep their parts of the business running while Sandra is gone, giving him the opportunity to fill in for Sandra as required.

Net score: 8

Option 3. Offer Grady the position.

Despite their apparent lack of sophistication, Safety Systems' screening techniques appear to have picked up some hint of the conflicts Grady was experiencing after Ed asked him if he was interested in the new group product manager job. At this point, while it is impossible to say what Grady's decision will be ultimately, there is still reason to believe that his work has validity and importance for him and that he will find a way of continuing both his marriage and his career at ConCom.

Even if Grady accepts the new job, Ed is still faced with replacing him as Italiano grouper. However, he does have two viable candidates, either of whom might be willing to accept Grady's old position.

Net score: 7

12

The Year Ends: The Challenge Goes On

December 31, 1987

Ed and Claire Cunningham snuggled up on the deep Victorian couch across from the roaring fire they'd just finished building. Outside the windows of the living room, they could see the snow falling with the kind of intensity winter usually reserved for February.

"Who made this wonderfully smart decision to stay home tonight?" asked Claire, leaning her head on Ed's shoulder. "We could have been out at the Wellingtons' worrying about whether we should risk a single glass of wine, and instead, here we are, a full bottle of Dom Pérignon to ourselves and all we have to do is stagger up the stairs."

"Actually, we don't even have to do that," said Ed as he took Claire's hand and started playing with her fingers, one at a time. "Since Richard is at Paul's and Katie is at Sandra's, no one would find out if we spent the whole night down here. All we have to do is cover our tracks before noon tomorrow."

"Cover our *lack* of tracks is more like it," said Claire lazily. "That's not such a bad idea, bedding down right here."

"Bedding down? What a mind you have, woman," Ed said, laughing. "It's New Year's Eve tonight! We've got to stay alert for another hour. We've got to replay every little thing that happened over 1987, figure out what we did right and what we did wrong, and make our New Year's resolutions. Bed down? Don't even think of it!"

"All right, Mr. Traditional." Very slowly Claire uncurled herself from beside Ed. She stood up, her slim height silhouetted against the heat of the fire, and walked across to an old dresser she'd refinished to serve as the living-room bar.

"You want delayed gratification?" she said, picking up the ice bucket. "You shall have it. But can we at least drink the champagne in the meantime?"

"By all means," said Ed. Claire walked back to the couch and put the ice bucket down on the coffee table. Ed took out the bottle of champagne and carefully began working the cork out. When it popped and flew across the room, Claire held out the two champagne glasses she'd picked up from the table and Ed filled them.

"What teamwork!" Claire said, handing Ed one of the glasses. "Years of marriage have put us into perfect harmony."

"Here's to more harmony," said Ed, clinking Claire's glass. They both sipped the bubbly wine appreciatively.

"And to think we could have been at the Wellingtons'," Claire mused again, sighing in satisfaction.

"Or worse," answered Ed. "I wasn't sure how I was going to make it back from that trip to California this week. Although I must admit, I was prepared to walk if I had to. I'd never miss a New Year's Eve with you."

"Not even to spend it with that goat lady?" teased Claire. "You've said she wasn't too bad."

"Not too bad for a goat farmer isn't exactly high praise." Ed laughed and put his arm around Claire. "But I have spent a lot of time away from home this year, haven't I?"

"I've seemed to notice your absence," said Claire ruefully. She leaned away from Ed's arm slightly and looked at him seriously. "I've assumed it was just because everything was so new and there was so much to do."

"I *think* that's it," said Ed, giving Claire a squeeze back toward him. "And you've got to admit, there have been some things that nobody would expect to see repeated."

"I thought *every* company like ConCom spent its corporate life buying businesses, selling businesses, buying equipment, selling equipment, hiring pople, firing people," Claire replied.

"But not in the same division in the same year!" Ed exclaimed. "It seemed as if they were just waiting for Specialty Foods to come into existence to get all these crazy things taken care of."

"There's probably more truth in that than ConCom would care to admit," Claire said, picking up her champagne glass. She took a long swallow. "The apple cider mill and that factory making the sauce in New Orleans—those probably needed attention years ago."

"That's certainly the situation when it came to reorganizing the sales force and putting Italiano advertising back on the air," said Ed wearily. "Those problems had my name on them." He leaned forward, picked up the champagne bottle, and refilled both glasses.

"Of course I got a crack at some positive things, too," he continued more cheerfully after another sip. "Two whole new businesses—goat cheese and Salsa! They offered me those on a silver platter. And, of course, I've had a chance to work closely with George and Ralph. Though"—his tone flattened—"I'm not sure I wouldn't have been better off at times if neither one of them knew who I was."

"That's it," said Claire decisively, taking Ed's glass and putting it down on the coffee table. She put both her arms around him and pushed him back on the couch. Just as his head touched the arm, she started tickling him ruthlessly. "No more second guesses," she said, tickling him under the arm. "No more regrets," she added before kissing him under the chin several times. "We've spent enough evenings with George Vulcani and Ralph Myerson as uninvited guests this year." She undid the top button of Ed's shirt. "Tonight it's New Year's Eve. Tonight I get you all to myself."

"I just wonder," said Ed, gazing off for a last minute over her shoulder. "I just wonder if somebody else would have done it all differently."

■ ■ ■

Who wouldn't have done it all differently, if we'd known before making each decision exactly what would happen? But that is the thrill and the frustraton of being a manager. The world is filled with unknowns and yet there are also the odds to be calculated, the rational thinking to be applied, the training and experience to draw on.

That's why there weren't any zeroes for the options Ed faced. Every possible answer had something in its favor and left the person choosing it with some hope for the future. And yet, it was possible to make a lot of mistakes or, at the least, inopportune choices.

What would have happened if you had chosen the lowest scoring option in each decision situation? How about if you'd chosen the best?

Now is the time to go back through your answers to the questions Ed faced and add up exactly how you did. To make it easy, there is a summary that follows with the scores for each option in each chapter. Use these together with your choices throughout the book to find out how you came out. Here's our assessment of how your future would look if you'd just spent 1987 living your version of Ed Cunningham's life.

—If you scored 23 to 25

This wasn't your year. Probably it wouldn't be a bad idea to spend New Year's Day bringing your résumé up to date.

—If you scored 26 to 40

Although this was not a sterling performance, you would probably get the chance to try to learn from your mistakes and spend another year as division president. The important question is did you manage—at least once—to come out on George Vulcani's good side? (Look back at the Apple Products chapter and the Nubian Network chapter, especially.)

—If you scored 41 to 59

Not bad at all for your first year in a corner office. You had to make some very good choices to move into this category. Next year should see Specialty Foods going for the $100 million mark!

—If you scored 60 to 69

Polish your shoes and buy a new suit. George Vulcani's going to be calling you in for a raise, a pat on the back, and probably the chance to pick up two or three wonderful new businesses he just happened to hear about at the Wellingtons' New Year's Eve party.

■ ■ ■

Summary of Solution Scores

Option	Score

Chapter 3—Italiano Advertising
1	4
2	5
3	6
4	10
5	3

Chapter 4—Sales Force Reorganization
1	5
2	10
3	2

Chapter 5—Salsa! Sourcing
1	7
2	4
3	9

Chapter 6—Italiano Production
| 1 | 3 |
| 2 | 8 |

Chapter 7—Nubian Network
1   1
2   9
3   4

Chapter 8—Managing Earnings
1   3
2   5
3   7
4   5

Chapter 9—Apple Products
1   1
2   8

Chapter 10—Hiring a Grouper
1   6
2   8
3   7